THE CHINA CONNECTION

DATE DUE

UNITED STATES FOREIGN POLICY SERIES
Peter Duignan, general editor

This series will provide expert analyses of U.S. interests and involvement in key countries, regions, and organizations.

THE CHINA CONNECTION: U.S. Policy and the
People's Republic of China
A. James Gregor

THE CHINA CONNECTION

U.S. Policy and the People's Republic of China

A. James Gregor

Hoover Institution Press

Stanford University, Stanford, California

To Sun Yun-suan,
who has served his people well

The Hoover Institution on War, Revolution and Peace, founded at
Stanford University in 1919 by the late President Herbert Hoover,
is an interdisciplinary research center for advanced study on
domestic and international affairs in the twentieth century. The
views expressed in its publications are entirely those of the
authors and do not necessarily reflect the views of the staff,
officers, or Board of Overseers of the Hoover Institution.

Hoover Press Publication 329

First printing, 1986

Manufactured in the United States of America

90 89 88 87 86   9 8 7 6 5 4 3 2 1

Library of Congress Cataloging in Publication Data

Gregor, A. James (Anthony James), 1929–
   The China connection.

   Bibliography: p.
   Includes index.
   1. United States—Foreign relations—China.
2. China—Foreign relations—United States.   I. Title.
E183.8.C5G73 1986   327.73051   86-7387
ISBN 0-8179-8291-4 (alk. paper)
ISBN 0-8179-8292-2 (pbk. : alk. paper)

Design by P. Kelley Baker

Contents

vi   *Contents*

Editor's Foreword

The United States Foreign Policy Series aims to provide clear, cogent analyses of U.S. interests and involvement in key countries and regions of the world. Each work will follow a common outline. Authors will be experts in the country or region they write about and will be expected to provide authoritative, perceptive, and readable essays.

As general editor I am pleased to introduce the first volume in this series, A. James Gregor's study of the relationship between the United States and the People's Republic of China. Gregor traces that relationship and the Chinese role in East Asia in order to provide a background for policymakers in Washington and for scholars and opinion makers elsewhere.

After discussing the land and people of China, Gregor sketches the history of U.S. involvement with China and the creation of the new China under Mao Zedong. Successive chapters deal with the PRC's foreign policy, rapprochement with the United States, the PRC as a security asset, the Taiwan issue, and the current reforms being undertaken in China. The final chapter discusses what U.S. policy should be toward China.

Gregor calls for greater realism in our policies toward China. Since 1949, U.S. assessments of the PRC have been frequently unrealistic—to the disservice of our national interests. Only recently has more sober and objective judgment begun to prevail.

China today faces enormous problems, many of them the consequences of policy failures on the part of its leadership. American leaders must recognize the complexity and intractability of those problems and plan accordingly. The PRC's military forces require modernization. The economic system remains grievously impaired and the outcome of the current reforms remains uncertain.

The United States shares certain security interests with the PRC, and a case can be made for continued cooperation with Beijing insofar as U.S. interests are concerned and present problems permit. The United States must recognize, however, that the PRC, while complicating Moscow's military planning, also constitutes a potential threat to its neighbors in Southeast Asia, especially to the ASEAN states and Vietnam. The United States should aim at reducing potential conflict between the PRC and its neighbors. Peace and stability throughout East Asia are in the interests of the United States.

The Washington policymaker's most difficult problem may turn on the policies that the PRC will adopt in the future. A fall back to the enormities of the Maoist past cannot be precluded. In the future, the United States may have to contend with the PRC's return to the world arena as a revolutionary state. In the past, both the domestic and foreign policies of the PRC have been subject to wild fluctuations. The passing of the present "pragmatic" leadership could trigger just such policy changes.

Americans must realize that China has not yet earned the trust of democratic nations and remains an international actor whose behaviors are largely unpredictable. Moreover, despite its pretentions, the PRC will remain only a regional power, of local military consequence and marginal international economic importance. The United States cannot invest much confidence in China's strategic significance in its rivalry with the USSR. More importance might well be assigned to the role of our firm regional allies.

All these matters are discussed in detail in Gregor's excellent monograph. I hope that the depth and breadth of his analyses will convince American leaders to pursue more realistic policies toward the PRC. In this book they have an illuminating synthesis and a comprehensive guide to understanding current events in China.

PETER J. DUIGNAN

Preface

Few intellectual pursuits are more hazardous and yet more compelling than political forecasting and the tendering of policy recommendations. Both involve procedures that are painfully inexact and lamentably judgmental. To pretend otherwise would be to deceive one's audience as well as oneself. Nevertheless, the making of political projections and the casting of policy recommendations are endeavors that must be undertaken. Decisions must be made that affect the most fundamental interests of humankind. Those decisions are best made in an environment where alternative interpretations are made available for public consideration, and where alternative recommendations can be publicly evaluated.

In the remainder of this century, those Americans charged with the responsibility of making foreign policy will face formidable tasks— particularly with regard to East Asia. There is reason to believe that the challenges to U.S. political, economic, and security interests will be greater there than in almost any other region of the world.

This brief work is intended as a modest contribution to the discussion that necessarily accompanies policymaking in Washington. It is a review of China's past, as well as an analysis of its present situation and future prospects, and how those prospects will influence U.S. interests in East Asia. To cover all that in such a brief study made it necessary to neglect a great deal. Nevertheless, the work is the product of an honest and sincere effort to contribute to an important dialogue on U.S. foreign policy. Its shortcomings are the consequence of my own inadequacies and the limitations of time and space.

The Pinyin system has been used for the transliteration of Chinese names throughout—except in those cases where the Wade-Giles transliteration has become so familiar that to provide an alternative would be pedantic. On the first mention of a name, the Wade-Giles transliteration is given in parentheses in order to facilitate recognition. In the Notes and Bibliography, the transliteration used in the original publication is retained for ease of reference.

It became clear to me while preparing the final version of this manuscript for publication that the work is in large part the product of the direct and indirect assistance of innumerable colleagues, most significantly Dr. Ramon Myers and Professors Thomas Metzger, Chalmers Johnson, and Jan Prybyla. Much of the book was written with the work of honest critics such as Dr. Harry Harding in mind.

In addition to these scholars, a number of institutions have provided valuable support and assistance: the Institute of International Studies at the University of California, Berkeley; the Hoover Institution on War, Revolution and Peace at Stanford University; and the Pacific Cultural Foundation. All sustained the work in important ways.

Finally, Professor Maria Hsia Chang provided the encouragement, affection, and understanding that made the work possible.

1

The Land
and the People

China, as a historic, political, and cultural entity, has long captivated the imagination of Westerners. During the sixteenth and seventeenth centuries, Jesuit missionaries brought back tales from the "mysterious East" that convinced Europeans that China's political and social order was a model to be emulated. The philosophers of the Enlightenment, from Leibnitz to Voltaire, saw special virtues in the thought and social practices of the Chinese. The system of examination that preceded entry into the ranks of China's bureaucracy, for example, was idealized by Enlightenment thinkers as the very epitome of the rule of right reason. Voltaire, otherwise cynical, was lyrical about the virtues of China. The religion of China, in his judgment, was "simple, wise, august, free from all superstition and all barbarity." The vast and populous empire was governed benignly like an extended family; the monarch was the father and the "legislative tribunals the elder brothers." China, for Voltaire, was a very special place. It had "subsisted in splendor" before the ancient Chaldeans' first efforts at social organization, when the Greeks were still illiterate savages.[1]

By the second half of the eighteenth century, however, Enlightenment critics—the revolutionaries, the conventional Christians, and the romantics—had set out to discredit the Chinese model. Reports of political despotism, widespread infanticide, and pandemic corruption had begun to filter into Europe as a consequence of increased systematic contact with China. As a consequence, the insistence by Chinese officials that Westerners acknowledge Chinese superiority was increasingly perceived as unmitigated arrogance.[2]

As late as the early nineteenth century, an imperial edict characterized foreigners as "depraved by the education and customs of countries beyond the bounds of civilization . . . and incapable of following right reason"[3]—a judgment hardly calculated to inspire goodwill among Europeans. So convinced was the emperor of China of his nation's importance that he thought the "barbarians" from the West could not survive a single day without China's products. He believed, for example, that he could threaten the very survival of Britain by imposing an embargo on what were then China's principal exports—tea and rhubarb—should the British fail to comport themselves properly.[4]

The predictable result of all this was mounting tension between the Westerners and the Chinese; Westerners were increasingly disposed to dismiss the Chinese as "backward" and China as a "retrograde nation." The Chinese, whom Voltaire in the early eighteenth century had described as "particularly superior to all the nations of the universe," were increasingly dismissed as "Chinamen."

Westerners have always tended to exaggerate both China's virtues and China's vices. They have perceived China as being either larger than life, or as suffering from deficiencies of epic proportions. Seemingly, everything about China is subject to exaggeration—its vast size and population, its commanding mountains and highlands, its history, which disappears into a legendary past more remote than anything with which Westerners are familiar, and its culture, which has endured with a continuity that is almost unfathomable to Europeans. But until recently, China remained shrouded in obscurity. In the United States, for example, in the mid-nineteenth century only sixteen works on China, Japan, and Korea had been published.[5]

Only since the late 1970s have Westerners begun to systematically collect information about the contemporary history of China, and whatever information they have is subject to reservation. The very immensity and complexity of China make information shortfall all but inevitable and contributes to the varied assessments of China, including its intentions and its significance for the West. The contemporary history of China has inspired so much enthusiasm and provoked so much bias that almost everything said must be discounted in some measure. Western visitors to China in the 1960s and 1970s, for example, delivered themselves of a veritable torrent of manifestly uncritical and reverential assessments of China's revolutionary accomplishments.[6] Since 1980, however, Western sinologists have tended to be severely critical.

THE GEOGRAPHY OF CHINA

China is a geographic unity of impressive size and oppressive population density.[7] Its legendary past began with the rule of the Yellow Emperor about two and a half millennia before the beginning of the Christian Era. The organized community we recognize as China extends from the central navigational channel of the Heilongjiang (Heilungkiang) in the north (53° north latitude) to the barren islets, reefs, and cays of the South China Sea in the south (4° north latitude), and from the Pamirs in the west (73° east longitude) to the Soviet border in the northeast (135° east longitude). China's land area is about 9.6 million square kilometers, making it the world's third largest nation (after the Soviet Union and Canada). China is 3 times the size of India, 18 times the size of France, and 26 times larger than Japan.

China's land boundary extends about 30,000 kilometers. China's neighbors are Korea in the east; the Soviet Union in the northeast, north, and northwest; the People's Republic of Mongolia in the north; Afghanistan, Pakistan, India, Nepal, Sikkim, and Bhutan in the west and south; and Burma, Laos, and the Socialist Republic of Vietnam in the southeast. Continental China is bordered on the east by the Gulf of Bohai, the Yellow Sea, and the East China Sea, and, on the southeast, by the South China Sea. China's coastline is approximately 18,000 kilometers long. About 5,000 islands are scattered throughout its offshore territorial waters.

China is the largest nation in the temperate zone; Beijing (Peking) has approximately the same latitude as New York and Canton has the same latitude as Mazatlán, Mexico. Because of China's location in the temperate zone, all of its land is theoretically suitable for agriculture. Unfortunately, although few regions of China are too cold for agriculture, much of its land surface is too high and much of its land is too dry for cost-effective exploitation. Mountains cover about two-thirds of China's land mass, and the Tibetan Highlands in the west constitute the highest and largest plateau on earth; they cover an area of about 2.2 million square kilometers and their average altitude is about 4,000 meters above sea level. Half of China's land surface rises about 2,000 meters above sea level.

The climate of China is largely determined by the movement of seasonal air currents. During the winter months, a massive movement of air from the northwest brings dry, cold monsoons into China. During the summer months, moist, warm winds from the southeast bring precipitation to the coastal plains of southeast, east, and northeast China.

Precipitation, which is almost nonexistent in the winter months, varies with the region. The southeast has the heaviest average annual precipitation (about 80 inches per annum); northwestern China, Inner Mongolia, and Xinjiang (Sinkiang) have no more than 10 inches of rain per year (sheltered as they are from the winds of the southeast by formidable mountain ranges). As a consequence, large areas in the northwest and the west are too high and too dry for extensive farming, and nondesert portions are generally used for pasturage. Thus, although China's land area exceeds that of the United States, the United States has four times the amount of prime agricultural land.

Given the geomorphology and climatic conditions, only 11 percent of China's total land area can be cultivated. The land that is cultivated is intensively farmed, with multiple cropping the norm in the regions along the eastern seaboard and in the river valleys and lowlands of the east and southeast—the Northeast China Plain, the North China Plain, the middle-lower Changjiang (Yangtze) Plain, and the Zhujiang (Pearl River) Delta—which are the regions most favored for agricultural production. The fertile plain located on both sides of the middle and lower reaches of the Changjiang is one of the major crop-producing areas of China.

In the southeast there is double or triple cropping of paddy rice. In the wheat-growing areas, such crops as corn, millet, oats, sorghum, and tubers are sown after the wheat harvest. The late-harvested grains comprise one-third of China's annual grain yield; the three annual rice harvests yield slightly less than half the country's total grain production. About 70 percent of China's effective labor force is employed in agriculture. As a result, China's population is concentrated in the cropping regions; 90 percent of the Chinese are resident on 15 percent of the land: the eastern and northwestern plains and the riverine systems of the major waterways.

According to the best estimates, China has abundant subsoil metal, nonmetal, and fossil fuel resources, and ample hydroelectric potential. Like almost everything else about China, estimates of its nonagricultural resources have varied dramatically over the years, and their extent remains a matter of dispute. At the turn of the century, the revolutionary Chinese nationalist Sun Yat-sen insisted that China was abundantly endowed with resources.[8] In the interwar years, foreign estimates of China's resource potential were far more conservative; their implication was that its endowments would not permit the Chinese anything more than a modest subsistence.[9] After the communist revolution, assessments became far more optimistic, and as late as 1976 China was said to be an "emerging world power" whose resource advantages would enable it to be a "leading, perhaps dominating, power in East Asia," capable of challenging the position held by Japan.[10] On the basis of reassessments made since the late 1970s, a reasonably accurate estimate of China's resource potential can be made.

China's reserves of most metal and nonmetal raw materials are apparently substantial. It has the world's largest reserve of antimony and tungsten and the world's second largest reserve of tin. It produces about 24 percent of the estimated world output of antimony, 30 percent of the world output of tungsten, and a large proportion of the world output of iron ore, molybdenum, mercury, and bismuth. It has substantial proven reserves of nonmetal resources, including magnesite, asbestos, fluorspar, graphite, and salt. Its reserves of metal and nonmetal natural resources compare favorably with those of the United States and the Soviet Union. Although estimates made since the late 1970s have been somewhat speculative, it is reasonably certain that China is endowed with a broad resource base capable of supporting industrialization. Improvements in the technology of extraction and the articulation of a suitable transport infrastructure should enhance its ability to exploit its potential.

China's fossil fuel resources are apparently plentiful. Estimates of both potential and recoverable reserves vary widely. China has been ranked both first and third in the world in terms of coal reserves, for example. Total coal reserves are estimated to be 1,500 billion tons— roughly comparable to those of the United States or the Soviet Union.[11] In 1981 China produced about 600 million metric tons of coal, making it the world's third largest producer of that resource.

The interwar estimates of China's potential oil production were significantly revised during the 1950s and 1960s, when a number of major oil-bearing geological structures were identified in Xinjiang, Shanxi (Shensi), Heilongjiang, and Sichuan (Szechwan). Moreover, substantial oil reserves were reported during the 1970s. Estimates of between 1.7 billion and 2.0 billion tons of total onshore natural petroleum reserves have been advanced, and it is speculated that anywhere from 4 billion to 20 billion tons of recoverable petroleum is to be found on the continental shelf.[12] In 1980 China produced about 106 million metric tons of crude oil.

The availability of natural gas and the potential for hydroelectric power generation supplement China's energy resources. China is the fifth largest natural gas producer in the world, with an output of about 1 million barrels per day oil equivalent and 100–150 billion cubic meters in reserves. China's hydroelectric power potential is estimated to be 14.5

percent of the world's total—the Changjiang River alone carries about 240 cubic miles of water to the sea annually. China's hydroelectric power potential translates into an estimated 536 megawatts of electrical energy.[13]

In absolute terms, China seems amply endowed with the raw material resources necessary for substantial, self-sustained economic growth. In relative terms, however, given its vast population, China is resource poor. In 1979 Hua Guofeng (Hua Kuo-feng) remarked that the "main problem" facing China was to maintain a rate of expansion of agricultural productivity that would enable the nation to meet the demands of its growing population. He added that "although the coal, petroleum, and power industries . . . have grown at a relatively swift pace, they still lag behind what is required."[14]

The Chinese constitute about 23 percent of the world's population, and China produces about 21 percent of the world's food grains. This suggests that China is just managing to keep its rate of increase of agricultural productivity constant with its rate of population growth. Since the late 1970s, the authorities in Beijing have concentrated on increasing grain production rather than the production of noncereal crops in an effort to satisfy the basic food needs of China's growing population. Nonetheless, the fact that China has been compelled to import grains is indicative of the population pressure with which China's leadership must contend.[15]

There is convincing evidence that the absolute increase in agricultural yield that has been recorded in China since 1949 has been accomplished without any increase in total factor productivity—it has been achieved almost exclusively through an increase in total labor input. Per capita labor productivity, however, has not increased. The trend has been to mobilize labor resources in order to accelerate the rate of increase of agricultural production.[16] As mentioned, the rate of agricultural productivity has, by and large, been constant with the rate of population growth. Nevertheless, the reports concerning household income and food availability in the Chinese countryside suggest that living conditions in the mid-1980s are comparable to those prevailing in China during the 1920s and 1930s, when 60 percent of family income was disbursed for food alone.[17]

The same picture emerges with respect to China's remaining resources. In 1978 the United States government's official estimate of China's petroleum reserves was 100 billion barrels (roughly 14 billion tons). Even granting that this is a relatively generous estimate, that amount would average out to 100 barrels of crude petroleum per capita for China's population in the mid-1980s.[18] Given even a relatively modest rate of industrial growth, China will need all its petroleum resources to satisfy its domestic needs—and will probably be a net importer of petroleum in the 1990s.[19] Similarly, if one considers the demands that would be made on the available subsoil resources should the Chinese make any effort to approximate the living standards of the Japanese by the year 2000 (which at one time was the professed goal of China's modernization drive), it becomes evident that those resources are totally inadequate.

It is estimated, for example, that the Japanese have used about 7 tons of steel per capita in constructing the buildings and transportation system of their economy in order to sustain their standard of living. China, with its thin transportation infrastructure and its relatively small industrial base, has utilized perhaps as little as one-tenth that amount of steel per capita. Should China attempt to approximate the level of Japanese development, its 1980 annual steel production of 30 to 35 million tons would have to be increased prodigiously. Since China produced in 1980 no more than about 25 percent of the steel produced in Japan, achieving Japan's level of production would be extremely difficult and would result in a rapid depletion of its domestic resources.

The constraints within which the Chinese must operate are revealed even more dramatically by a comparison of the two nations' installed electrical power generation capacities. At the end of the 1970s, Japan had a total installed generating capacity of 108,000 megawatts of electricity. Given its population of about 114 million, Japan had a capacity of about 950 megawatts per million inhabitants. China, at that time, had a total installed generating capacity of about 50,000 megawatts. Given its population of about 1 billion, China could provide about 50 megawatts per million inhabitants. Should China attempt to approximate the per capita electricity consumption of Japan by the year 2000, its power generating system would have to produce about ten times the amount it is capable of generating in the mid-1980s. To achieve the output required, each year China would have to increase its generating capacity by an amount slightly less than its present total productive capability.

These circumstances explain why commentators have described China's resource base as inadequate to the task of comprehensive modernization. In per capita terms China is not resource rich; it ranks below almost all of the world's second-ranking powers with respect to raw-material availability. For example, if China consumed petroleum at a rate equivalent to the per capita consumption rate of Japan in the mid-1980s, its known reserves would last less than six years.[20]

In order to exploit its available resources effectively, China requires vast investments of capital. Agricultural yield can be increased (Japan's rice yield per hectare is about twice that of China), but only with massive investments in skill acquisition, farm implements, fertilizers, herbicides, and insecticides; water conservancy, irrigation, and cultivation of marginal lands; as well as exploitation of subsoil resources and identification and extraction of supplementary recoverable supplies. All of this will be required to do little more than to meet the needs of China's growing population. One of China's most fundamental problems is the size of its population.

THE POPULATION OF CHINA

There is suggestive (if disputed) evidence that China has always had a relatively high population density.[21] For whatever reason—the people's attachment to the soil, conservative family patterns, restrictive property relations, or labor-intensive economic pursuits—China's governing elite has always had access to vast amounts of locally resident manpower for the construction of public works. Early in the Shang dynasty (circa 1700 B.C.), thousands of Chinese labored to fabricate a city wall of stamped earth, about 6 kilometers in circumference and 9 meters high. Three thousand years later the walls of Nanjing (Nanking) and Beijing were still being built of stamped earth. During the Ming dynasty (circa 1368–1644 A.D.), hundreds of thousands of Chinese massed to construct walls that were 12 meters high and 32 kilometers long. The Great Wall and the Grand Canal were the consequence of the efforts of a mass of conscripted labor. China is the longest continuous civilization that has been able to employ massed manpower for such purposes.

At about the time of the birth of Christ, the population of China was estimated to have been 60 million persons. In the ninth century, toward the end of the Tang dynasty, there were an estimated 80 million Chinese; in the twelfth century, during the reign of the Song (Sung) dynasty, the population increased to 110 million. By the sixteenth century (late Ming period), there were 150 million Chinese. In the nineteenth century, China's population was estimated to have been over 300 million—and it almost doubled in the next century. Between 1949, when the communist government assumed power, and 1985, the population has doubled once again; in 1981 the population of China was estimated to be more than 1.1 billion persons—with an expected annual increment of about 15 to 18 million.

The pressure of China's population on the limited amount of arable land has been, and is, very great. In the mid-1980s, sown land averages out to about 0.4 acres per capita, and there is little additional land that is potentially suitable for farming. Most of the noncultivated portion (89 percent) of China's land area consists of mountains, desert, grassland, and urban conglomerations. A major land reclamation effort could, at great expense, add only approximately 1.5 percent more acreage to the cultivated land.

China has improved its agricultural land by carefully regulating the use of water, meticulously maintaining drainage and irrigation canals, and systematically supplying the soil with nutrients in the form of natural fertilizers (animal and human excreta, green manure, mud from rivers and ponds, and animal and plant refuse). The collection, transportation, and distribution of these fertilizers (annually amounting to 6 to 7 metric tons per acre) has traditionally required a significant amount of rural manpower—perhaps as much as half the man-days available. Because of the fragility of the system, the dependence upon the availability of water, and the lack of political stability that would make massive employment of manpower possible, China has periodically suffered the effects of catastrophic declines in agricultural productivity. During the 2,162 years that observations have been recorded, China has endured 1,031 years of floods and 1,060 years of drought. Political unrest has further limited the ability of China's agriculture to satisfy the most fundamental needs of the population.

Part of China's present agricultural problem is attributable to the disposition of its rulers to increase the amount of land cultivated as the population expanded. It has been estimated that in the course of this agricultural expansion, 670 million acres of China's forests were cut down. The rimlands and lowlands are now almost entirely devoid of trees. Because there is nothing to bind the earth, millions of tons of topsoil have been swept down the great rivers of China, thus raising the riverbeds and causing floods.

More important has been the reluctance or inability of China's rulers to limit population growth. In the past, the only constraints on the reproductive capacity of the Chinese were disease, famine, and war.

During the millennial use of China's agricultural land, parasites have gradually accumulated and now permeate the soil. Disease has also been spread by the extensive use of human and animal waste. As a consequence, China's population has long been afflicted with intestinal parasites. The eggs of parasites have been carried in swirls of dust and are found in the waters that surround the peasants' habitations. It is estimated that liver parasites are responsible for the debility currently suffered by more than 20 percent of the population. As recently as 1960, 90 million cases of tapeworm were reported, but perhaps 90 percent of the rural population was so infected. In the same year, 30 percent of all deaths were reported to be attributable to these parasites (4 million annually); parasites have caused twice as many deaths per year as have China's wars during the twentieth century.

Historically, the ultimate constraint on population growth in China has been famine, which, as recently as 1958–1961, claimed the lives of perhaps as many as 20 to 30 million Chinese. In 1981, the authorities in Beijing acknowledged the existence of widespread hunger in the North China Plain and requested international aid. In 1980 a multitude of peasants from Hebei (Hobeh) Province descended upon the urban centers of that region to beg and to scavenge. China has been able to provide food for its population only by importing from 4 to 6 million tons of grain annually from the grain-exporting countries of the West.

War has also curtailed the growth of the Chinese population. Every dynasty in the long history of China was founded by the sword. Under strong governments—the Han, the Tang, the early Ming and the early Qing (Ch'ing) dynasties—military expeditions consisting of millions of Chinese ventured into Vietnam or Korea, or across the mountainous areas and plateaus of Central Asia. In some decades, an endless succession of rebel hordes and alien armies left unnumbered dead strewn across China. As recently as the war in Korea, the "human wave" assault tactics of the Chinese armies proved to be costly in terms of battle casualties.

However, despite disease, famine, and war, since 1900 the Chinese population has grown prodigiously. With the advent of nationalism, in fact, China's leaders strongly encouraged procreation. Sun Yat-sen, the "Father of the Chinese Revolution" of 1911, was convinced that China faced racial extinction at the hands of foreign imperialists and advocated sustained population growth. The communist leadership did little to change that policy.

Classical Marxists had always maintained that Malthusian admonitions concerning the dangers of unrestricted population growth were part of a capitalist plot against humanity, or simply necessary because of capitalist mismanagement. Both Karl Marx and Friedrich Engels had insisted that "the productive power at the disposal of mankind is immeasurable. The productivity of land can be infinitely increased by the application of capital, labor and science."[22] They argued that a "large family" was therefore a "desirable gift to the community." Engels confidently asserted that "we are forever secure from the fear of over-population."[23]

As a consequence of their commitment to Marxist orthodoxy, the communist rulers of China chose not to impose any restrictions with regard to reproduction. For two decades after their accession to power in

1949, over 20 million births were recorded annually—an increment approximately equal to the entire population of East Germany or California. In 1952, *People's Daily* denounced birth control measures as a means "of slaughtering the Chinese people without drawing blood"—and as recently as 1960, one observer concluded that "there is . . . no incentive to limit families [in China] as a necessity. . . . With a higher standard of living, and since a large family is an inconvenience, the majority of China's people may demand family planning as a convenience, but at present this is still a minority."[24]

Mao Zedong (Mao Tse-tung) seems to have been convinced well into the 1950s that birth control was unnecessary for the Chinese, for each new stomach came "with two hands attached." Nonetheless, it soon became evident that constraints would have to be introduced, and China's leaders instituted draconian measures. As a consequence, since the early 1970s there has been a continuous decline in the nation's birth rate; the goal is to reduce that rate from 2.3 percent per annum (1971) to 1 percent in the late 1980s. At the present (mid-1980s) rate of approximately 1.2 percent real growth per annum, it will take China almost 60 years to double its population.

The present leadership uses public meetings to arouse sentiment in favor of restricting births. If suasion proves insufficient, economic sanctions are imposed. Couples producing more than their quota of children are punished. The names of "excess" children are not immediately entered into the official household register, and during the time such children are not so registered, they are ineligible for rice, cloth, or other rations. The parents must satisfy the new children's needs, usually at disabling expense, by purchasing items in the black market. If the officials become aware of a pregnancy that will result in an "over-quota" child, a deduction is made from the prospective parents' wages, beginning with the second trimester of the pregnancy, to induce the woman to submit to "voluntary" abortion. As a final recourse, if the woman insists on carrying the excess child to term, she is dismissed from her work unit. Because Chinese families must manage with limited incomes, unemployment is, for most, intolerable. As a consequence of peer pressure, public admonition, and economic sanction, millions of prospective mothers in China submit to abortions. Monetary rewards are given those women who opt for tubal ligation, and everyone is expected to delay marriage and space their two "allotted" children appropriately.

Westerners are cognizant of the magnitude of China's problem. "The problem," they are prepared to grant, "is simply this: too many people relative to land (especially farmland) and capital."[25] Nonetheless, many remain "puzzled by the absence of opposition" to the methods employed by authorities to reduce the rate of population growth. There are no "fiery confrontations" in which the Chinese insist that "women be free to make individual decisions on abortion privately and without pressure," and that individuals be allowed to choose the time and circumstances of their marriage, as well as to make decisions with regard to family planning.[26]

But if Westerners are puzzled by such passivity in response to government policies concerning birth control, they should be equally mystified by similar behavior in other instances of extensive governmental interference in the private lives of citizens. Such interventions have been commonplace during the three decades of communist rule in China.

When the forces of Mao Zedong acceded to power in 1949, more than a decade of civil war and foreign invasion had resulted in large-scale devastation and a weakening of the Chinese economy. About 40 percent of the arable soil lay untilled. Consequently, it was necessary to rehabilitate vast tracts of land. The restorative programs also included reforestation of millions of acres of China's rural landscape and impressive water conservancy and irrigation projects. These efforts required the mobilization and spatial redistribution of millions of Chinese laborers. Since little material incentive could be offered them, and since the economic system lacked free-market mechanisms, the government was compelled to use normative appeal and simple coercion to achieve the regional allocation of labor. (The administrative transfer of labor has been used systematically over the years as the primary means of achieving objectives determined by the central government.)

Millions of peasants and urban dwellers were marshaled to plant industrial trees and shelterbelts. Under the First Five-Year Plan (1953–1957), 28.2 million acres were afforested. In 1958, under the "Great Leap Forward" movement, 69 million acres were transformed into forests. In 1959 an area almost as large as France was planted with trees in a period of about fifteen months. The long-term plan was to double the forested area of China by the year 1968. The scale of the undertaking is indicated by the plan to have 700,000 workers complete the afforestation of a thousand-mile-long shelterbelt in Northern Gansu (Kansu) in one season.

The program of irrigation and drainage of arable land to which the communist government had committed itself was equally vast. By 1957, at the end of the First Five-Year Plan, China had increased its irrigated acreage from about 21 million hectares to nearly 35 million hectares, and thus had surpassed the prewar level of available irrigated acreage. After 1958, labor-intensive methods were utilized on an even larger scale in the effort to irrigate all of China's available acreage. The government reported that the total irrigated acreage increased from 35 million hectares to 67 million hectares between 1957 and 1958. However exaggerated the official claims might have been, the enterprise was a dramatic example of what could be accomplished by essentially compulsory effort.

What is now reasonably clear is that as a result of faulty plantings and inadequate maintenance by masses of workers largely untrained in even the most rudimentary silvicultural procedures, those efforts were largely unproductive.[27] In many areas where afforestation was attempted, the survival rate of young trees proved to be as low as 10 percent. The attempt to increase the amount of irrigated farmland was also unsuccessful. Ten years after the program was begun, the amount of irrigated land had not been significantly increased.

The construction methods employed in the irrigation projects did not control the flow of water as required. Many of the rivers in the most intensively worked areas carried a great deal of silt. Such sediment clogged irrigation conduits almost immediately upon their completion, thus rendering them useless. As a consequence, much of the new irrigated land eventually returned to its original condition.[28]

The social and economic costs of the redistribution of laborers were disheartening. Redistribution often necessitated separation of families for extended periods, the transfer of urban dwellers to rural areas, and the relocation of peasant labor from their home province to border regions. Redistribution interrupted not only the lives of peasants and urban workers, but those of teachers, students, medical and health personnel, and industrial workers as well.[29] During the Great Proletarian Cultural Revolution (1966–1969), millions of urban youths were "transferred down" (*xia xiang*) to rural communes, state farms, and provincial enterprises. This almost always involved the disruption of education or the interruption of a career, separation from the nuclear family, and transportation to a totally unfamiliar and often threatening environment.

The government of Communist China worked "miracles" in the mobilization and site transfer of millions of workers. There is no evidence that its demands for sacrifice met with organized resistance, even when those programs were incompetently planned, indifferently executed, and to very little purpose. In part, this is because in China the masses have traditionally had certain expectations concerning the political system and made certain assumptions about the prerogatives of the ruling elite as well as their own obligations to that elite. In effect, the political culture of dynastic China included the imposition of a pattern of appropriate behaviors calculated to render the masses manageable. However much the "new China" differed from the old, it seems reasonably certain that the new leaders of China exploited the obedient behavior of their subjects.

THE POLITICAL CULTURE OF DYNASTIC CHINA

In terms of the continuity of its culture and its political institutions, China is unique. Two centuries before the beginning of the Christian Era, China's basic political institutions had already been established. Those institutions, and their underlying philosophy, would remain essentially unchanged for the next two millennia. By 221 B.C., Qin Shi Huang (Ch'in Shih Huang) had founded a multinational empire, governed by a bureaucratized and centralized authoritarian elite. Thereafter, virtually all rulers of China would utilize similar institutions and appeal to a similar rationale.

Having defeated his regional competitors in the attainment of impe-rial power, Qin Shi Huang proceeded to create a two-tiered system of control. By making appointments at the prefectural and county levels, he ensured his dominance of the system. He then standardized weights and measures, devised a common calendar, introduced a uniform currency, and initiated the instruction of a unitary Chinese script. In order to minimize dissidence and reduce the threat of local resistance, he pro-scribed the existence of "contending schools." Education (including ideological instruction) was to be controlled by the central government, and private libraries and nonauthorized texts were to be destroyed by fire. If scholars ignored the constraints specified in royal decrees, they were executed. In the most famous instance of suppression, 460 scholars were buried alive for "glorifying the past to oppose the present." In the judgment of the ministers of Qin, "All matters under heaven, important or unimportant, are to be decided by the sovereign."[30]

Qin Shih Huang initiated massive public projects that included con-struction of the Great Wall of China and of a system of roads that connected the major regions of the empire. Countless laborers were conscripted to build that road system, and 300,000 Chinese were mobi-lized to work on the defensive wall. In addition, 500,000 were dispatched to garrison fortifications in the South and 700,000 were employed in the construction of imperial palaces. More than 0.5 million, serving as corvée labor, worked on the construction of Qin Shih Huang's mausoleum.[31]

Thus long before the modern era, the ruling elites of China mobilized corvée labor on a large scale to perform monumental tasks. Such an undertaking required a general submissiveness and passive obedience. Such compliance could be obtained through coercion and (or) moral suasion. China's leaders have employed both in varying measure throughout the nation's long history. The earliest history of China is the story of the gradual occupation of arable land by countless generations of agricultural families whose settlements spread outward from a core region in the valley of the Huanghe River. The villages that would become part of China were apparently already thickly populated in the Neolithic period. These early inhabitants, who worked the easily tilled loess, were remarkably sophisticated; domesticated dogs, pigs, sheep, and cattle were common throughout the region. By 1500 B.C., a Bronze Age civilization flourished in the Huanghe region. Gradually hundreds of small city-states developed, each ruled by a warrior hegemon. Each city-state initially occupied a defensible position at a river basin or alongside a marshy area; only gradually did the Chinese elite begin the process of building a unified and centralized state. With increasing regularity, large bodies of forced labor were committed to elaborate irrigation and terracing projects. As these efforts became more systematic, intensive, and extensive, the city-states merged through conquest or amalgamation. The more extensive projects required managerial control, complex organizational planning, engineering skills, and systematic integration. As early as the western and eastern Zhou (Chou) dynasties (circa 1100 B.C. until the advent of the Qin), the semiarid conditions and topography of the territorial domains, the summer inundations, the attendant silting of rivers made "hydraulic agriculture" (the extensive use of flood control, drainage, and irrigation) a necessity.[32] Hydraulic agriculture requires organized cooperation, a large population base, and centralized control of localities strung out on a river system.

Maintenance of such a system also required complex population control mechanisms. One of the most effective means of population management would be provided by evolving Chinese political thought. During the reign of the Zhou dynasty, when China was becoming unified in the Spring and Autumn period (770–476 B.C.) and the Warring States period (475–221 B.C.) (that is, before the unification of China under the Qin), the major schools of Chinese political thought—Confucian, Daoist (Taoist), Mohist, and Legalist—began to develop. Both Confucius and Laozi (Lao Tzu) were probably contemporaries in the sixth century B.C., and Mozi (Motze) was born a few decades later. Mengzi (Mencius) was born at about the beginning of the fourth century B.C.; Han Fei was born a century later (circa 280 B.C.).

With the exception of the quasi-anarchism of the Daoists, almost all the political thought of this period was concerned with the principles of statecraft. Much of the literature that antedated the golden period of early Chinese intellectual development included, or was later interpreted as including, an assessment of the nature of the state and its relationship to society. The *Book of Changes,* parts of which date back as far as three millennia before Christ, was devoted to, or has been understood to be devoted to, the nature and origins of the state.

In the commentaries that are now appended to the *Book of Changes* (and attributed to Confucius), the origin of society and the state are said to be revealed in nature. Because society and the state originate in nature, they are considered perfectly natural. In the *Book of Changes* there is no suggestion that society or the state are contrivances, the result of a contract among self-sufficient individuals. Society and the state "followed the rule of all under heaven," and that rule was exemplified in patterns of compliance, commencing with the relationship of submissiveness and obedience of wife to husband, of filial piety of son to father, of loyalty of minister to ruler—all in "arrangements of propriety and righteousness."[33]

For the Confucians, the relationships within the family were paradigmatic of those in society.[34] For Confucius, the proper governance of the state is anticipated in familial relationships, for where there is filial piety, there the sovereign will be served, and where there is "fraternal submission," there will elders and superiors find obedience.[35] The admonition to foster and maintain hierarchical proprieties appears throughout the Confucian "Analects," which inform us that "filial piety and fraternal submission" are the basis of all laudable actions.[36] The righteous man exerts his "utmost strength" in serving his parents and "devotes his life" to the service of his ruler.[37]

The Confucians believed that the ideal state was one in which all segments of the population have found their proper places, the just ruler rules, and the "relation between superiors and inferiors is like that between the wind and the grass. The grass must bend when the wind blows across it."[38] Where good government prevails, authority resides with the ruler; the people remain content in their several places, and "there will be no discussions among the common people."[39]

Neglecting, for the sake of exposition, all the subtleties of Confucian ethics, it seems evident that a basic principle of Confucian thought is the maintenance of hierarchically ordered social control. For Mengzi, perhaps the most renowned follower of Confucius, "great men" had their "proper business," just as "little men" had theirs. "Those who labor with their minds," he maintained, "govern others; those who labor with their strength are governed by others. . . . This is a principle universally recognized."[40]

Mengzi, like Confucius, asserted that the ruler ruled because he possessed paradigmatic virtue—and the ideal rule was a rule of benevolence and humanity. But rule was hierarchical, and one of the principal responsibilities of the ruler was to inculcate in his subjects a regard for fraternal and filial duties in order to ensure the integrity of the state.[41] Only in a well-ordered state could the individual achieve fulfillment as a moral agent. In effect, the Confucian ideal state is a reflection of a bureaucratized and centralized "hydraulic" society in which subjects discharge their obligations without resistance. In a society whose survival is contingent upon the maintenance of complex irrigation canals and other water control structures, an intricate system of constraints is necessary to ensure the compliance of massed labor. Ideally, such compliance is the consequence of internalized norms and the dictates of felt obligation; members of society are bound by common interests.

It seems clear that the political philosophy of the early Confucians included principles of statecraft that sustained a populous, hydroagricultural society, with its vast public works, its centralized, bureaucratic controls, and its dependence on an obedient and responsible population. The early Confucians believed that such a society was sustained by a political order that was guided by the elite's virtuous and paternalistic concern with the masses.[42] There was a conviction that in one sense or another, the ultimate interests of each individual were essentially identical to, or at least compatible with, those of his fellowmen of whatever rank. In general, Confucians maintained that in striving to "establish himself," the individual, whatever his station, invariably "established others."[43]

To these ancient Chinese philosophers, man was by nature a creature destined to live in association—governed by rules of appropriate conduct that included obedience, fidelity, and selflessness. Compliance was the result of careful inculcation and systematic education. Effortless conformity and obedience, frugality, and labor were by-products of this effort to instill functional virtues in a citizenry on whom history and circumstances had imposed demanding social obligations.

Throughout the history of dynastic China, these themes common to the schools of ancient Chinese philosophy influenced the rationale of governance, public instruction, and the examination system. In periods of more emphatic autocracy, simple obedience, respect, and service of the subjects were emphasized. In periods when power was less centralized, the benevolence and paternalism of the established elite were emphasized. But in almost all instances there was an insistence upon deference, labor, frugality, conformity, and sense of responsibility to others.

Central to these themes was a conception of man as part of a network of reciprocal obligations—a heterocentric creature who was naturally and inextricably a member of a historic community possessed of an organic unity—rather than an egocentric individual originally found in a "state of nature." Outside that community, the individual would be a shadow of a moral agent, incapable of survival much less of fulfillment.[44]

Membership in such a community required assumption of multiple responsibilities, ranging from filial and fraternal responsibilities to responsibilities to the leadership of the larger community. In discharging them, the individual evinced propriety, obedience, diffidence, and conformity to prevailing social and cultural norms. In such a system, the model individuals were the obedient child, the faithful sibling, the responsible head of household, and the law-abiding and responsible subject. The model individual endured privation, assumed responsibilities without demur, and sacrificed stoically. Minimally such an individual was eminently adaptable to the demands of a vast, centralized, and bureaucratized hydraulic civilization.

The traditional political culture of China thus contributed to the ruler's ability to control his subjects in circumstances that required management of vast territories, comprehensive planning, and the massive deployment of conscript labor.[45] As long as such circumstances prevailed, the functional necessity for the induced compliance of the populace would remain. The necessity for such behavior has existed so continuously throughout China's history that the political ideas that originated long before the beginning of the Christian Era have persisted into the twentieth century. Thus, the reformers of the last of China's dynasties and the first rulers of the first dynasties have invoked the same ideas, and those ideas found similar expression in the revolutionary statements of both Sun Yat-sen and Chiang Kai-shek.[46] Even the iconoclastic ideology of Mao Zedong, so emphatic in its Marxism-Leninism, retains much of the substance of traditional Chinese political ideas. Why this should have been so is not difficult to understand.

Modern China has retained some of the most prominent features of the hydraulic society of the past. About 70 percent of its labor force is still bound by obligations imposed by the need to cultivate the "soil and grain" of China. The same dikes, levees, and dams control today, as they did in the past, the threatening waters of the mountains and plains. Irrigation remains essential to the agriculture of China, and it is agriculture (specifically, hydraulic agriculture) upon which the survival of the masses depends. Conscript labor still affords the reserves of energy that renders the nation capable of survival. Millions of bureaucrats administer a productive community; an exiguous elite devises integrative plans and imposes onerous tasks—and requires compliance in their execution. Today's communist leadership argues that Qin Shi Huang's use of conscript labor, at a frightful human cost, for the construction of massive walls, ceremonial monuments, and a communications infrastructure was "progressive and in the people's interests."[47]

Today's China

What might be called the "modal character" of the Chinese has been influenced by a millennial political culture—the "peculiarly persistent qualities of the traditional Chinese social and political order."[48] The central values of Chinese political behavior have always been loyalty, reliability, conformity, compliance, and steadfastness under privation and in the discharge of obligations. The Chinese have also stressed bureaucratic hierarchy and have recognized the central role of elites in shaping a society, determining its purposes, and defining collective obligations.

The evolution of this "national political personality" has taken place in a vast geographic area over a period that humbles the Western sense of history. Beginning in the nineteenth century, imperial China attempted to adapt the national character to the demands of the modern world. The intrusion of the industrially advanced Western powers tested the survival capacities of dynastic China. Between 1839 and 1842, Britain and imperial China fought the First Opium War, at the conclusion of which a humiliated China was made subject to the first of the "unequal treaties." The Second Opium War (1856–1860) opened the coast of China to foreign contact, and the imperialist powers exacted more sacrifices from the prostrate nation. In the interim between the First and Second Opium Wars, the Chinese peasantry staged the Taiping Rebellion, which lasted almost fifteen years (1851–1864).

War and insurrection undermined the viability of the Central Kingdom; by the end of the nineteenth century it was clear that China could survive only if major reform or systemic revolution rendered it capable of resisting both foreign impostures and domestic upheaval. However, during the first half of the twentieth century, revolution and reform seemed to help but little. Weakened by internal strife and savaged by Japanese invasion, China survived the Second World War only to face the advent to power of the revolutionary forces led by Mao Zedong.

2

The "New China" of Mao Zedong

During the nineteenth century, China was compelled to contend with the overwhelming commercial and military influence of the industrialized powers. Great Britain had gained control of India, and British merchants invested their capital in, and devoted their energies to, the opium trade. This century saw the extension of European control over the trade and external relations of the Qing dynasty and the gradual erosion of Chinese imperial power.

In the century between the beginning of the First Opium War and the termination of the Second World War, China suffered a series of humiliating defeats. The Revolution of 1911, inspired by Sun Yat-sen, brought an end to the Manchu dynasty, but it did not result in the establishment of a Chinese republic capable of sustaining itself in the competitive environment of the early twentieth century. For almost two decades after the abolition of the dynastic system, provincial military authorities dominated domestic politics; the chaos of the "Warlord Period" rendered China too weak to exercise any international influence.

After 1928, when China was nominally reunited under a government controlled by Sun Yat-sen's revolutionary party, the Kuomintang, the nation endured one crisis after another. Party factionalism initially undermined the developmental intention and nationalist aspirations of Chiang Kai-shek (who had inherited Sun Yat-sen's mantle after Sun's death in 1925). Subsequently, revolutionary activity organized and directed by the Chinese Communist Party (CCP) and Japan's imperialist aggression threatened China's survival. By the mid-1930s, it had become clear that

Sun Yat-sen's program could not be implemented until the problems of national integration and foreign imperialism had been resolved. The protracted war against communist insurgency and the Japanese invasion exhausted the energies of the revolutionary party that had sought to realize the vision of Sun Yat-sen. At the end of the Second World War, the Chinese Communist Party, supported by the Soviet Union, undertook to defeat the Kuomintang and to create a "socialist republic."

Between 1945 and 1949 the Republic of China was torn by civil strife; the Nationalists of Chiang Kai-shek struggled against the Communists of Mao Zedong. The United States remained ambivalent, but was half disposed to assist the Nationalist government in its resistance to communist initiatives. However, there were those in Washington who considered the followers of Mao Zedong to be "progressive agrarian reformers" who sought nothing more than to rebuild China's economy and to reassert China's sovereignty in the face of Western imperialism. Washington proved incapable of resolving its indecisiveness, and ultimately the Kuomintang was left to contend with the revolutionaries led by Mao Zedong without U.S. support.

By the last half of 1949, the forces led by Mao had overwhelmed the armies of Chiang Kai-shek, and on October 1 of that year the birth of the People's Republic of China (PRC) was proclaimed. From that moment until his death on September 9, 1976, Mao Zedong was the single most important influence on his nation's development. During the quarter century prior to the establishment of the PRC, Mao had risen from the ranks of China's revolutionaries and had achieved dominance over the Chinese Communist Party. He was to become the most powerful political leader in China's recent history.[1]

MAO ZEDONG

Born in 1893, Mao Zedong was to witness the disintegration of the Qing dynasty and China's anguish over the incursions increasingly made by the industrially advanced Western powers. Japan defeated imperial China in 1895, then extended its influence into Korea and annexed Formosa—the island of Taiwan. Mao's adolescent preoccupation with his nation's future led him to familiarize himself with the reformist and revolutionary literature of his time. He admired Kang Yuwei (K'ang Yu-wei) and Liang Qichao (Liang Ch'i-ch'ao), the advocates of constitutional monarchy, as well as Sun Yat-sen, the proponent of revolutionary republicanism. The differences between them did not overly concern the young Mao. What was important was that they all were committed to the goal of national salvation—the strengthening and renovation of the Central Kingdom. Mao was concerned less with the subtlety of ideas than with the accomplishments of men of action—warriors and nation builders such as Washington and Napoleon. He had become convinced that whatever strategy might be employed to regenerate China, "great men" were required who were disposed to struggle in the service of their oppressed nation.[2]

By the time Mao Zedong reached maturity, he had already begun to articulate a program for China's salvation and regeneration. Like many of his contemporaries, Mao sought to strengthen China's ability to resist Western imperialism; to this end, he advocated the modernization of China's economy and China's social system.

To Mao, it seemed clear that the hopes of Sun Yat-sen had been dashed after 1912 by the blandishments and the corruption employed by Yuan Shikai's (Yüan Shih-k'ai's) authoritarian rule. In 1915, the Japanese attempted to impose the infamous Twenty-One Demands on China, which would have reduced the nation to a Japanese dependency. Students and workers organized to resist those demands in what came to be known as the May Fourth Movement. Ultimately, that movement expanded and became known as the New Culture Movement, which sought the redemption of China through the abandonment of all traditional constraints on modernization. In 1916, Chen Duxiu (Ch'en Tu-hsiu) and Li Dazhao (Li Ta-chao) assumed the leadership of that movement.

The Bolshevik Revolution of 1917 had a peculiar fascination for the iconoclasts of the New Culture Movement. The October Revolution in Russia had seen a poor and economically backward nation rise up against its "imperialist" tormentors. Very soon the magazine *New Youth*, the organ of the New Culture Movement, began to carry commentaries that reflected the renewed interest in Marxism expressed by Chen and Li.

Prior to the October Revolution, Chinese revolutionaries had dismissed Marxism as entirely inappropriate to the conditions that prevailed in retrograde China. The interpretation given Marxism by V. I. Lenin, however, seemed to make the ideology of interest to those who sought to modernize their nation.

Lenin spoke of revolutions in economically backward areas—the "weakest links" in the chain of imperialist domination. Whereas Karl Marx and Friedrich Engels had anticipated revolution in the industrially advanced West, Lenin foresaw resistance and revolution in the economically backward East. In July 1918, Li Dazhao counseled Chinese revolutionaries to greet the new tide of revolution that had arisen in Moscow and St. Petersburg. He conceived the Russian Revolution as the harbinger of China's salvation and the opening phase of a world revolution that would conclude with the total victory of Communism.

At almost the same time that Li's article appeared, the young Mao Zedong arrived in Beijing. At the university he obtained a position as a librarian's assistant under the supervision of Li himself. Almost immediately he began to participate in the meetings of the Marxist Study Group that Li had founded the previous spring. Under the ministrations of Li, Mao "rapidly developed towards Marxism."[3] It was a development that was to change the history of modern China.

THE IDEOLOGY OF SINICIZED MARXISM

The "Marxism" of Li Dazhao was substantially different from the Marxism of Marx and Engels, although Mao could hardly have understood that at the time of his conversion. In 1919, few works on the subject of Marxism were available in Chinese. Before that time, Mao had apparently read only the first section of the *Communist Manifesto*, a selection from Karl Kautsky's *Karl Marx's ökonomische Lehren*, and a book on the history of socialism by Thomas Kirkup. Consequently, Mao's "Marxism" bore little resemblance to classical Marxism when he joined the newly organized Chinese Communist Party in 1921. At that juncture his political ideas were a curious collection of idealist, populist, nationalist, and voluntarist notions. Whatever coherence they displayed was probably largely attributable to Li, who was perhaps the most rigorous intellectual in any of the small groups that, at that time, made up the nucleus of the CCP.

In May 1919, in a lengthy article entitled "My Marxist Views," Li clearly stated his reservations concerning classical Marxism. As a Chinese intellectual familiar with China's long traditions, Li refused to renounce his convictions concerning the importance of ethical and "spiritual" factors in the making of history.[4] Whatever else the class struggle might have been in Marxist theory, for Li it involved ethical issues. The revolutionary assessments of Marxism must, in his judgment, necessarily involve "ethical adjuncts" that found expression in the "willed activity" of participants. According to Li, the major defect of the European revolutionary parties was that they had failed to invoke, up until that time, the moral sentiments of the masses. They had not engaged the "will" of the "people"—the real agents of revolution.

For Li, class consciousness was not identified with any socioeconomic class. It was essentially a product of moral reflection, and the revolution it inspired was a function of the ability of a self-selected minority of declassed intellectuals to arouse the latent energy of the masses. As early as 1920, the expression "revolutionary vanguard," referring to the intelligentsia, appeared in Li's writings. An abiding faith in the ability of self-directed intellectuals to fashion political and social reality in accordance with their convictions and determination became an integral part of Li's Marxist world view.

For Li, nonproletarian intellectuals could serve as the vehicle for the class consciousness that both Marx and Engels thought could only be the product of a specific class under specific material conditions. Li rejected the fatalism and determinism that he found in classical Marxism. His conviction was that the consciousness requisite for revolution could be generated by declassed intellectuals and conveyed to the nonproletarian masses of China. Li held that class distinctions, so laboriously drawn by the theoreticians of classical Marxism, were of relatively little immediate consequence for China, which was a "proletarian nation"—oppressed and impoverished as a result of foreign exploitation. Like Chen Duxiu, Li maintained that China's enemy was not its "capitalist class," but foreign imperialism. Since imperialism was China's enemy, all anti-imperialist Chinese potentially constituted the "revolutionary masses."[5]

Li conceived the entire population of oppressed and exploited China as the recruitment base for the regenerative revolution that would save the nation. His elitism allowed him to assign the task of organizing and directing this "anti-imperialist" revolution to a minority of determined intellectuals.[6]

There was probably as much Confucianism in the elitism and the voluntarism of Li Dazhao as there was Marxism or Marxism-Leninism. The persuasiveness of the central theme of anti-imperialism is as attributable to the history of modern China and Chen Duxiu as to Lenin's lucubrations. But whatever their source, these notions lent coherence to the loosely structured thought of the young Mao Zedong and would continue to do so for the remainder of his life.

That Mao found populism, elitism, and voluntarism congenial is easy to understand. Fascinated as an adolescent by the heroic novels of dynastic China, and impressed in his early maturity by stories of the warriors and statesmen of China and the West, Mao viewed history as shaped by the will and determination of exemplary individuals—a notion not incompatible with the standard view of Chinese historiography.

Even before his conversion to Marxism, Mao had spoken of influencing the "subjective attitudes" and mobilizing the "will" of the masses, to inspire them to perform acts of heroism. In 1923, the need to mobilize that will, and to inspire heroism, arose out of the imperialists' irrepressible desire to "squeeze . . . the fat and blood of the Chinese people."[7]

Mao had long held anti-imperialist sentiments, but by the mid-1920s he was expressing his objections in theoretical terms—the most important of which was the notion that imperialism was impelled by the felt necessity to exploit the less-developed countries. That China's woes could be attributed to the rapacity of external enemies allowed Mao, following Li, to advocate a "great union" of all the Chinese people in a revolutionary enterprise aimed at restoring the "glory of the Han."[8] Those who did not rally around the standard of "Marxist revolution" were not only "counterrevolutionaries," they had betrayed the vision of a renascent China. Those who supported imperialism in any way automatically distinguished themselves as "enemies." The parameters of the domestic class struggle were to be established in the struggle against foreign enemies. For Mao, the task of the revolution was to overthrow the foreigners and those whose "traitorous acts" served the interests of foreigners. Not only peasants and workers, but "merchants, peasants, students and teachers"—all who suffered a "common oppression"— were potential allies in the anti-imperialist revolutionary mission.[9]

This primitive matrix of ideas formed the basis of "Mao Zedong Thought." Throughout the remainder of his life, Mao would elaborate on these themes, drawing out seeming implications as circumstances demanded. As early as 1928, elitism and voluntarism were implicit in Mao's conviction that he could "proletarianize" his guerrilla forces (composed of individuals who were not proletarians) simply by subjecting them to "political training so as to effect a qualitative change in [them]."[10] In its most mature expression, this meant that "men . . . are not the slaves of objective reality. . . . [The] subjective activity of the popular masses can manifest itself in full measure, overcome all difficulties, create the necessary conditions, and carry forward the revolution. In this sense, the subjective creates the objective."[11] The "broad masses" needed only to grasp Mao Zedong Thought to acquire an "inexhaustible source of strength and a spiritual atom bomb of infinite power."[12] The populism, elitism, and voluntarism so prominent in his thought received their fullest expression in the peculiar dominance of the Thought of Mao Zedong throughout the history of the Communist revolution in China.

Political training, education, the "remolding of consciousness"—not the material forces of production—would be the critical factors in revolution and national regeneration.[13] The morale, elan, and consciousness of the actors, and not the objective economic circumstances of any given environment, were of importance to Mao. For him, history was determined by "superstructural" elements—the philosophy, convictions, and attitudes of men—rather than their "material life conditions."[14] To shape history, the masses required "remolding"—infusion with the "invincible power" of Mao Zedong Thought. "Rectification" of personal convictions, "movements" for "remolding" the masses, "thought reform," and "study groups" came to characterize the political style of Maoist political culture. The Thought of Mao Zedong became the definitive guide in every enterprise.[15] At the peak of the enthusiasm for ideological rectitude, applicants to institutions of higher learning in the People's Republic of China were admitted and advanced largely on the basis of examinations that reflected their commitment to the Thought of Mao Zedong.[16] The various constitutions of the PRC embodied the conviction that revolution, and the very salvation of China, could only proceed along the "road indicated by Marxism-Leninism–Mao Zedong Thought." "All of the victories in revolution and construction" were "won" only under the "guidance of Marxism-Leninism–Mao Zedong Thought."[17]

Whatever was unique in Mao's conception of the party, the notion that the leader's "thought" was determinant resulted in the familiar substitutions that typify all hegemonic and unitary political systems in the twentieth century: the masses are led by the "vanguard party," and that party's directives are informed by the infallible thought of the inspired leader. Such a system is dominated by a party that is charged, in principle, with implementing those directives. In China, party members were admonished to remember that the "interests of the Party and the people are one" and that the "Party is a united militant organization, welded together by discipline which is obligatory on all its members."[18] They were also reminded that "comrade Mao Zedong's works are the highest directives for all our work. The line of demarcation between Marxism-Leninism and revisionism, between revolution and counter-revolution, lies in whether one supports Mao Zedong Thought and acts in accordance with it or whether one resists it and refuses to act in accordance with it."[19] "At no time," party members were informed, "is it permissible for us to depart in the slightest from the path of Chairman Mao's thinking."[20] The enlightened leader, possessed of "the greatest truth ever known since time immemorial,"[21] took it upon himself to "remold" the thinking of both the party members and the people and thus to shape the nation's future.

In all of this there was more than a little traditional Confucianism. Ancient Chinese philosophers had conceived the relationship between the ruler and those he ruled as paternal, benign, and didactic. The ruler was the moral guide for a population whose interests he incarnated. The ruler, through exemplary virtue, instilled in the people the dispositions that sustained the hierarchical system.

The singularly modern feature of Maoism was the concept of unqualified commitment to the anti-imperialist struggle, which was fundamental to Mao's thought and inspired his political activity. There was little, if anything, in classical Marxism pertaining to the subject of anti-imperialism. For both Marx and Engels, colonialism was simply the mechanism by which industrial capitalism came to invest the world. By introducing capitalist productive processes throughout the world, colonialism was doing "history's work."[22]

It was Lenin who assigned imperialism an entirely different historical role. Because of its depredations, imperialism would shift the axis of world revolution from the advanced industrial countries of the West to the backward economies of Asia. The founders of sinicized Marxism-Leninism theorized that since the retrograde nations of the East did not have a class-conscious proletarian population, the revolution would have to be undertaken by a nonproletarian mass led by a vanguard party of declassed revolutionaries. The revolution would be detached from any specific economic circumstance and would have no determinate class base.[23]

What motivated the revolutionaries was their outrage at the incursions of the imperialists. Influenced by this kind of reasoning, Mao became an advocate of revolution in nonproletarian environments and an opponent of imperialism in whatever guise. For Mao, the "monster imperialism"[24] was China's implacable enemy. "Imperialism [was] the foremost and most ferocious enemy of the Chinese people."[25]

Because of the centrality of the anti-imperialist struggle, Mao enlisted and excluded elements of the Chinese population from the revolution not on the basis of their class membership, but on the basis of their position with regard to imperialism. Thus the "comprador big bourgeoisie," which served the "capitalists of the imperialist countries," was deemed an enemy of the revolution. The "national bourgeoisie," which episodically found itself opposed to foreign capitalists, would be a sometime ally. The "landlord class," which in Mao's judgment constituted "the main social base for imperialist rule in China," was the "target" of revolutionary violence. The peasants, because they were understood to be a "firm ally" of the anti-imperialist proletariat and constituted 80 percent of the total population, were considered revolutionary.[26]

None of this bore any relationship to the complex notions of Marx and Engels, and although it shared some affinities with Leninism, its principal features were more characteristic of reactive nationalism than of Leninism; Western Marxists have long been prepared to grant as much.[27] Soviet theoreticians have insisted that "Maoism has nothing in common with scientific communism, with the teaching of Marxism-Leninism."

They see Maoism as a mélange of "traditional Confucian philosophy," nationalist sentiment, "petty bourgeois revolutionism," "ahistorical utopianism," elitism, and voluntarism.[28]

However one chooses to interpret Maoism, it seems clear that it provides the ideological justification for a hierarchically structured, highly centralized, elite-dominated system. As a doctrine concerned with population management, it conceived human beings as capable of transforming their environment if they were appropriately inspired by instruction and demonstrative example. Because "correct modes of thought" constitute "magic weapons" with which the "people" could "perform miracles,"[29] there was an institutionalized insistence on doctrinal conformity. Finally, because Maoism was the only doctrine that could save China from imperialism—its foremost enemy—anyone who failed to conform was not only an enemy but a traitor. The ideological disputes that were part of Mao's revolution and subsequent rule revealed the passion with which China's Communists sought to defend their nation against the machinations of foreign imperialists and of those "bourgeois" Chinese, of whatever objective class, who were understood to have entered into collusion with them.

THE POLITICAL SYSTEM

Ideologies are invariably ambiguous concerning operational specifics. Moreover, reality has an intractability that often tests the most coherent and consistent ideological convictions. Many aspects of the political system established by the Maoists upon their defeat of the Nationalist armies had not been described in the doctrinal literature produced so prolifically by Mao prior to his accession to power. Nonetheless, for all its novelties and vagaries, the system clearly was Maoist.

In June 1949, on the eve of the proclamation of the establishment of the People's Democratic Republic, Mao announced that the state system of the "People's Democratic Dictatorship" would serve as "an instrument for the oppression of antagonistic classes." It would be a government of the "broad masses," and it would deny the most elementary civil and political rights to the "running dogs of imperialism—the landlord classes and the bureaucratic bourgeoisie as well as the representatives of those classes." The unregenerate would be suppressed with violence.[30]

The government would be dominated by a dedicated cadre of the Chinese Communist Party, whose membership then constituted less than 1 percent of China's total population. That minority party, possessed of the thought of "Marx, Engels, Lenin, and Stalin," would "arouse" and "remold" the population, thus ensuring that China would enjoy the "Great Harmony" anticipated in traditional Chinese social and philosophical thought.[31]

For Mao, there could be no alternative to his program. China could not have "a bourgeois republic because she [was] a country suffering under imperialist oppression"—and the bourgeoisie was the natural ally of foreign oppressors. As a consequence, "all Chinese without exception must lean either to the side of imperialism or to the side of socialism." They were either "bourgeois" or "proletarian"; there were no other options. Because imperialism still existed, and because imperialists recruited "lackeys" and "running dogs" from among the Chinese "bourgeoisie," the Chinese must "strengthen the people's state apparatus—mainly the people's army, the people's police and the people's courts"—in order to guarantee the public defense and internal security. "To counter imperialist oppression," and the subversion it suborned, revolutionary China required a "powerful state apparatus" disciplined by a "revolutionary vanguard."[32]

The communist party, as the vanguard of the revolution, was "the harbinger of enlightenment, [composed of] the only people capable of helping the less enlightened." Only the revolutionary party could "successfully raise the people's consciousness, lead their actions and serve them well." To ensure the proper discipline and the correct orientation, the party's work was to be guided by the Thought of Mao Zedong, for "Mao Zedong [was] not only the greatest revolutionary and statesman in Chinese history, but also its greatest theoretician and scientist."[33]

The government was composed of executive, legislative, judicial and administrative agencies whose functions frequently overlapped. Control by the party was assured by party functionaries' concurrent occupation of key offices in public institutions. Mao Zedong, for example, was chairman of the party, chairman of the Central People's Government, and head of the People's Revolutionary Military Council. Liu Shaoqi (Liu Shao-ch'i) was vice-chairman of the Central Committee of the party and of the Politburo (the central directive agency of the party), as well as one of the vice-chairmen of the Central People's Government, one of the vice-chairmen of the People's Revolutionary Military Council, honorary chairman of the All-China Federation of Trade Unions, and a leader of the PRC Committee on National Elections and Committee on the Drafting of the Constitution.

Party leaders, however, never considered this kind of control adequate to their tasks. They intended party influence to extend throughout society, not simply dominate the state machine. In 1954, when the PRC finally formulated its first Constitution, it institutionalized party penetration into every aspect of Chinese life by establishing "democratic central-ism," the operative directive that governed party discipline, constitutive of the state.

The democratic centralism of the CCP was predicated on the convic-tion that the strength of the "revolutionary proletariat" was a function of disciplined organization. That organization was based on the "principle of the subordination of the individual to the organization, the subordina-tion of the minority to the majority, the subordination of lower organiza-tions to higher organizations, and the subordination of all the constituent Party organizations to the Central Committee. . . . [Thus] the Party as a whole has a . . . unified discipline which all Party members must observe, and a unified leading body which must be obeyed by the entire membership."[34] Prior to 1954, that kind of discipline had been expected only of party members; thereafter, all the citizens of the "New Democ-racy" were expected to be disciplined to the same extent and in the same way as party members. Democratic centralism was employed as a device to articulate and implement a factitious "popular will" that was supposed to represent the true desires and interests of the Chinese people.[35]

To ensure discipline, a multiplicity of state and semi-state organiza-tions was created, all governed by the requisite democratic centralism. At the lowest level of the state administrative hierarchy were People's Con-gresses, party domination of which was ensured by a system of nomina-tions and the presentation of slates. These bodies were charged with the responsibility of "transmitting orders, reporting results and guiding the work."[36] The Congresses were supplemented by a plethora of state and semi-state "mass organizations" such as the New Democratic Youth League, the Young Pioneers, the All-China Federation of Democratic Youth, the Sino-Soviet Friendship Association, the All-China Democratic Women's Federation, the All-China Federation of Trade Unions, and the All-China Federation of Industrial and Commercial Circles. Under the direction of the central organs of the party, the mass organizations mobi-lized, "remolded," and "provided guidance" in campaigns launched to accomplish some end and to bring under party control all persons not directly supervised by it. Overlapping and continuous campaigns fea-tured banners, the chanting of slogans, declamations by party leaders, and massed marches accompanied by patriotic songs. There were cam-paigns to achieve "fiscal economy," to defeat "commandism," to pro-mote "resist-America and aid-Korea," and to "rectify" thinking and augment production. This tactic was supposed to release a torrent of human energy that would be utilized to achieve the national purpose, as construed by the party leadership.[37]

Whether these campaigns are understood as a technique designed to eliminate the barriers between leaders and masses, or as a reflection of a notion of participation that emerged out of the experiences of guerrilla warfare, the fact is that the effort to increase participation and community action was premised on a recognition of the difference in the power of the party cadres and the population. To be effective, mass participation had to be organized, and mass organizations had to be made subject to party control. Whatever was accomplished by the party cadres in terms of democratizing their work style and eliminating the traditional show of deference to status and position, it was clear that basic structural inequalities in power between the rulers and the ruled remained. Mass participation was never allowed to result in the establishment of an alternative source of political power capable of limiting the initiatives and prerogatives of the state.

The concept of state power, as defined by the leadership of the People's Republic of China, is radically different from the concept as understood by the citizens of "bourgeois republics." To Mao Zedong, government was not created as a result of a grant of power by a sovereign people, to be regulated by checks and balances intended to protect individual inalienable and natural rights. These notions have been regularly dismissed as "bourgeois fictions" by the theoreticians of Mao's China. To Maoists (and to all Marxists-Leninists), government—state power—is an "instrument of class rule," to be used for the suppression of "class enemies." A constitution is not a charter for the defense of individual rights; it is a shield for the protection of the "people's state."[38] The minority communist party proclaims not only that "Marxism-Leninism–Mao Zedong Thought is the theoretical basis guiding the thinking of our nation," but also that it is the "fundamental duty" of citizens "to support the leadership of the Communist Party of China" and to "support the socialist system."[39] The Constitution of 1978 stated that "the working class exercises leadership over the state through its vanguard, the Communist Party of China," and that "the guiding ideology of the People's Republic of China is Marxism-Leninism—Mao Zedong Thought." Moreover, "the state upholds the leading position of Marxism-Leninism–Mao Zedong Thought in all spheres of ideology and culture. All cultural undertakings must serve . . . socialism." The state also "safeguards the socialist system, suppresses all treasonable and counterrevolutionary activities, punishes all traitors and counterrevolutionaries, and punishes new-born bourgeois elements and other bad elements." All citizens were required to "support the leadership of the Communist Party of China" as well as "the socialist system."[40] Article 1 of the Constitution promulgated in 1982 specifically states that "sabotage of the socialist system by any organization or individual is prohibited." As though that were not sufficient, Article 51 states: "The exercise by citizens of the People's Republic of China of their freedoms and rights may not infringe upon the interests of the state."

In effect, the rights and freedoms granted citizens by China's "proletarian" state have always been carefully circumscribed and defined by the interests of the Chinese Communist Party and the "socialist system" it dominates. As a consequence, whenever China's masses have been mobilized in campaigns or movements, their participation has always been carefully monitored to ensure party control. The party leadership issues political directives, allocates resources, makes final administrative decisions, and attempts to resolve conflicts. This it accomplishes by penetrating the chains of command within the state and semi-state organizations. The ancillary mass organizations have never been given any measurable political autonomy. They are (and have been) primarily schools for political education and a means of grass-roots control.

The complex array of interlocking (and sometimes overlapping) institutions that constituted the Maoist state were imitations, and in some cases replications, of Soviet institutions. Thus the Maoist state system shared the inegalitarian, hierarchical, and bureaucratic features of the Soviet system, which were reinforced by the inegalitarian, hierarchical, and bureaucratic principles inherited by the Chinese as part of the imperial tradition. The system was a result of the obvious necessity to stabilize society and maintain basic public services at the conclusion of a destructive international and civil war; it was also influenced by Mao's convictions concerning the relationship of a qualified elite to the restive and potentially responsive but "unenlightened" masses.

An extensive bureaucratic network administered the political, productive, educational, and communications systems of the People's Republic of China. Soon after establishment of the Maoist state, China's bureaucrats found themselves united in hierarchical organizations that set them apart from the rest of the population. They had no personal assets, yet as a group they soon exercised allocative control over the principal resources of the entire nation. They were not producers, yet they superintended production; they made and administered decisions that affected the economy at both the local and national levels. Bureaucrats enjoyed status and material advantage in the form of high salaries, better rations, servants, and automobiles and telephones. As early as 1955, government bureaucrats were consuming about 10 percent of the national budget, almost twice the originally planned allocation of 5 percent.[41]

During the first decade of communist rule, the bureaucracy expanded at an impressive rate. In 1949, there were 720,000 bureaucrats in government service. By 1958, that number had increased by over 1,000 percent to 7,920,000—largely because of the traditional aspiration to achieve the status of an "official" and the obvious salary and prestige advantages of government employment.

The evidence is overwhelming that although the bureaucracy that was created with the establishment of the Maoist state was reasonably honest and efficient by the standards of Third World polities, it fostered and perpetuated institutional inequality and administrative authoritarianism. Bureaucrats, using their positions of authority, gained privileged access to scarce goods and welfare benefits for themselves and their clientele. They acquired special access to housing, preferential working conditions, educational institutions, government subsidies, travel and entertainment, and special medical treatment. The more assertive citizens voiced their objections to what they characterized as the institutionalization of "feudal fascism." They complained that complex, self-serving patron-client relations sustained the entire bureaucratic apparatus and that patriarchal ruler-vassal relations determined the distribution of assets throughout the system.[42]

Such criticism, which had become prevalent by the early 1970s, actually reflected some of Mao's early reservations concerning the burgeoning bureaucracy that was part of the system he had created. In the early 1950s he had explicitly complained of "corruption and waste" in the bureaucracy. The campaign that was consequently launched against the "Three Evils" was a calculated attack against waste, privilege, and corruption in the party, the government, and mass organizations.[43] In 1956, in an effort to control the expanding bureaucracy, Mao advocated that "the Party and government organs should be thoroughly streamlined and cut by two-thirds."[44] That suggestion could only strike fear into the hearts of bureaucrats, whose life circumstances were determined exclusively by their positions in the system.

Since individuals in the People's Republic of China were (and are) proscribed from accumulating wealth or property, the nation's bureaucrats enjoyed material comforts only so long as they remained in office. Unlike the traditional mandarinate, the bureaucrats of Mao's China were extremely vulnerable. The mandarin who offended his superiors might very well lose his official position, but he could fall back on his holdings in land and (or) his accumulated assets. The bureaucrat in Mao's China who was divested of his official position found himself devoid of resources— his sole asset was his state office. In consequence, bureaucrats became abjectly dependent upon the state because it provided employment. Lack of personal security led them to seek the patronage of more powerful officials who, in turn, were motivated to weave a network of dependency relations that might offer them a potential defense against the attack of still more powerful officials. The result was the creation of intricate and constantly changing personalistic factions.

Officials who had been denied both their positions and the option of retreating to private life because of a lack of personal resources united with others similarly circumstanced to press for rehabilitation and vindication. Unstable coalitions of convenience resulted. Rightist and leftist factions circulated in office; each faction sought the patronage of a major official, and major officials attempted to build alliances among themselves. The disputes were frequently marked by such savagery and vituperation that they threatened the continuity of the system.[45]

Bureaucrats, because of their vulnerability, argued for a system that was more rule-governed and predictable. They pointed out that organization is a primary necessity for effective governance and that the measure of "truth" of any particular strategy is its pragmatic effectiveness.[46] They emphasized that because of their special qualifications, they were important to effective governance, for without such "experts," organizations would suffer functional impairment and production would decline.

FACTIONAL DISPUTES AND POLICY DIFFERENCES

These kinds of argument surfaced in the internecine struggle between Mao and his first heir apparent, Liu Shaoqi. Whereas Mao, who conducted his revolutionary campaign with the assistance of guerrilla warriors, saw mass mobilization as a consequence of inspiration by a self-selected leadership, Liu, who established communist organizations in the areas dominated either by the Nationalist government or by Japanese invaders, viewed party work as involving deliberate action by disciplined and responsible agents.[47] Mao's formative experiences had been in situations where leadership and masses mingled in the excitement of mutual commitment. Liu's experiences had led him to invest confidence not in personal enthusiasm and demonstrative display, but in impersonal organization. For him, it was not inspiration (neither individual nor collective) that promised success in the areas under anticommunist control, but rather organizational integrity, often requiring anonymous participants to follow established rules of conduct. For Liu, the party was a largely impersonal organization that was staffed by those who qualified in some serious sense as professionals. For Mao, the party was a transmission belt for the inspired directives of the vanguard. Given this conception of the party, Mao considered the bureaucratic structures necessitated by the governance of postrevolutionary China an annoying hindrance to his revolutionary purpose. He gave early evidence of his lack of confidence in an impersonal and rule-governed bureaucracy.[48]

These two conceptions of party function and party organization produced tensions that sometimes threatened the soundness of the political system. For an extended period, the "mass line"—"from the masses to the masses"—was used to conceal the differences in emphasis and operational procedures. That bureaucrats should not allow arrogance or selfishness to adversely affect their relationship with the masses was an early "mass line" admonition that would not necessarily threaten the security or well-being of the rank and file. Only when the system malfunctioned and there were threats of mass dismissal in accordance with some obscure political or ideological criteria were the bureaucrats galvanized into action. Unfortunately, these circumstances occurred with some frequency in the People's Republic of China. In such cases, malfunctioning was attributed to ideological "deviation"—to failure to follow the "correct line." More frequently than not, in those instances of system failure, Mao chose to assign blame to party functionaries for having failed to adequately mobilize mass support rather than to planning errors at the center.

A series of catastrophic failures in the 1950s led to increased tension between the proponents of each of these conceptions of party function and party organization. In the course of that increasing tension, in 1959, Mao stepped down as chairman of the People's Republic of China.

In significant measure, Mao's successor represented the interests of the established functionaries. Liu was identified with the effort to "regularize" and "institutionalize" the state system. He was methodical and project oriented, and he viewed consistency and predictability as essential to effective functioning. His work methods have been described as cautious and practical. All these dispositions directly or indirectly served the interests of the functionaries.

The need to proceed systematically in planning and administration implied the employment of trained and knowledgeable personnel—a consideration that contributed to the institutional importance of place holders. Governance by established rules, competence, and organizational efficiency were the criteria used to measure institutional worth. All of this would tend to make bureaucratic employment more secure, less subject to the vagaries of political and ideological moods. The contribution of these "experts" to system maintenance and goal attainment would be respected. By the early 1960s, bureaucrats in the People's Republic of China had every reason to give passive or active support to the organizational policies of Liu Shaoqi.

Whatever the relationship between Liu and Mao between 1959 and the advent of the Great Proletarian Cultural Revolution in 1965–1966, it seems clear, in hindsight, that Mao had become increasingly restive and disapproving of the evolving system. Mao and his followers ultimately confronted Liu with objections to "bourgeois" and "counterrevolutionary" artistic and literary production. By the end of August 1966, it had become clear that Liu, and those functionaries in the party and the government who supported him, were the principal objects of Mao's attack. In 1967, Mao seized the initiative and launched a campaign to destroy the autonomous bureaucracy with its claims to professional competence and its appeal to organizational imperatives. In the course of the campaign, all "scholars," "authorities," and "specialists" were subjected to verbal and physical attack. In many areas local officials were tortured and killed. Nonparty organizations were established to attack "enemies" within the party and the government. At the peak of the conflict, 90 percent of the nation's senior cadres were identified as "red bourgeoisie"—"those in authority who [had] wormed their way into the Party and [were] taking the capitalist road." It was announced that the "revolution [had] suddenly turned all [power] from the hands of the bureaucrats into the hands of the enthusiastic working class," who had discovered that "without the bureaucrats they could not only go on living, but could live better and develop quicker and with greater freedom. . . . [Without] the bureaucrats and bureaucratic organs, productivity was greatly liberated."[49]

The Maoist call to "Bombard the Headquarters" was an injunction to assault the bureaucratic organs of the party and the state. The Maoists dismantled party committees, the leading organs of the Young Communist League and of the All-China Federation of Trade Unions. They also seized the central and local media and the provincial organs of authority. Two-thirds of the party members who had been elected to the Central Committee in 1956 were denounced and removed from office. Eleven of the 15 members and alternative members of the Central Committee's Secretariat, including the general secretary (and ally of Liu), Deng Xiaoping (Teng Hsiao-ping), were identified as "black bandits," and more than 50 percent of the members and alternate members of the party Politburo were stigmatized as "enemies of the Thought of Mao Zedong." Only three members of the Politburo—Mao, Lin Biao (Lin Piao), and Zhou Enlai (Chou En-lai)—escaped vilification.

The Maoists perceived this course of action as necessary to destroy anything that obstructed communication of the Thought of Mao Zedong to the people. The principal charge leveled against Liu Shaoqi and the "capitalist roaders" was that they allowed the entire apparatus of the state to become task oriented to the "exclusion" of Mao's "Thought."

Once bureaucratic impediments were removed, Mao Zedong Thought could again become the "moral atom bomb of colossal power" and "take hold of the masses."[50] The charge imposed on the "revolutionaries" was to "arouse the enthusiasm of the people and broaden their horizon . . . by means of the great Thought of Mao Zedong."[51] "With the invincible Mao Zedong Thought," Mao's followers were informed, "we have the highest criterion for judging right and wrong" and for distinguishing "between revolutionaries and counterrevolutionaries, genuine revolutionaries and sham revolutionaries."[52]

The Great Proletarian Cultural Revolution was an effort to substitute indoctrination with the "Thought" of the leader for all the bureaucratic control mechanisms laboriously devised by Liu Shaoqi and his supporters and thus to shape history by infusing millions with the supreme will of a single "world historical" figure. The effort was motivated by the conviction that "as the Chinese people master Mao Zedong Thought, China will be prosperous and ever-victorious. . . . [Then] they are sure to win their emancipation, bury imperialism . . . and realize communism throughout the world."[53]

In all of this, there was more Mengzi than Marx, and more Confucianism than Marxism-Leninism. It involved conceptions of social dynamics and revolution that were essentially pre-Marxian, and had more affinities with the populism, voluntarism, and elitism that had appealed to the young Mao than with any of the theoretical subtleties of Marx or Lenin. Mao perceived China as "poor and blank." Its poverty rendered its masses receptive to revolutionary indoctrination. It was "a clean sheet of paper" upon which the "newest and most beautiful words can be written."[54] The population of China was raw material to be fashioned by a master craftsman to revolutionary purpose. That purpose was to make of a weak and poor nation one that was strong and prosperous—one that would conquer imperialism and assure China its rightful place in the world—and herald the advent of the long anticipated Great Harmony.[55]

Mao grappled with the problems of poverty and vulnerability to foreign invasion that had afflicted China in the late nineteenth century. His solution consisted of an artful combination of Western techniques, a Marxist rationale, Soviet instrumentalities, and traditional Chinese elements. By the end of 1952, he had attained his immediate objective, the seizure and retention of political power, by effecting the violent liquidation of the "reactionary classes" that had conspired with the imperialists to reduce China to the status of a "semicolony." In early 1953, the Central Committee of the Chinese Communist Party inaugurated the second phase of what was to be "permanent revolution": a "socialist transformation" of agriculture, handicraft production, and industrial enterprise. The First Five-Year Plan was initiated the same year in an effort to accomplish what the Qing modernizers were incapable of doing, and what the Nationalist revolutionaries had not had the time or opportunity to seriously attempt.

THE ECONOMIC SYSTEM

Modernization of China's economy[56] was necessary if Mao was to achieve his principal goal of making China a strong and prosperous nation.[57] China required the material wherewithal to construct and maintain a modern military establishment, and that required an extensive and complex industrial base. Industrialization could not be accomplished without fabrication of a suitable infrastructure: roads, rail systems, energy grids, and communication networks. It also necessitated exploitation of natural resources and a rapid improvement in technology and technical skills, mechanization of the work process, and a sustained increase in agricultural yield to provide the requisite intersectoral flow of assets from the traditional to the modern sectors of the economy.

When the Chinese Communist Party gained control of mainland China in 1949, the national economy had almost ceased to function—in part because of intense conflict that had lasted for more than a dozen years. The Nationalist government was bankrupt and the national economy was wracked by a spectacular rate of inflation that made normal commercial transactions virtually impossible. The communist authorities immediately commenced a program to stabilize the national currency by centralizing control of the financial system and balancing the national budget.

The Communists also inaugurated a program to effect a "socialist transformation" of the economy. Land reform had already been initiated in the areas dominated by the communist armed forces before the final defeat of the Nationalist armies and had involved perhaps as many as 160 million peasants. In 1952, the remaining 300 million rural inhabitants were drawn into the reform, and 43 million hectares of land changed hands. In the urban areas, the government nationalized almost 3,000 industrial enterprises, including the major banks, railroads, and shipping establishments, in order to create a "state sector" in the economy. Between 1949 and 1952, the war-ravaged economy was rehabilitated; industrial production increased by 145 percent and agricultural yield increased by 49 percent. During that same interval, the economy was largely "demarketized" and was well on the way to becoming totally "deprivatized." Production, resource allocation, wages, profits, and distribution were no longer to be governed by market mechanisms but rather by centrally made, planned decisions. To ensure control of the processes involved, private ownership and, by implication, the opportunity for entrepreneurial initiative and decision making, were abolished. Even the small private sector of the economy, which had survived confiscation, was locked into joint state-private ventures in which production, marketing, and profit were controlled by the state.

Originally, Mao had suggested that the communist government proceed with its socialist transformation with self-imposed constraint. He said that his intended "new democratic revolution" differed from a "socialist revolution" in that it would "overthrow the rule of the imperialists, traitors, and reactionaries in China but [would not] destroy any section of capitalism which is capable of contributing to the anti-imperialist . . . struggle." Mao suggested that because the principal aim of the revolution was to "oppose imperialism," it would "preserve capitalist enterprise in general . . . to help in the rapid industrialization of the economy." The new democratic revolution would, in fact, "clear the way for capitalism."[58] Although the "state enterprises" of the revolutionary government would be of "socialist character" and would "constitute the leading force in the whole national economy," the "republic will neither confiscate capitalist private property in general nor forbid the development of such capitalist production as does not 'dominate the livelihood of the people'."[59]

All this notwithstanding, by 1956 all of China's industries were state controlled, only 4 percent of the total value of retail sales was still in private hands, and no more than 7 percent of the total national income was generated by the private sector.[60] In that year less than 4 percent of the peasant households qualified as "private." Ninety-six percent of the rural population was organized in agricultural collectives patterned after the Soviet *kolkhozy*. By the mid-1950s, the Maoists had created a state-controlled, hierarchical national economy on the model of that of the Soviet Union. A few years earlier, Mao had announced that "the Communist Party of the Soviet Union is our best teacher and we must learn from it."[61]

The Maoist mimicry of the institutions of the Soviet Union is easily comprehensible. Neither Mao nor his entourage had ever given evidence of competence in economic theory or planning. On more than one occasion, Mao had commented on his ignorance of economics.[62] With the decision to embark upon the socialist transformation of China's vast and complex economy, the Maoists began to consult Soviet textbooks and Soviet technicians, a large number of whom assisted in the articulation of a control and planning structure. The transition was then made to a system in which resource allocation was controlled by the state, not determined by the market. In the new system, neither traditional patterns nor the market supplied information, coordination, or incentives. The central government established a "planned purchase and planned supply system" to ensure creation of virtual monopolies of the trade in essentials. Key productive inputs were distributed throughout the system by allocations devised by state planners and supervised by the State Bureau of Material Supplies. This rationing system, composed of "material balances," was gradually expanded to include all raw materials and capital goods. In 1952 there were 28 such balances. In 1956 the number had increased to 235. By 1980, despite the vicissitudes suffered by the system, the number of material balances was about 1,000.

Nationwide rationing of food grains and basic consumer goods was instituted in 1955 and is still in effect. The state also began to fix industrial wholesale and retail prices and workers' wages, to assign workers to specific employment, and to control mobility. Farmers of collectives were paid according to the Soviet work-point system. By the end of the First Five-Year Plan (1953–1957), the economy of mainland China was functioning in much the same way as that of the Soviet Union.[63]

The annual real rate of growth of the gross national product between 1953 and 1957 was a commendable 6.2 percent. In that five-year period, the gross value of industrial output increased by 128 percent and that of agriculture increased by 24.8 percent. These accomplishments seem to have inspired Mao to implement a policy of mass mobilization that he imagined would accelerate economic growth. China's masses were to be infused with ideological incentives and made to "dare to produce."[64] In September 1958, Mao insisted that "I have witnessed the tremendous energy of the masses. On this foundation it is possible to accomplish any task whatsoever."[65]

In late 1957, encouraged by Mao, the Eighth Congress of the Chinese Communist Party revised the growth goals of the Five-Year Plan that had been proposed in 1956. The growth targets for the Second Five-Year Plan (1958–1962) would be a 650 percent increase in industrial output (at an annual growth rate of 45 percent) and a 250 percent increase in agricultural yield (at an annual growth rate of 20 percent). Steel output was anticipated to grow from 5.5 million tons to 80–100 million tons. The output of coal would increase to 700 million tons—a 540 percent increase. Electric power production would increase to 240,000 kilowatt hours—a 1,240 percent increase. In five years, the economic productivity of the People's Republic of China was to surpass that of Great Britain.

By late 1957, mobilization of the peasants had already begun. Over 100 million peasants were mobilized to construct 11,000 irrigation projects involving seven times as many man-days in one year as had been employed in all the years between 1953 to 1957. Sixty million peasants were mobilized to construct 6,000,000 primitive "backyard" blast furnaces for the production of steel in rural areas. Approximately 7,500,000 small blast furnaces were in operation by the end of 1958 (including 1,500,000 furnaces that were constructed in urban areas). China had clearly embarked on its Great Leap Forward.

The first official reports gave the impression that China had achieved astonishing economic success. In 1957, the grain harvest of the PRC was about 187 million tons—the equivalent of all of China's harvests prior to 1937. In 1958, the harvest was reported to be 250 million tons—an increase of 35 percent. One hundred million acres of land were reported to be under irrigation in 1959. In the same year, the output of steel was reported to have increased 100 percent, from 5.35 million tons to approximately 10 million tons. Unfortunately, these statistics proved to be grossly inflated. The 1958 increase in grain yield had not been 35 percent, but 2.5 percent—just about equivalent to the rate of population growth. Moreover, the vast waterworks project that had been undertaken produced extensive ecological damage, and large sections of the irrigation and water conservancy system did not function. (The sections that did function disrupted the water table and the distribution and drainage of the natural rivers.) These factors, coupled with unsuitable weather, grievous errors in planning, and simple incompetence reduced the grain harvest in 1961 to about 150 million tons—below the level of tolerance. It is estimated that at least 10 million peasants died in the famine that followed.

The effort to initiate "backyard" steel production was an economic disaster. The small factories and blast furnaces, jerry-built by unskilled labor, produced tons of material of poor quality, at a high cost. Resources were diverted from efficient plants and dissipated. It is estimated that about $800 million in materials alone was wasted in 1958–1959. During the Second Five-Year Plan, the annual growth rate of the gross value of industrial and agricultural output was only 0.6 percent—significantly below the rate of population growth in the same period. The economy of Communist China was at the brink of collapse.

A policy of "readjustment, consolidation, and . . . raising the standards" was initiated in 1961. There was clear retreat from the notion that national production could be increased by inspiring masses with the Thought of Mao Zedong. Mao had stepped down as chairman of the

People's Government in 1959, and Liu Shaoqi and the "professionals" around him began to readjust the economy. Those, who in 1956, had underwritten a relatively orthodox Stalinist Five-Year Plan for 1958–1962, were restored to favor. They attempted to rehabilitate the economy's productivity—which had declined 31 percent between 1958 and 1961—by returning planners, statisticians, administrators, managers, and other "nonproductive" and "bourgeois oriented" workers to their tasks. Mao's revolutionary line had been that the "specialists" and "authorities" in the system should involve themselves directly in the productive process in order to contribute to the collective enthusiasm that was expected to spontaneously increase industrial and agricultural productivity. The more calculating leadership, sobered by the failures of the Great Leap, advocated strict assignment of bureaucratic tasks and responsibilities within a technically managed program of ordered growth.

According to Mao's revolutionary line, increased productivity was the direct result of political motivation—the creation of "new men." The masses, inspired by moral and political incentives, would be transformed and would transform China. Motivation, for the Maoist revolutionaries, meant remolding the minds of men—teaching them the value of selflessness, egalitarianism, intensive labor, and dedication. Whole populations would thus be rendered "red," and capitalism would finally be overcome. In Mao's judgment, that would be the day when China would be "completely free of the influence of capitalist ideology. At that time the qualitative changes of ideological remolding will have ended."[66]

The failure of the Great Leap Forward confirmed the conviction of those identified as the "capitalist roaders" (led by Deng Xiaoping and Liu Shaoqi) that an economy could not function without competent functionaries and a rational plan for resource allocation, production, and distribution. A reasonable amount of predictability was also necessary. "Permanent revolution," and the Maoist interpretation of the "mass line," militated against all that. Mao's populism and voluntarism had not only threatened the security of the capitalist roaders but had seriously disrupted the national economy and had weakened China. By 1960 Liu Shaoqi and Deng Xiaoping could expect, and did receive, the support of important strata in the party and the government. Mao briefly retreated to the "second rank." But by 1965, he had reorganized his support and was ready to launch the Great Proletarian Cultural Revolution. The rehabilitation of 1961–1964 was rapidly undone, and by 1967 the value of industrial output had declined by 13.8 percent. In 1968, it fell another 5 percent. Agricultural productivity decreased 2.5 percent in 1968. Although the Great Proletarian Cultural Revolution displayed some of the features of the Great Leap Forward with a substitution of "moral" as opposed to "material" incentives, and a wholesale dismissal of the "experts" who were obstructing Mao's direct contact with the masses, in general the economic plans of 1966–1969 were less counterproductive than those of 1958 and 1959. As early as 1971, it became clear that something would have to be done to halt the decline in industrial and agricultural productivity; Zhou Enlai was given the responsibility of restoring the faltering economy. In 1973 the People's Republic of China contracted for the purchase of more than $2 billion in whole productive plants from Japan and Western Europe. By 1974, $1.7 billion in machinery and equipment had been imported—double the acquisitions of 1973. At the same time hundreds of administrators and technical experts who "struggled" during the Great Proletarian Cultural Revolution were rehabilitated. Among them was Deng Xiaoping. (Liu Shaoqi died in disgrace in 1973.)

The death of Zhou in January 1976, and the demise of Mao in September of the same year, left the Maoists, led by Jiang Qing (Chiang Ch'ing), Mao's widow, face-to-face with the capitalist roaders under the leadership of Deng. The People's Republic of China had entered the post-Mao period. Mao's chosen successor, Hua Guofeng (Hua Kuo-feng), gained control for a brief time but was supplanted by Deng Xiaoping in 1977.

THE LEGACY OF MAO

Between 1949 and 1978, the People's Republic of China underwent a radical political, social, and economic transformation. Millions perished as both a direct and an indirect consequence. At least 5 million were killed in the suppression and antilandlord campaigns of 1949–1952. Anywhere from 10 million to 30 million perished as a result of the politically contrived shortages of the Great Leap Forward. As many as 1 million died as a consequence of the anarchic violence of the Great Proletarian Cultural Revolution. The number who died in the "thought reform" labor camps is impossible to estimate.

The economic accomplishments of Mao's regime were not without luster. The annual average real economic growth rate between 1950 and 1980 was 5.6 percent. The tendency to "put politics in command," however, created serious instabilities and there were substantial fluctuations in the rate of real economic growth, which was three times as variable as that of India or Japan, and four times as variable as that of the Republic of China on Taiwan or the Philippines.[67]

After almost 30 years of revolutionary government, the People's Republic of China was still a low-income country; its annual per capita income in 1980 was estimated at $256—about the same as that in Haiti or the Central African Republic.[68] Approximately 70 percent of the population was still involved in agricultural pursuits—about the same proportion as in 1950. The failure of the bulk of the nation's labor force to make a transition from agricultural to industrial employment reflects the low per capita productivity and helps explain the relative lack of improvement in living standards. Between 1957 and 1978, for example, the per capita availability of food grains, the main staple of the rural Chinese, declined 3.2 percent, and per capita availability of edible oils fell 33.3 percent; the supply of cotton cloth was reduced by 2 percent.[69]

The paradox that China should have a relatively unchanging living standard, yet also have a productive system that is growing at an appreciable rate is explicable in terms of the dispositional characteristics of command economies. Because of the nature of centralized control, the budgetary structure, and the organizational incentives of nonmarket economies, there is a tendency toward excessive capital accumulation. In such systems, those in positions of authority have an interest in economic expansion—as that expansion is reflected in aggregate statistics. As a consequence, there is a frenetic search for capital for investment. State ministries and factory managers appeal to the central government for resources to enable them to meet and surpass their assigned quotas. Since there is nothing in the system that acts as a constraint, the state budget tends to extend allotments to the various ministries to ensure their fulfillment of planned quotas. As a result of such incentives, the ratio of capital investment to the gross domestic product (GDP) in the PRC increased from 7.5 percent in the pre–Second World War years to 24 percent in 1953–1957, the years of the First Five-Year Plan. In substance, less was distributed in terms of consumer purchasing power and more was transferred to the state coffers as capital accumulation for subsequent allocation to the component ministries.[70] In 1959, when the economy was at the brink of collapse, the state siphoned off 40 percent of the GDP as investment capital. Between 1970 and 1978, the ratio of investment to GDP remained at 33 percent.

In a market governed economy, it would be difficult to sustain such a rate of capital accumulation unless capital investments proved to be profitable. In a command economy, there is no such constraint. Whether an enterprise is profitable or unprofitable, the state is committed to its survival. There is a tendency for enterprise managers to expand plants and to collect resource and capital inputs in anticipation of future needs. Unused capacity increases, inventories expand, and storage costs escalate.[71] The productivity of capital is low, unnecessary projects are undertaken, and projects are begun but not completed. In effect, the people's assets are used nonproductively; hence the peasants and workers of China are exploited by the proletarian state.

Coupled with the excessive capitalization of the system, labor productivity has remained remarkably low—so low that some Western estimates indicate that improved efficiency might reduce the PRC's industrial work force by as much as 50 percent. Because of technical backwardness, there is also inefficient utilization of energy and raw materials, which is compounded by persistent imbalances between upstream and downstream industries. In the steel industry, for example, the output of pig iron lags behind the needs of steel furnaces, and steel finishing lags behind the output of crude steel. In 1978 only 65 percent of crude steel output could be fashioned into finished steel products, necessitating the importation of 8 million tons of finished steel and the expensive warehousing of unused crude steel. In addition, onshore energy production in the People's Republic of China reached a plateau in 1980 and subsequently began to decline. Inefficient energy utilization, combined with an energy shortage, have severely limited industrial productivity.

The problems of industry are relatively insignificant in comparison with those faced by the rural sector. Because of the high reproductive rate of the rural population and the limited availability of arable land, there has been no change (and a possible decline) in the rural standard of living since the mid-1960s. In 1957 the average annual real wage of persons employed on collective farms was 98 yuan. In 1976, it was 111 yuan. The subsistence income of an average rural family in 1976 was estimated to be 95 yuan. In effect, the agricultural economy of the PRC has remained at the threshold of tolerance since the revolution of 1949. As recently as 1977, the authorities in Beijing admitted that about 100 million people, or about one-tenth of China's total population, did not have enough to eat.[72]

Attempting to manage these problems is a vast bureaucracy animated by a loosely articulated set of notions identified as "Marxism-Leninism–Mao Zedong Thought." Like dynastic China, the "new China" is ruled by a bureaucracy whose distinguishing virtues are loyalty, submission, and a contrived selflessness that gives every appearance of timidity.[73] But whereas the nineteenth-century Qing required about 40,000 officials, and their several million retainers, personal secretaries, clerks, and police personnel to administer the empire, the Chinese Communist Party has engaged approximately 20 million cadres in a similar enterprise. The neo-Confucian Qing leadership expected to induce conformity by using moral injunction, appeals to rectitude and personal example; the Chinese Communist Party of China has attempted to do nothing less.

The emperors' legitimacy derived from the "Mandate of Heaven." Under Mao, the leaders' legitimacy was derived from the Thought of Mao

Zedong, incarnated in the chairman.[74] The leadership of post-Maoist China continues to appeal to that source of legitimacy—incarnated not in a man, but in the party bureaucracy.[75] This effort to make not a "sage-ruler," but an institutionalized party, the source of all morality is influenced more by certain Chinese traditional attitudes than by any Western source of inspiration. The resultant political system is fundamentally different from liberal democratic political forms.

Mao left his heirs a multiply dysfunctional system, as well as a record of violence, injustice, capriciousness, incompetence, waste, and no small measure of stupidity. For almost three decades China was ruled without a system of laws; sanctions were imposed in conformity with communist party dictates. During almost that entire period, China's intellectuals were abused and alienated, creating the dearth of talent that continues to disable the system. Millions of Chinese suffered discrimination because their families had a "bad class background." Children whose parents had owned property were denied access to institutions of learning. Persons whose grandparents had been "landlords" were considered forever suspect and denied equal opportunity at work or in life itself.

By the time Mao died, cynicism had infected an entire generation of young persons. They, their brothers, and their fathers, had been manipulated by a callous party leadership. The differences between party rhetoric and the realities of Maoism had become all too evident.

The post-Maoist leadership, seeking to realize the political and economic vision of the pragmatists around Liu Shaoqi, found itself still trying to modernize a basically retarded economic system. They were compelled to deal with the fateful problem of the pressure of the growing population on the limited support capacity of the soil. Moreover, they had inherited the problems of a nation beset on every side by external threats that were a by-product of Maoist foreign policies. Just as the Maoist economic system reflected Maoist convictions, Maoist foreign policy was in significant measure a reflection of Mao's interpretation of the political motives of the principal actors in the world community.

3

The Foreign Policy
of the People's
Republic of China

However one chooses to interpret China's foreign policy and its behavior in the international arena (and interpretations vary widely), almost every analyst is prepared to grant that Communist Chinese ideological beliefs determine Beijing's policy decisions in some way. Just as frequently, analysts will grant that ideological convictions are only one of the many and varied influences that affect those outcomes—and that the prominence of ideology seems to vary with time and circumstance. Given the complex mix of factors involved, few contemporary scholars and policy analysts pretend to be able to predict Beijing's behavior with any precision.

The undertaking is rendered less difficult, however, if one recognizes that the concerns that have preoccupied China's leaders since Mao have been shared by all nations in a world community composed of sovereign states. The Chinese interpretation of the world at the beginning of the nineteenth century allowed foreigners only tributary relations with the Central Kingdom; the "new China" of the twentieth century has been "socialized" to the complex international system of independent and nominally equal political communities. Whatever pride the traditional sense of cultural and historic superiority might generate among the Chinese, the hard realities of the contemporary world have mitigated against its overt expression. In a significant sense, China since Mao, unlike dynastic China, has been an orthodox actor in the international community. Some of its evident concerns have been protecting national security (and to this end, maintaining the integrity of its borders) and maximizing its ability to act independently in pursuit of what the leadership in Beijing conceives to be the national and international interests of the People's Republic of China. Threats to security and independence must be averted if revolutionary China is to survive and prosper. The cardinal importance of such an elementary truth is as obvious to the leaders of modern China as it is to the leadership of any modern nation.[1]

In retrospect, therefore, much of the PRC's foreign policy might be explained in terms of competition between domestic interest groups, each having a different notion of how the PRC might enhance its national security, protect its geographic integrity, and ensure its freedom of maneuver. In that sense, much of Beijing's international conduct has been similar in many respects to that of similarly circumstanced nonsocialist and nonrevolutionary nations. Beyond that, however, the People's Republic of China is a revolutionary power. In principle, the authorities in Beijing advocate a radical redistribution of the world's political and material resources. Whether any particular individual in that leadership has personally committed himself to achievement of such purpose is not of particular consequence. The fact is that the claim to legitimacy made on behalf of the revolution by the government it brought in its train is based on an ideology of radical redistributive change. The government in Beijing claims to represent the real and ultimate interests of the world's "oppressed" and "powerless" against their "oppressors." However cynical any of the leadership of the PRC might be, it is necessary that the articulation of revolutionary rhetoric remain a prominent aspect of the PRC's overt international behavior.

Actually, there is persuasive evidence that, for the Maoist revolutionaries of China and their heirs, the appeal to national and international revolution was, and remains, something more than a cynical or manipulative maneuver to achieve power, control the masses, and legitimize the system. The Maoist and post-Maoist leadership most responsible for the domestic and foreign policy conduct of the PRC have given every indication of being convinced of the substantial truth and justice of their revolutionary ideology. In that sense, their commitment to revolutionary internationalist purpose recommends that their intentions be considered part of any adequate explanation of their conduct.

The explanation and anticipation of the behaviors of the leadership in Beijing is no longer simply an academic exercise. Since 1949, the People's Republic of China has become a major regional actor on the international scene, and the United States has found it necessary to enter assessments of potential Communist Chinese conduct into its foreign policy calculations. In some measure, the convictions of the leadership in Beijing concerning the nature of other international actors, have necessarily become part of Washington's assessments.

THE FOREIGN POLICY CONVICTIONS
OF MAOIST CHINA

When China's radicals, at the end of the First World War, turned to the Bolshevik Revolution as an instructive guide, they took up a collection of ideas that was to significantly influence the foreign policy of modern China. Among the notions that shaped their domestic revolutionary strategies were Lenin's convictions concerning the nature and dynamics of international relations.

As has been suggested, by that time China's experience with the industrialized powers of the West had generated an anti-Western disposition that was fully compatible with the anti-imperialist orientation of Leninism. Lenin's arguments in *Imperialism, The Highest Stage of Capitalism* were incorporated into the doctrines of Mao Zedong almost without remainder. Although there was little serious discussion of the analysis that underlay the arguments, Lenin's central contentions surfaced and resurfaced in Maoist doctrinal literature. "Monopoly," Lenin said, constituted "the basic economic feature of imperialism." By the turn of the nineteenth century, Lenin argued, competition in the West had reduced the number of capitalists. Those who remained had concentrated production in vast trusts and cartels. Financial institutions had undergone the same concentration; consequently, a nation's entire economy could be dominated by a few banks. Those banks "integrated" their efforts, and what resulted was "the domination by financial oligarchy of all spheres of social production and public life." The state ultimately submitted to the will of this oligarchy and came to represent their exclusive interests.[2]

The dominance of this financial oligarchy deepened the "contradictions of capitalism." The vast accumulations of capital that resulted from monopoly control required investment supplements if profitability were to be sustained. Advanced industrial countries had become capital saturated. In a capitalist national economy, because of the exploitative impoverishment of the masses, the domestic market could no longer profitably absorb the production of the prevailing cartels. Trade outlets and investment opportunities were sought in other countries. The oligarchy that dominated the capitalist state apparatus began a drive to attain external hegemony, thus transforming capitalism into imperialism. Each advanced capitalist nation sought to dominate wider and wider spheres of economic influence to ensure its economic survival. "The capitalists divide the world, not out of any particular malice, but because the degree of concentration which has been reached forces them to adopt this method in order to obtain profits."[3]

The predatory nature of imperialist states was understood by Lenin to be a consequence of imperialism's economic requirements. Because each imperialist state is governed by the same requirements, what results is an intense and fratricidal competition. Imperialist states not only strive to dominate dependent and underdeveloped communities, but are compelled to struggle among themselves in their effort to survive.

In each imperialist state, an exiguous minority of "financial oligarchs" determines national policy. Possessed of "super profits," they surround themselves with suborned social elements—petty bourgeois functionaries, declassed intellectuals, and members of the "labor aristocracy"—that collectively constitute a "bourgeoisified privileged stratum."[4] This is the stratum that mobilizes public sentiment, marshals the nation's forces, and executes detailed plans for foreign aggression.

In penetrating foreign economies, the imperialists enlist the assistance of local capitalists—monopolists, merchants, landowners, and "petty bourgeois intellectuals"—to serve as intermediaries and as a domestic support base for their policies. Those who seek monopolistic advantage in the local markets targeted by imperialists establish close ties with foreign financial and productive establishments. Compradors, domestic merchants who act as agents for foreign firms, find local market outlets for foreign monopoly capitalism's productive surplus. Local landowners who find themselves with a surplus of capital invest in foreign financial institutions or underwrite the activities of compradors. Dependent intellectuals provide the rationale for all these activities.[5]

As a critical conclusion to this kind of analysis, Maoists identified imperialism as the "most ferocious enemy" of the Chinese people, and the "running dogs" of imperialism as the revolution's most immediate domestic opponents.[6] In the course of the domestic revolution against foreign oppression, the local monopoly capitalists, the compradors, the landowners, and the venal intellectuals would be singled out as irremediably "counterrevolutionary" and the appropriate objects of revolutionary violence. The "national bourgeoisie" struggling to create a domestic industry, the working class exploited by foreign and domestic monopoly capitalism, and the peasants languishing under the oppression of the landlord class constituted the recruitment base of the anti-imperialist revolution.

The victory of the revolution in 1949 meant that China had defeated, at least temporarily, the "running dogs of imperialism." The problem that remained was to devise a strategy for dealing with foreign imperialism.

Because of the peculiarities of the Chinese civil war, Mao Zedong and his followers, relatively early in their history, found it necessary to formulate a foreign policy. In the mid-1930s, the "base areas" controlled by the Chinese Communist Party began to function as organized governments—Maoists communicated with, and received responses from, foreign governments. By 1946, Mao had articulated a set of basic foreign policy directives. There could not be the least doubt on the part of China's friends or foes that the primary imperative of Chinese communism was to combat imperialism in whatever form it manifested itself. China's identification with the Soviet Union followed from Mao's conviction that "mankind can free itself . . . only by the road pointed out by Stalin and with his help."[7] In 1940, Mao maintained that the major international forces that were destined to shape contemporary events had divided into two "fronts": the "counterrevolutionary front of world capitalism" and the "revolutionary front of world socialism." The two fronts would struggle to gain control of the disintegrating colonial empires.

In all colonies and former colonies, liberation movements were inspired, organized, and directed by the "democratic bourgeoisie." In both colonies and former colonies—whose industrial development had been delayed—only the "national bourgeoisie" was disposed and equipped to resist the depredations of international imperialism. Mao maintained that these movements, although led by the bourgeoisie, were directed against the interests of world capitalism and consequently were "objectively" part of the "new world revolution, the proletarian-socialist world revolution." Thus it could be argued that "no matter what classes, parties or individuals in an oppressed nation join the revolution, and no matter whether they themselves are conscious of the point or understand it, so long as they opposed imperialism, their revolution becomes part of the proletarian-socialist world revolution and they become its allies."[8] The litmus test for identification as allies of the proletarian-socialist world revolution was the conscious or unconscious, explicit or implicit, opposition to world imperialism. By 1940 Mao was convinced that whatever their class origins or political persuasion, the enemies of China's foremost enemy were China's friends.

At the same time that Mao tendered these assessments, he counseled his followers to remember that although world imperialism was slated for ultimate destruction, it remained a formidable, if decadent, foe. Therefore, it was still necessary to direct revolutionary energies against the most overtly threatening imperialists, while isolating them from their

"class" allies. Communists were admonished to exploit the "contradictions" that obtained among the various imperialist powers in the service
of the socialist revolution. The "progressives" should insinuate themselves into any conflicts resulting from the competition among the imperialist powers for markets and spheres of influence "to make use of
[the] contradictions, win over the many, oppose the few and crush our
enemies one by one."[9] Although Communists opposed "all imperialism," it was the imperialism that most directly threatened the immediate
interests of the nation that was the proper object of opposition. When
Japan attacked China in a war of aggression, for example, the communist
forces made common cause with "British and U.S. imperialism," thus
helping to defeat Japan. Once Japan no longer posed a direct threat, the
United States became the proper object of resistance. As long as the
United States remained the major imperialist antagonist of the new
China, the minor imperialist powers, pursuing their own peculiar interests, might be encouraged to serve China's purpose by obstructing
U.S. policy. In that sense, Mao's anti-imperialism was pre-eminently
flexible to changing circumstances. It could be used to exploit whatever
opportunity might be presented in the course of international political
exchanges.

These ideas constituted the nucleus of a hard core of foreign policy
conceptions that Mao Zedong brought with him through the years of
struggle that ultimately led to power in 1949. In 1946, in an interview with
Anna Louise Strong, Mao repeated what were essentially the same
themes he had advanced six years earlier. The two major forces in the
world were imperialism and socialism, represented by the United States
on the one hand and the Soviet Union on the other. An "intermediate
zone" was composed of "many capitalist, colonial and semicolonial countries in Europe, Asia and Africa."[10] The United States was attempting to
bully the nations of this vast zone into conforming to its policies, but Mao
was convinced that all the countries menaced by Washington would soon
unite against it. In the interim, however, the forces of "proletarian-
socialist world revolution" would have to make careful "compromises,"
including "certain important ones," not only to limit the damage that
U.S. imperialism might cause, but to attain as much success as possible
given the existing configuration of forces.[11]

Thus, by 1946, Mao Zedong had articulated the basic outline of what
was to be the foreign policy of the People's Republic of China. The
principal aim of Mao's nascent foreign policy was the absolute destruction of world imperialism, represented in 1946 by the United States. In
order to accomplish that, the PRC would have to recognize and exploit
the major "contradictions" that influence the course of international

events. The principal contradiction, of course, was that between the imperialist and socialist "camps." There was also the contradiction between the "oligarchic clique," which dominated the imperialist nations, and those nations' oppressed subjects; the contradiction between the imperialist powers and the newly emerging liberation forces in the colonial and semicolonial countries in Africa, Latin America, and Asia; and the contradictions among the imperialist powers themselves.

Beijing maintained that it was the "socialist camp," led by the Soviet Union, that constituted the "main force" of the world revolution. The "democratic and progressive forces" in the very heartland of imperialism, driven by their own class interests, would resist the plots of their domestic class oppressors. The colonial and semicolonial peoples, seeking their sovereign independence, would further weaken imperialist strength. Finally, the imperialist powers, driven by the irrepressible needs of their own economic survival, would debilitate themselves in the course of fracticidal strife. The foreign policy establishment of the People's Republic of China would be required to operate within this complex constellation of opposing forces in order to finally rid mankind of the scourge of imperialism forever.[12]

THE APPLICATION OF MAO'S DOCTRINE

Having formulated the general doctrine that was to govern the PRC's foreign relations, Mao regularly enjoined his followers (in a variety of contexts) "to be firm in principle," but also to "have all the flexibility permissible and necessary for carrying out our principles."[13] However sensible such an admonition appears, it is not particularly helpful as a guide to predicting Beijing's behavior in any particular circumstance. Any number of alternative behaviors are theoretically possible (many of which may be permissible) in any attempt to take advantage of all the major and minor "contradictions" that exist in the contemporary world.

Immediately upon assuming power, Mao announced that "all Chinese without exception must lean either to the side of imperialism or to the side of socialism." The PRC predictably identified with "the side of the anti-imperialist front headed by the Soviet Union."[14] Irrespective of the clear position of the PRC, there is considerable evidence suggesting that between 1947 and 1950, Washington remained confused about what the nature of Sino-American relations ultimately would be. By 1947, the United States had demobilized the military forces that had been marshaled to fight the Second World War. The United States Army had been reduced from the wartime high of 89 divisions to barely 15 ill-trained and ill-equipped divisions. The U.S. Air Force, which had deployed 217 active air groups during the war, was now ready to deploy 2 such groups. There had also been a drastic reduction in the number of combatants operative in the U.S. Navy. Washington hardly appeared prepared for confrontation.

While demobilization proceeded, a decision was made in Washington to disengage from the Chinese civil war. At some point in the effort to establish a viable coalition government for China composed of both Nationalists and Communists, General George Marshall, constrained by agreements with the Soviet Union, and influenced by the advice of State Department specialists, had written off the survival of Nationalist China. The U.S. white paper of August 1949, which charged that the Nationalists had been responsible for their own failure and defeat, simply provided the public with a rationale for a policy that had already been decided upon.

With the ultimate victory of Mao's forces, the United States waited for clear signals from the new regime. U.S. consular offices remained open as Mao's armies swept over China. On January 5, 1950, President Harry Truman announced that the United States would not interfere in any Communist Chinese attempt to invade Taiwan—to which the remaining forces of Generalissimo Chiang Kai-shek had retreated after the defeat on the mainland. On January 12, 1950, Secretary of State Dean Acheson informed the world that the U.S. defense perimeter in the Pacific excluded both the Korean peninsula and the island of Taiwan.[15]

Only with the invasion of South Korea by the armed forces of communist North Korea on June 25, 1950, was there a reactive shift in U.S. West Pacific policy. Washington perceived the North Korean attack as the result of Soviet instigation—as part of a communist program of postwar expansion. The Western response to that attack was to pursue a prudent policy of containment. Under the circumstances, it was unclear what the authorities in Beijing might do. Washington's policy, in 1949, had been to gamble on the notion that a China united by the Maoists might resist the temptation to ally with the Soviet Union. However fondly wished, there appeared to be little to support such a conjecture at that time. Despite the tentative gestures toward the United States made by "liberals" in the Chinese Communist Party, it seems abundantly clear that by 1949 Mao was adamantly opposed to "U.S. imperialism," and there was little that Washington could do to alter that fact. As we have seen, Mao had made his position absolutely clear as early as 1940, and in 1948, Liu Shaoqi, in his "On Internationalism and Nationalism," had insisted that, in the judgment of the Chinese Communist Party, the world was inescapably divided into two mutually antagonistic camps, that of imperialism and that of socialism. As though to confirm the antagonism, in April 1949 local Communist Chinese officials in Mukden arrested U.S. Consul General Angus Ward and four of his aides. There seems to be little doubt that the Maoist leadership had decided that the United States government was an enemy of "China reborn."

Irrespective of all that, when the United States authorities decided to intervene in the Korean conflict on June 27, they dismissed the possibility that the new government of China would mobilize and dispatch its military forces to engage those of the United Nations. In 1950, the People's Republic of China was understood to be burdened by grievous economic problems, suffering from military inadequacies, inhibited by logistical problems, and threatened by domestic resistance. That it would choose such an occasion to test the armed might of the United States appeared to be highly improbable.[16] Nonetheless, in October and November 1950, the leadership in Beijing put together an initial intervention force of 30 divisions of the People's Liberation Army (PLA) to confront the troops of the United Nations. By mid-April 1951, the PRC had committed 19 armies and 57 divisions to the conflict on the Korean peninsula.[17] From then until the armistice of 1953, the Americans and Chinese, for the first time in their respective histories, remained locked in mortal combat on the Korean battlefield.

Most Americans had not expected that eventuality. U.S. officials felt that they had signaled Beijing of Washington's intention to enter into normal relations with Maoist China.[18] To the Communist Chinese, however, every U.S. overture constituted one more instance of duplicity, covert aggression, and malevolence. To Mao, the United States was only the most recent in the long series of Western imperialist predators that had succeeded in unhinging the life of China. Thus, when the military forces under the command of the United States crossed the 38th parallel on the Korean peninsula and proceeded toward the Yalu River, which marks the boundary between Korea and the People's Republic of China, Mao interpreted the move as a mortal threat to the survival of China. He called upon the Chinese people to resist the imperialists. Approximately 500,000 Chinese were thrown into unequal combat against the firepower of U.N. forces. In just two weeks of heavy ground operations (May 15–31, 1951), for example, the PLA sustained about 100,000 casualties.

China's decision remains something of a puzzle to analysts. Why, with such economic, logistical, and political problems, and with so little to gain, would the leadership in Beijing commit some of the nation's crack military formations to fight a qualitatively superior enemy? It seems evident that Beijing considered the struggle on the Korean peninsula a threat to the territorial integrity of the PRC—and, indeed, to the survival of the nation.[19] The question is, Why did Mao and his entourage consider the threat so fearful that they were prepared to risk nuclear retaliation?[20] Beijing was convinced that if the United States were not stopped on the Korean peninsula, Washington would proceed with a land invasion of continental Asia.

The failure on the part of policymakers in Washington to take seriously Beijing's threat of intervention in the Korean War was at least in part the consequence of their inability to understand Maoist China's perception of the political, social, and economic system of the United States, even though Mao had been very candid in expressing his views. In 1947, for instance, during the civil war between the Nationalists and the Communists, Mao maintained, "after the victorious conclusion of the . . . Second World War, U.S. imperialism and its lackeys . . . stepped into the shoes of German and Japanese imperialism and formed a reactionary camp against . . . the liberation of the Chinese people."[21] A year later, he repeated this contention: "Since the victory of World War II, U.S. imperialism and its running dogs in various countries have taken the place of fascist Germany, Italy and Japan and are frantically preparing a new world war and menacing the whole world."[22]

By the time of the founding of the People's Republic of China, Mao's perception of the United States as a "fascist" aggressor was an integral part of the belief system of China's communist leadership. This image of the United States, and its implications with respect to the American political character, influenced the Maoist deliberations that ultimately led to the decision to massively intervene in the conflict on the Korean peninsula. There is no credible evidence that Beijing's decision to intervene was influenced by the Soviet Union. Beijing decided to enter the conflict because it deemed its entry vital to the survival of the nation.[23]

That the United States, having only recently emerged from the most devastating war in its history, war-weary and demobilized, intended a land invasion of China's vast territory is so bizarre a notion that only the most well-entrenched prejudgment could prevail against it. It was just such a prejudgment that Mao entertained. He had decided that "U.S. imperialism and its running dog Chiang Kai-shek have replaced Japanese imperialism . . . and adopted the policies of turning China into a U.S. colony. Confronted by these reactionary policies of U.S. imperialism . . . the Chinese people have no way out except through struggle. . . . As far back as April 1945, our Party's Seventh National Congress foresaw the possibility that U.S. imperialism . . . would carry out these reactionary policies and formulated a complete and fully correct political line to defeat them."[24] Given these convictions, Beijing's intervention in response to

U.S. involvement in the Korean conflict was certainly a possibility that U.S. policymakers should have anticipated.

There seems to be a tendency among U.S. officials charged with the formulation of foreign policy to dismiss such "ideological" considerations from their deliberations. Even though they are frequently shown to be wrong, they tend to deal "pragmatically" with many issues. In familiar contexts, such a disposition may be helpful in efforts to reduce the level of emotion and to expose "real" as opposed to "seeming" disagreements that arise in negotiations. In dealing with "ideocratic" political systems, however, such "rational choice" assessments may not be entirely functional.

Ideocratic political systems are unique in that they are predicated on a reasonably well articulated set of formal emotive and substantive beliefs. The rationale of the "revolution" as well as its very legitimacy turn on the "justice" and "truth" of its belief system. In their relations with others, such systems make appeal to some determinate set of moral and substantive beliefs in order to vindicate their position. They assume certain postures, for example, because "all of history is the history of class struggle"—a conflict between oppressors and oppressed. The world consists of imperialist and proletarian nations locked in overt or covert moral, political, and sanguinary conflict. "Principle" requires the assumption of support for one position or another.

Between 1947 and 1950, U.S. officials dealing with Sino-American policy seem to have underestimated the extent of Communist Chinese apprehensions concerning U.S. policies in East Asia. China's Maoists entertained substantive convictions about the intentions of the U.S. that were extremely resistant to counterevidence. Beijing perceived the U.S. rehabilitation of Japan and the presence of U.S. military forces in the Philippines and the islands of the Pacific as part of an elaborate plot to attack continental China and to reduce it to a colony, an additional opportunity for trade and investment.

Washington officials seem to have harbored a sense of grievance, not because Maoists held such views but because the Maoist revolutionaries had not respected the procedural rules that govern international conduct. Authorities in Beijing had seized some U.S. properties in contravention of the established rules for the protection of property. The arrest of U.S. consular officials in Mukden was also a transgression of proper conduct and common usage. Because they focused on these procedural infractions rather than on Maoist substantive beliefs, U.S. officials thought it likely, irrespective of prevailing tensions, that the United States and the Communist Chinese regime would eventually commence normal relations.

U.S. policymakers remained convinced that the leadership of the PRC would not directly intervene in the Korean crisis, even after the commitment of United States forces to combat. Such an action did not appear to them to be in China's best interests. But when United Nations forces approached Manchuria, Beijing considered China to be in mortal peril (given the Maoist conviction that all intentions of the "imperialist" United States were malevolent) and opted to enter the war.

In retrospect, there is every reason to believe that U.S. policy in the period immediately preceding the outbreak of hostilities in Korea was primarily directed not against Maoist China, but against what was seen to be growing Soviet influence in China. A clear indication by Beijing, at the close of the civil war in China in 1949, that China under Mao's rule would not automatically align itself with Moscow would probably have elicited positive responses from Washington.[25] Instead, Beijing chose to "lean to one side." Its unremitting hostility to "U.S. imperialism" and its unqualified commitment to the "proletarian-socialist world revolution" under the leadership of the Soviet Union drove it to enter the armed confrontation in Korea.

The conflict in Korea shaped U.S. policy toward Maoist China for the next two decades. Washington was thereafter determined to halt the spread of communism and to more resolutely aid the forces of anticommunism in Asia. In effect, Beijing's doctrinal beliefs contributed to the fulfillment of prophecy: "imperialist America" must necessarily be the enemy of revolutionary China.

EVOLUTION OF THE FOREIGN POLICY OF THE PEOPLE'S REPUBLIC OF CHINA

In 1949, the PRC was prepared to assume a "revolutionary" posture that was perhaps even more radical than that of the Soviet Union. Not only was Mao prepared to "lean to one side" in the conflict between imperialism and socialism, but officials in Beijing became vocal advocates of "anti-imperialist wars of national liberation" in the colonial and semi-colonial areas of Asia, Africa, and Latin America. At the Asian and Australian Trade Union Conference in Beijing in November 1949, as though to celebrate the establishment of the People's Republic, Liu Shaoqi called upon the foreign delegates in attendance to return to their respective countries and proceed along the "Chinese road" to liberation from the trammels of imperialism.[26] Liu employed the argument advanced by Mao in 1940: "Unless there is a policy of alliance with Russia, with the land of socialism, there will inevitably be a policy of alliance with imperialism, with the imperialist powers."[27] There was apparently "no third way."[28]

One unfortunate consequence of this interpretation of Maoist declaratory doctrine was Beijing's involvement in a costly military conflict with United Nations forces on the Korean peninsula. Moreover, Mao, confident as a result of his recent victory on the mainland of China, overestimated the revolutionary possibilities afforded by the virtual collapse of Western colonial power in Asia. The armed insurrections that occurred during this period in Malaya, Burma, Indonesia, and the Philippines, and that flared briefly in India, were all suppressed. With the ominous exception of Vietnam, the policy of armed insurrection, as part of the world revolutionary struggle, was a signal failure. Beijing, in fact, was in no position to provide other than propaganda support for most of these efforts. Whatever material assistance was provided was limited by Beijing's marginal resources and its remoteness from the revolutionary scene.

The failure of revolution in Asia, and the sobering experience of the Korean conflict, led the foreign policy establishment in Beijing to reconsider the nation's alternatives. Originally, Beijing had expected that North Korea would cancel the "imperialist" enclave in South Korea and that the armed forces of the PRC would finally liquidate the remnants of Chiang Kai-shek's forces in the Taiwan redoubt. The success of national liberation movements in Malaya, Burma, Indonesia, the Philippines, and India would have completed a major part of the world revolution anticipated by Mao.

Washington's response to the invasion of South Korea, Beijing's abandonment of its assault on Taiwan, the Soviet Union's evident hesitancy in directly engaging the armed forces of the United States, and the suppression of revolutionary efforts along China's southeastern periphery led to a marked shift in Beijing's foreign policy. The PRC resorted to the diplomatic flexibility that had been enjoined by Mao and that had been held in reserve.

It seemed evident to Beijing that the struggle with imperialism would be more protracted than had been anticipated. Maoist China was prepared to acknowledge the strategic usefulness of the "neutral" nations in such a conflict. States following a "third way" might yet be made to serve the purposes of the revolution. Consequently, Beijing initiated a campaign to foster normal diplomatic relations with such nonaligned nations as India, Pakistan, Indonesia, and even Egypt—which but a few months previously Beijing had identified as a "fascist military dictatorship."[29] By

1960 the PRC had concluded agreements that defined its borders with Nepal, Pakistan, Afghanistan, and the Mongolian People's Republic to the north.

Beijing reminded its international audience that Mao had always advocated the normalization of diplomatic relations with "any nation" prepared to reject the Nationalist Chinese and to engage in "friendly" interaction with Beijing. If the world were not to be transformed immediately, the PRC recognized the usefulness of establishing its own international legitimacy. That concern was supplemented by what had apparently become a serious preoccupation with the integrity of the nation's boundaries.

In the international arena, Beijing seems to have been impressed by the fact that many reactionary governments, previously dismissed as "lackeys of imperialism," displayed considerable policy independence in the United Nations, distinguishing their positions from those of the "oligarchic masters" of U.S. "imperialism." Moreover, Beijing's new conciliatory spirit seemed to accord well with the international strategy of Moscow—to pursue "peaceful coexistence" with the nuclear-armed enemy.

By the time of Josef Stalin's passing in 1953, Beijing had decided to qualify the aggressive policies it had pursued since the effective termination of the Chinese civil war. Only the conflict in Vietnam remained a promising instance of resolute anti-imperialist armed struggle—and in the spring of 1953 Beijing began to accelerate the deliveries of military equipment to the insurrectionary Viet Minh. In 1954, the French forces were defeated at Dien Bien Phu. Estimates vary, but the Communist Chinese are generally credited with providing artillery, ammunition, and other equipment, supported by about 2,000 personnel, to strengthen General Vo Nguyen Giap's successful operations against the French fortress.

The Vietnam connection involved Beijing's contacts with the Pathet Lao in Laos, and the revolutionaries profited from the PRC involvement in Viet Minh operations. The complex situation prompted the major powers to convene an international conference in Geneva in 1954 in an effort to mitigate the tensions in Asia, and specifically in Indochina, through negotiations. The Geneva Accords that resulted were more notable for being breached than for being observed. The United States was clearly opposed to the increased communist activity in Laos, as well as to the dominant position enjoyed by the communist leaders in Hanoi, who threatened to transform all of Vietnam into a "proletarian-socialist state." Beijing continued to support the Laotian insurgents and the

Vietnamese infiltrators, who remained active in Laos throughout the entire period.

By 1954, Beijing had begun systematic efforts to elicit the support of the nonaligned states in Asia, the Middle East, and Africa. The Asian neutrals were perceived as potential candidates for incorporation into an anti-imperialist united front "from above"—a union of states whose mutual interests were essentially anti-imperialist. Beijing sought to establish relations with these states and evidenced an almost calculated indifference to their domestic policies. The Indonesian government, for example, was courted by Beijing even though it had suppressed an effort by the Indonesian Communist Party to overthrow it in 1948. The government of Pakistan, an Islamic state, was anticommunist in principle, and Egypt under the military rule of Nasser had suppressed the Egyptian Communist Party. Nonetheless, Beijing refused to criticize Pakistan's domestic policies and established trade relations with Cairo that were clearly calculated to seduce.

The shift away from the aggressiveness explicit in the "two camps" doctrine of 1949 allowed Beijing to enter into relations with "feudal-capitalist," but tendentially "anti-imperialist," states that promised to oppose U.S. policies in East Asia. In April 1955, Zhou Enlai formally enunciated the new policy at the Bandung Conference, and in doing so elaborated on themes he had articulated as early as 1951.[30] The PRC's new policy was based on the "Five Principles of Peaceful Coexistence": respect for each nation's territorial integrity, nonaggression, noninterference in another nation's domestic affairs, equality among states, and peaceful coexistence.

Between 1951 and 1954–1955, the leadership in Beijing clearly abandoned its commitment to overt incitement of subversion and revolution in the newly independent nations of Asia, Africa, and the Middle East. In general, Beijing accepted the tactical necessity of working with these nonaligned, noncommunist nations without attempting to foment rebellion. Beijing seems to have made an effort to allay the suspicions of its Asian neighbors; for example, it ordered a cessation of incitement to antigovernment activity by the pro-PRC Chinese in Indonesia. Beijing remained convinced, nonetheless, that the world balance of power could be significantly altered if the PRC assumed the leadership of an anti-imperialist political bloc. Moreover, whenever the PRC's vital interests were affected, the leadership in Beijing did not hesitate to violate the Five Principles of Peaceful Coexistence in interfering in the domestic affairs of any nation—including those with whom it had formal diplomatic ties. Therefore, since the PRC's security interests were presumably engaged in

Laos and Vietnam—nations with whom it shared borders—Beijing continued to support the antigovernment Pathet Lao and to arm the revolutionary forces of Ho Chi Minh throughout this period.[31]

In Cambodia, where Beijing had similar security concerns, but where there was no local communist organization with which it might collaborate, it employed threats and blandishments (in the form of promised economic aid—the first such offer extended by the PRC to a noncommunist nation) to prompt Norodom Sihanouk to sign a friendship treaty with the PRC.

Beijing also extended offers of trade to both Djakarta and Pakistan. This period (1951–1955) marked the commencement of Beijing's systematic use of foreign trade as "a weapon for international political struggle."[32] Within one year of the Bandung Conference, Beijing had signed ten trade agreements with Arab countries including Egypt, Syria, and Lebanon. The trade agreement with the "military fascist regime" in Cairo resulted in one of the largest cotton sales in Egypt's history, as well as the sale by the PRC of 60,000 tons of steel to Egypt—at prices that were 20 percent lower than those on the world market—although the steel was desperately needed in China. This agreement was among the most important because in May 1956, Egypt became the first Arab nation to enter into formal diplomatic relations with Beijing. The PRC's diplomatic offensive in the Middle East had brought it its first significant international diplomatic recognition in six years. In November 1956 Egypt, Syria, and Yemen opposed, for the first time, the U.S.-supported postponement of the debate on whether the PRC should be admitted to the United Nations.

Beijing's success signaled the end of the PRC's political isolation and marked a lessening of support for the West by Arab nations of the Middle East. The consequence was that the Arab countries became increasingly dependent upon the socialist countries for economic, military, and political support. Relations between Egypt and the Western powers worsened in 1956 with Cairo's nationalization of the Suez Canal, and Beijing supported Nasser. Beijing was apparently convinced that the Arab world had finally recognized that its principal opponent was "Western imperialism," and if that were true, the Arab nations could be drawn into a "united front from above" directed against U.S. imperialism. In spite of their "feudal" domestic policies, the Arab nations were "progressive" in their potential anti-imperialism. When the British, French, and Israelis intervened in the Suez crisis in 1956, Beijing seemed certain that Mao's theory of an inevitable conflict between the imperialist powers and the nations that formerly constituted the colonial world had been confirmed, and that in the world struggle between imperialism and socialism, a series of revolutionary wars of national liberation would precede the dissolution of Western (particularly U.S.) power in the "intermediate zones."

In 1957 Beijing hailed the launching of the first artificial earth satellite by the Soviet Union. Given this technological accomplishment, Beijing anticipated that Moscow would no longer fear U.S. nuclear arms and would therefore play a more aggressive role in the anti-imperialist struggle. Mao overlooked the lackluster performance of the Soviet Union during the Suez crisis, and the crisis in Syria in 1957–1958, and announced that "the East Wind has prevailed over the West Wind"—an allusion to socialist superiority in the balance of world power—and that the worldwide success of socialist revolutions was imminent.

Thus inspired, in 1958 Maoist China embarked on the ill-fated Great Leap forward—an effort by the PRC to match the Soviet Union's recent technological accomplishment in space with a spectacular development of industry and agriculture.

At the same time, the PRC's foreign policy became increasingly aggressive. Beijing prepared to launch an attack against the Nationalist-garrisoned offshore islands in the Taiwan Strait—part of its calculated policy of "engaging the enemy on as many fronts as possible."[33]

The provision by the United States of support for the Nationalist defenders on Kinmen (Quemoy) and Matsu, the loss of numerous PRC combat aircraft over the Taiwan Strait, and Moscow's continued reluctance to directly confront the United States once again created serious tensions in Beijing. At the same time, a crisis in Sino-Indonesian relations began to develop over Djakarta's treatment of its resident Chinese population.

By 1959, relations between the People's Republic of China and the Soviet Union had already begun to show signs of tension. Nikita Khrushchev's "deStalinization" campaign, for example, had precipitated a reaction in Beijing. At the Eighth Congress of the Chinese Communist Party in September 1956, a decision had been made (apparently by Mao's critics) to delete all references to the "Thought of Mao Zedong" from the party Constitution, and there were intimations that Mao was expected to withdraw from active party leadership. The report of the outgoing Central Committee was delivered not by Mao, but by Liu Shaoqi. The Hundred Flowers campaign (May 1956–June 1957), an effort to elicit the critical thought of China's intellectuals, brought forth a torrent of complaints directed at the nation's leadership, including the communist party.

These bitter challenges to Mao reinforced his decision to call for a domestic "Great Leap Forward," to re-establish his unchallenged leadership and to make the PRC a major actor in the international arena. The apparent determination of the United States to "contain" Beijing's initiatives by entering into military alliances with compliant Asian states, providing support against the PRC's military actions in the Taiwan Strait, and increasing its involvement in Indochina and Indonesia contributed to Mao's decision to once again modify his tactics.

On the domestic scene, Mao undertook to accelerate China's economic development by mobilizing the masses, inspiring them with his "thought," and substituting moral incentives for bureaucratic planning. An expanded economic base was seen as a prerequisite for a more assertive foreign policy. In 1958, Beijing announced its decision to develop its own nuclear deterrent. It was clear that Maoist China was entering a new phase of its inevitable struggle against "U.S. imperialism."

THE COMMENCEMENT OF THE SINO-SOVIET DISPUTE

There is considerable evidence indicating that difficulties between the People's Republic of China and the Soviet Union arose in the early history of their interaction. It seems equally evident that there were disagreements between Mao and the highest authorities in Moscow. Soviet pretentions, a disposition to meddle in Chinese affairs, and a general lack of concern for Chinese sensibilities contributed to the difficulties. But beyond that, there were profound ideological and foreign policy disagreements between the leaders of the world's two largest communist powers. By 1960, the Chinese Communists had begun to carefully document the differences that were slowly unravelling the "proletarian internationalism" that had been the basis of the "lasting and indestructible eternal friendship" between the PRC and the USSR.[34]

Beijing's polemic against Soviet "revisionism" began with a Communist Chinese rehearsal of Lenin's interpretation of imperialism. Lenin's "truths" were irrefutable. A "financial oligarchy" in the capitalist countries sought a redivision of the world in order to assure themselves access to "world markets, sources of raw materials and fields for investment." So long as "capitalist imperialism exists," Beijing reminded Marxist-Leninists, "the source and possibility of war will remain."

Beijing's leaders concluded that the imperialists, in their frantic attempt to repress revolution, might launch a nuclear war—but even if they do, "it will certainly not be the so-called annihilation of mankind. . . . The victorious people would very swiftly create a civilization on the ruins of imperialism a thousand times higher than the capitalist system and a truly beautiful future for themselves."

Actually, the Maoists neither anticipated nor advocated such a conflict. They argued that the "socialist camp" had achieved military and political superiority over the "imperialist camp" and as a consequence, had effectively foreclosed the imperialist's nuclear option. Moreover, the contradictions among the imperialist countries made their recourse to nuclear weapons increasingly unlikely. Finally, to compound the problems that faced the imperialists, the nations of the Third World, in resisting imperialism, were limiting the capitalists' international markets and denying them access to raw materials. In Beijing's judgment the imperialist nations, with limited markets and investment outlets, as well as mounting domestic economic problems, and in constant competition among themselves for a declining share of the world's resources, were in an irreversible state of decline.

Their analysis led the leadership in Beijing to formulate several foreign policy conclusions: (1) nuclear peace was reasonably certain (and in any case, nuclear war was not to be feared); (2) ultimately, peace could be guaranteed only by the total destruction of imperialism in all its forms; (3) in the interim, compromises with the imperialist powers were "entirely permissible and necessary. . . ," for although there "should be firmness in principle," there must be "flexibility in tactics in revolutionary struggle"; (4) tactical compromises should not obscure the reality that all "methods of revolution and forms of struggle should be employed against imperialism . . . including the illegal and the 'legal,' the extraparliamentary and the parliamentary, sanguinary and bloodless, economic and political, military and ideological"; and (5) although the principal contradiction in the contemporary world is that between socialism and imperialism, the contradiction between the imperialists and the developing countries of Asia, Africa, and Latin America will determine the outcome of the struggle.

In substance, Beijing argued that there should be peaceful coexistence between states with different social systems, but that the international "class war" between oppressors and the oppressed should continue unabated. "We Communists," the Maoist ideologues contended, "fight in defense of world peace and for the realization of the policy of peaceful coexistence. At the same time, we support the anti-imperialist revolutionary wars of the oppressed nations and the revolutionary wars of the oppressed peoples for their own liberation and social progress, because all these revolutionary wars are just wars. . . . [The] replacement of capitalist imperialism by socialism and communism is the final goal of our struggle. We must not conceal our principles from the masses."[35]

Beijing's objections to Moscow's policies turned on what the Maoists considered "revisionism's" dilution of Lenin's revolutionary principles. Beijing saw Moscow's exclusive emphasis on peaceful coexistence not only a betrayal of its revolutionary heritage, but a fundamental error in international political strategy. The Maoists held that the compromises reached with capitalist states served the ultimate interests of the revolution by ensuring the maintenance of international peace. But the "class struggle within the capitalist countries and the revolutionary anti-imperialist struggles of the oppressed nations" belonged to a "different category" and should not be compromised.[36] Such struggles were part of the revolutionary process that was taking place, and it was the obligation of all revolutionaries to support such efforts in the service of the "historical mission of the proletariat."

Beijing maintained that "the whole cause of the international proletarian revolution hinges on the outcome of the revolutionary struggles of the people of [Asia, Africa, and Latin America]. . . . Therefore, the anti-imperialist revolutionary struggle of the people [of these areas] is definitely not merely a matter of regional significance, but one of overall importance for the whole cause of proletarian world revolution."[37] For Beijing, "the contradictions of the world are concentrated in Asia, Africa and Latin America."[38]

The Communist Chinese took their Soviet counterparts to task for not supporting Nasser during the Suez crisis, for failing to support the Algerian "national liberation struggle" against France, for supporting U.N. intervention in the Congo in collusion with U.S. imperialists, and for allowing themselves to be humiliated by the United States during the Cuban missile crisis. To Beijing, Moscow had failed to provide the "fraternal" revolutionary support for the wars of liberation in the developing countries.

In the early 1960s, Beijing decided to provide the missing support for the national liberation movements in the Third World. It had already accorded diplomatic recognition to the Algerian National Liberation Front—something the Soviet Union had been loath to do. Closer to its own borders, the PRC increased its material assistance to the "White Flag" communist revolutionaries in Burma and to the Pathet Lao insurrectionists in Laos, and it was continuing its flow of arms to the insurgents in Vietnam. In 1958, Beijing had offered to send "volunteers" to Indonesia in an effort to strengthen Djakarta's "anti-imperialist" foreign policies.[39]

At about the same time, Beijing began to evince increased interest in the revolutionary potential of sub-Saharan Africa. Documents that have since become available indicate that Beijing had become convinced that Africa was "both the center of the anti-colonialist struggle and the center for East and West to fight for the control of the intermediate zone, so that it has become the key point of world interest."[40]

This was a conviction that matured at a time when more and more of the former colonies of sub-Saharan Africa were being granted independence. Between the end of the Second World War and 1960, only six African nations south of the Sahara had achieved formal independence. In 1960, however, sixteen states in sub-Saharan Africa became independent. Almost immediately, an international meeting was convened in Conakry, Guinea, from which the "imperialist powers" were excluded. Zhou Enlai sent messages of greetings, and the head of the Chinese delegation to the conference delivered a speech in which he emphasized the relevance to Africa of the Chinese "path to national liberation."

Beijing was convinced that the African states would seize the initiative against foreign imperialism. In doing so, they would develop a new consciousness of "proletarian obligation," and "the whole African continent, and the 200 million and more Africans [would] advance to the forefront" of the world revolution. Beijing expected to supplant the Soviet Union as leader of the new wave of revolution in the expanding "intermediate zone."

To give concrete expression to its militancy, Beijing began training African guerrillas to participate in wars of liberation. Training camps for Africans were established near Nanjing, and clandestine operations were subsequently undertaken on the African continent, financed and supported by Beijing. Such camps were ultimately established in at least five African countries (Burundi, the Congo, Ghana, Tanzania, and Zambia), and arms for African rebel forces were transshipped not only through Burundi and Tanzania, but through Uganda as well.

The bases in Ghana and Tanzania were particularly notorious. By 1965, Chinese instructors were training individuals from Portuguese Angola, Niger, Zaire, Nigeria, Gabon, Upper Volta, Cameroon, Rwanda, Zambia, Malawi, and Tanzania in guerrilla warfare tactics.[41] It soon became evident that they were to be used not only against the colonial regime in Portuguese Angola, but against "reactionary bourgeois" regimes throughout Africa, including independent Kenya, Cameroon, the Congo, and Burundi.[42]

Given China's limited resources and its distance from the African continent, PRC support for an African revolution was more rhetorical than material. Beijing's policies were dictated by its assessment of the world situation, its own immediate interests, its perception of the "inevitable struggle" between imperialism and socialism, and its effort to supply the support in the intermediate zone that the Soviet Union was either unwilling to provide or incapable of providing. Beijing had interpreted the events on the continent—the Suez crisis, the uprisings in Algeria and the Congo—as harbingers of the "wave of revolution" that would result in the final defeat of imperialism.

While all this was transpiring, the differences between the PRC and the USSR had become public knowledge. In mid-1963, the Chinese Communist Party openly identified the policies of the Soviet Union with "revisionism." In 1964, Beijing argued that the leadership in Moscow was preparing for the "restoration of capitalism" in the Soviet Union. "Degenerate elements" from the party and the bureaucracy had come to constitute a "privileged stratum" opposed to the workers and had made profit the basic principle of national production. To gain support for their position, Soviet leaders were "peddling bourgeois ideology, bourgeois liberty, equality, fraternity and humanity, inculcating bourgeois idealism . . . and the reactionary ideas of bourgeois individualism, humanism and pacifism among the Soviet people and debasing socialist morality."[43]

More ominous than these doctrinal differences were the growing intimations that the leadership in Beijing had begun to regard the boundaries between the PRC and the USSR as a matter of dispute. China had long considered Outer Mongolia part of its territory. In 1949, and again in 1954, Mao apparently raised the boundary issue in discussions with Soviet representatives. By 1960, the Soviet Union was officially protesting what it described as "systematic violations of the Soviet border" by elements of the PRC military. In March 1963, the *People's Daily* raised questions concerning the "unequal treaties" of Aigun (1858), Beijing (1860), and St. Petersburg (1881), which had established the boundary between tzarist Russia and imperial China. The clear implication was that the boundary arrangements were intrinsically unjust. In July 1964, Mao made pointed reference to the territories that tzarist Russia had acquired at the expense of a debilitated China during the nineteenth century. To a group of visiting Japanese socialists, Mao reflected on the fact that "about 100 years ago the region east of Baikal became Russian territory and since then Vladivostok, Khabarovsk, Kamchatka and the other places have been added to the Soviet Union. We have not yet made our claims against this list."[44] He also alluded to the territories wrested by the Soviet Union from Japan, Finland, East Germany, Poland, and Romania at the end of the Second World War—as though he were suggesting the possibility of political cooperation between those nations for the purpose of effecting a revision of the territorial settlements made at the termination of that war.

Whatever his intentions may have been in introducing the subject, the impact on Moscow was electric.

Mao Zedong seemed only dimly aware that at that time, the Soviet Union had already commenced what was to become the most awesome arms buildup in history. Moscow had always assessed the military capabilities of the United States far more realistically than did Beijing. Sometime in the early 1960s, a decision was made in Moscow to achieve, at a minimum, conventional and nuclear arms parity with the United States. The Soviet Union began rapidly accelerating its military procurements and extending its forward deployments into its Far Eastern provinces. In 1962, the first Soviet armored and infantry divisions appeared along the Chinese border, and Moscow initiated collateral development of an infrastructure in these provinces. Hard-surfaced roads were constructed over thousands of miles of permafrost, and work began on the Baikal-Amur Main Line Railway. Command posts, airfields, and supply depots were constructed, and critical structures were hardened against the effects of nuclear blast. It was obvious that the Sino-Soviet border dispute had the potential of becoming a fundamental security problem for Beijing.

COLLAPSE OF THE FOREIGN POLICY OF THE PEOPLE'S REPUBLIC OF CHINA

While the crisis was developing in the North, Beijing's policies in Southeast Asia began to falter. For years Beijing had attempted to enlist Indonesia's support against "U.S. imperialism" and to reduce Soviet influence in the region. By 1963, Beijing was stating that its relations with Indonesia had reached a "new stage." The PRC supported Indonesia's claims against Malaysia, and in 1964 a leader of a Chinese friendship delegation hinted that the PRC might directly support Indonesia in the event of war. At the same time, President Sukarno explicitly referred to the United States as one of the "imperialist" powers obstructing his nation's just cause.

By September of that year, the PRC's commitment to Indonesia seemed firm. The Soviet Union had been equivocal concerning its support for Djakarta's initiatives against Malaysia, and Indonesia had fallen in arrears in its debt repayments to Moscow. Djakarta drew closer to Beijing at about the time that the People's Republic of China exploded its first nuclear device and Khrushchev was deposed. Sukarno made an unscheduled visit to Beijing and was promised extensive economic and military assistance. It was during those negotiations that Zhou Enlai advised Sukarno to concentrate on conducting a guerrilla war against Malaysia and urged the formation of a "fifth force" or "people's militia" in Indonesia.

Apparently the plan was to initiate a "combined Sino-Indonesian thrust against Malaysia" to achieve a tactical linking with the Vietcong in South Vietnam, in order to finally eliminate the remaining "imperialist" bases in Southeast Asia. This was to be achieved with the increasing involvement of the Indonesian Communist Party, the *Partai Komunis Indonesia* (PKI), under the leadership of D. N. Aidit who, since 1963, had begun to assume a more and more pro-Beijing orientation. In accordance with the PKI's increasing rapprochement with Beijing, Aidit announced that "revisionism" constituted a "main danger" to communist aspirations in Asia. He emphasized the inevitability of a split between the domestic Indonesian "national bourgeoisie" and the native "progressive forces" led by the Indonesian Communist Party. Whatever else this may have meant, Aidit's call for a people's militia suggested that he might, with Sukarno's acquiesence, put together an Indonesian equivalent of the Red Army that would be used both against Malaysia and to secure domestic power.[45]

At about this time, Lin Biao's famous *Long Live the Victory of People's War!* was published.[46] Lin specifically invoked the Chinese model of the anti-Japanese and anti-Nationalist revolutionary campaign as paradigmatic for all "revolutionary struggles of the oppressed nations and peoples throughout the world." "The seizure of power by armed force," Lin reminded his audience, "the settlement of the issue by war, is the central task and the highest form of revolution. This Marxist-Leninist principle of revolution holds good universally, for China and for all other countries."[47]

Such statements could only sound singularly ominous to the various noncommunist and anticommunist factions in Indonesia. Beijing had recommended that Sukarno organize a fifth force in the islands, a force that would doubtlessly threaten the capability of the professional military to control what was becoming an increasingly volatile situation. The Communist Party of Indonesia had a broad popular base; what it lacked was an independent military capability. The notion that a people's militia might be organized aroused criticism and created apprehension among the military and the more conservative elements in the population.

Tensions mounted until the end of September 1965, when "left-nationalist" dissident army officers and members of some of the PKI's youth organizations attempted, unsuccessfully, to stage a coup. The extent to which Beijing was directly involved in inciting and arming the revolutionary forces in Indonesia remains unclear. What is clear is that

Beijing had counseled the leadership of the Indonesian Communist Party—and much of Aidit's behavior is traceable to Communist Chinese influence.

The rapid suppression of the coup attempt (in which a number of high-ranking Indonesian army officers were assassinated) led to the accession to power of the more conservative, U.S.-oriented army officers and culminated in the physical extinction of the core of the Indonesian Communist Party. Hundreds of thousands of Indonesian Communists paid with their lives for having joined Beijing in its advocacy of "armed struggle" against the "national bourgeoisie," "people's war," and "anti-imperialist revolutionary war." Beijing not only suffered a massive ideological setback, but it had to forfeit whatever diplomatic gains it had made in Indonesia over the years.

Beijing suffered similar (but less calamitous) failures in its effort to incite a people's war in Malaysia, Thailand, and Kashmir. In 1965, U.S. ground forces made their appearance in South Vietnam and gave every indication of being determined to remain. Fifty thousand Communist Chinese troops were deployed in North Vietnam to secure control of the transportation facilities, and Beijing made munitions and rice available to the revolutionary forces in Vietnam. The people's war in Vietnam was rapidly becoming more complex and perilous; it was also worsening the already strained relations between the PRC and the USSR.

In 1966 Mao himself urged Japanese communist leaders to incite guerrilla warfare in Japan, an idea that was immediately dismissed by Japanese radicals—leading to an open rupture between the Japanese and Chinese communist parties. As the People's Republic of China lapsed into the revolutionary frenzy of the Great Proletarian Cultural Revolution, the incitement to armed revolution became more hysterical. Beijing became increasingly involved in the insurrectionary efforts of the White Flag Communists in Burma—efforts that took many lives but did not succeed in undermining the Burmese government. Beijing also extended moral and material support to the Maoist New People's Army in the Philippines, to foster a peasant rebellion that accomplished little except to prompt the Philippine government to invoke martial law in 1972.

Beijing's revolutionary efforts were no more successful in sub-Saharan Africa. Its endeavors to establish revolutionary bases on the continent were dealt serious setbacks by military coups in Dahomey and the Central African Republic, which immediately broke diplomatic relations with Beijing on the grounds of attempted subversion and incitement to rebellion. Worse still, in early 1966 President Nkrumah of Ghana, who had served as a major conduit for Communist Chinese influence in Africa, was overthrown by a coup, the leaders of which proceeded to expose Beijing's efforts to involve the African states in a series of people's wars directed against both the existing black governments and "U.S. imperialism." In the same year, the Sudanese government denounced Beijing's interference in the domestic politics of the Sudan. In 1967, the vice-president of Kenya denounced the PRC for interference in Kenya's internal affairs, and Nigerian authorities charged the PRC with involvement in the Nigerian civil war.

Beijing also suffered defeats in the Middle East and North Africa. In January 1965, President Habib Bourguiba of Tunisia maintained that the PRC, "under the cover of nationalism and in the name of waging a struggle against imperialism . . . has been trying its utmost to encroach on other nations."[48] In March 1968 the king of Morocco complained of Beijing's interference in the domestic politics of his kingdom. After the failed coup in Indonesia, Egypt's reservations concerning the connection with Beijing increased. Nasser suppressed the pro-Beijing communist elements in Egypt, who had refused to join his Arab Socialist Union. The Egyptian government intimated that the Communist Chinese had provided financial assistance to antigovernment pro-Beijing forces and that relations between the two governments had deteriorated. Although Beijing attempted to disassociate itself from antigovernment elements in the Arab states in a desperate effort to maintain effective relations with those states, the extremism of the Great Proletarian Cultural Revolution did have an effect on those relations. Moreover, Communist China's admonitions to the Arabs to seek resolution of their problems by waging a people's war were largely ignored in Arab capitals. By that time, Beijing had fully identified with the Palestinian Liberation Organization; however, few Arabs were disposed to abandon the strategy of conventional warfare in the Middle East for the kind of guerrilla war advocated by Beijing.

The fact is that neither the Africans nor the Arabs could comprehend Beijing's dual anti-imperialist and antirevisionist strategy. To accept Beijing's foreign policy strategy would have cut off the African and Arab states from both the United States and the Soviet Union, the only powers that could provide the economic and (or) military aid all of them so assiduously sought. The People's Republic of China could offer little of either. Beijing's economic assistance was limited, compared with that made available by Washington and Moscow, and its arms shipments were composed of small arms and obsolescent equipment. By the late 1960s, Beijing's revolutionary efforts in Africa and the Middle East were largely counterproductive.

Beijing's involvement in the Vietnam War succeeded only in establishing that the leadership of the People's Republic of China was long on revolutionary rhetoric but short on material support. Beijing's insistence that achieving national liberation by means of a people's war required "self-reliance" seems to have been an indirect admission of the PRC's inability to provide little more than moral support.[49] As a consequence, Hanoi became increasingly dependent upon Moscow's largesse in order to maintain its troops on the fighting fronts. The Soviet Union was becoming more entrenched in Indochina. Beijing had committed itself to a strategy that could only endanger what were becoming its increasingly critical security concerns.

Beijing's continued belligerence with respect to India after the Sino-Indian border war of 1962 had driven New Delhi to seek greater rapprochement with Moscow and had all but ensured a permanent Soviet presence in South Asia. By the end of 1966, most of the members of Communist China's diplomatic corps, including nearly all its ambassadors, were recalled to the homeland to receive indoctrination with the "Thought of Mao Zedong." Between 1967 and 1969, the People's Republic of China had nearly no foreign representation. In March 1969, clashes took place between armed troops of Communist China and the Soviet Union along the Ussuri River—and for a time there was a threat of war. The military authorities in Moscow had apparently made preparations for a pre-emptive strike against PRC nuclear installations. By the late 1960s, Maoist China found itself threatened by a manifestly superior and increasingly hostile enemy to the North. The heavy commitment by the United States in the South meant that Communist China could very likely become involved in another conflict that would deplete its limited resources and destroy the stability of its government.

Beijing attempted to maintain diplomatic relations with foreign nations whenever doing so served its national interests—for example, with Nepal, Afghanistan, Pakistan, Zambia, and Tanzania. Nonetheless, in sub-Saharan Africa the number of nations that entered into formal diplomatic relations with Beijing declined from seventeen to thirteen. The alienation of Fidel Castro resulted in an almost complete reduction of PRC influence in Latin America.

The Great Proletarian Cultural Revolution had disrupted China's economic development program, interrupted the training of critical personnel, forced the military to assume increasingly onerous burdens of population control and production management, and weakened the entire party apparatus. It seemed clear, to even the most committed, that the policies of the leadership in Beijing were inconsistent with the domestic, regional, and global goals of the revolution.

For all its tactical flexibility, the People's Republic of China had pursued its policy of world revolution with a single-mindedness that jeopardized not only its economy and security, but ultimately, its capacity to maneuver. The single most important factor that influenced Beijing's foreign policy was the international policy being pursued by any given country's government.[50] The anti-imperialist struggle—the conflict with the United States—was the core of PRC foreign policy. The United States constituted its prime enemy in achieving a redistributive world revolution. Those nations that assumed explicit and forceful opposition to U.S. policy could expect to receive Communist Chinese support. Conversely, the Soviet Union's effort to foster détente between the two superpowers was the point of departure for Beijing's increasingly hostile remonstrances.

In its assault on the international status quo, Beijing made common cause with anyone, be they representatives of tribal monarchies, Gaullist capitalists, or communist rebels in the rain forests of Vietnam. In pursuing its "dual revolutionary" policy, Beijing attempted to sustain peaceful coexistence with foreign governments while at the same time exhorting them to join the "armed struggle" and attempting to move them into positions of confrontation with the United States. However well- (or ill-) conceived that policy, Beijing had neither the resources nor the cunning (and was not sufficiently geographically proximate) to adequately orchestrate all the moves necessary to sustain such a complex enterprise. For a time, many noncommunist governments were so sufficiently insecure in their power, and consequently so responsive to Beijing's blandishments, that they were susceptible to the PRC's pressures to adopt policies or issue pronouncements that accorded with its general Maoist program. For a time it also appeared that some nationalist leaders, such as Ben Bella of Algeria, Sukarno of Indonesia, Ne Win of Burma, and Cuba's Fidel Castro, might bring their nations into an effective, Beijing-sponsored, anti-U.S. united front. The coups that unseated Ben Bella and Sukarno, the intransigence of Ne Win, and the ultimate pro-Soviet defection of Castro, undermined any such expectation.

By the spring of 1969, the Great Proletarian Cultural Revolution was over, and it was evident that the threats to the stability and security of the "new China" had led Beijing to search, once again, for an alternative foreign policy. When Secretary of State William Rogers visited Pakistan in May 1969, he was informed by President Yahya Khan that Beijing had communicated to him that "China now considers the USSR and not the U.S. as her enemy number one."[51] The way had been opened to the fateful rapprochement between the United States and the People's Republic of China.

4

Beijing's Rapprochement with the United States

By 1969, all of Beijing's foreign policy interests were being threatened. The Soviet Union had marshaled a multi-purpose military force along the Sino-Soviet border that was fully capable of severely mauling the relatively primitive People's Liberation Army. In March and again in August of that year, Soviet armed forces meted out "firm rebuffs" to Communist Chinese units in border conflicts. Along the Ussuri River and at the Dzungarian Gates in western Xinjiang, several hundred Chinese troops were savaged by Soviet forces. The firefights also involved armored units and helicopter gunships. There is persuasive evidence indicating that the Soviet Union was then planning a pre-emptive strike against Chinese nuclear emplacements and facilities in northern China.

Beijing had not only failed to maintain amicable relations with the Soviet Union, its erstwhile "proletarian-socialist" and "eternal" ally, but it had failed to mobilize and control the international "revolutionary forces" it perceived emerging in the nations that composed the intermediate zone between socialism and imperialism. Mao Zedong seemed to have been mistaken in identifying the Middle East and sub-Saharan Africa as "world centers" of revolutionary contradictions. The most important Arab states remained pro-Western in orientation, and the rest looked to Moscow and not Beijing for support. The newly independent African states pursued policies equally unanticipated by Beijing. Some pursued manifestly pro-Western policies—or fastidiously maintained their "nonalignment." What revolution there was took the form of military-sponsored and military-dominated coups rather than Maoist inspired wars of national liberation. Almost all the African governments that emerged after domestic military coups were totally indifferent to the ideologically motivated policies of Beijing.

The authorities in Beijing did little to repair the damage to PRC's international status and reputation. The increasingly irresponsible radicalism of Beijing's foreign policy was driving the nation further into isolation. Only in Indochina did the armed "revolution" against imperialism appear to be making progress—but even there, the success of "people's war" seemed to redound almost exclusively to the advantage of the Soviet Union. By 1968, Moscow had begun an ambitious policy of expansion into South Asia and Southeast Asia. Also in 1968, Great Britain announced its decision to withdraw the British military presence from the region by the end of 1971. At about the same time, the United States began to give evidence of a desire to extract itself from the Vietnam conflict. In 1969, Nixon announced his plans to withdraw U.S. ground forces from Asia, restricting forward deployment to naval combatants and aircraft.

In effect, by 1969 the Western "imperialists" were creating a power vacuum in Southeast Asia that the Soviet Union seemed prepared to fill. For the first time in its history, the Soviet Union was asserting that the world balance of power had finally shiften in favor of the "socialist bloc." Moscow's initiatives in 1968 and 1969 clearly indicated its decision to increase its influence in East, Southeast, and South Asia. Soviet trade exhibits were opened in Singapore and Kuala Lumpur. Soviet Foreign Ministry representatives made trips to Burma, Laos, Cambodia, and Japan. In 1969, Moscow made its first allusions to the benefits regional alliances would provide the countries of Southeast and South Asia, with the cooperation and support of the Soviet Union.[1] By 1970 Beijing was clearly anticipating armed attack by the USSR.

These were the general circumstances with which the PRC was compelled to deal at the beginning of the 1970s. The leadership in Beijing began to realize that the attempt to oppose both imperialism and revisionism during the late 1960s—while inciting worldwide revolution—had very little to recommend it as a national policy. Mao had always advised isolating one's strongest opponent by encouraging the defection of his real and potential allies from his "camp." That was precisely the purpose of the "united front." Uniting with one's lesser opponents—however briefly and with whatever reservations—could only undermine the strength of one's principal opponent. In the war against Japanese aggression, for example, Mao advocated a union of revolutionary China with its lesser enemies—the United States, Great Britain, and France—against Tokyo. With the defeat of Japan in 1945, the United States emerged as the principal enemy. Mao once again advocated a policy of uniting with China's lesser foes—the Western European capitalist states—to weaken the United States. Beijing should exploit the contradictions among its enemies to serve its own purposes.

Just as the defeat of Japan in 1945 had signaled the appearance of another threatening antagonist, necessitating a new realignment of "united front" forces against imperialism, the apparent defeat of the United States in Southeast Asia meant that Beijing would have to devise a new strategy to deal with yet one more foe.

Throughout 1970, despite the real and imminent threat of war with the Soviet Union, Beijing remained unable to settle on a specific foreign policy strategy. At first, there was an apparent effort to appease the Soviet Union. Declamations against the United States increased measureably. The PRC military, under the leadership of Lin Biao, apparently believed that the purposes of the revolution would best be served by pursuing détente with the Soviet Union and engineering the military defeat of "U.S. imperialism" in Southeast Asia.

The opposing views of the civilian (and party) bureaucracy, which had been largely influenced by Zhou Enlai, could hardly hold sway during the Great Proletarian Cultural Revolution, for the political effectiveness of the civilian bureaucracy had been seriously impaired as a result of the domestic disturbances. The highest-ranking members of these administrative units had been humiliated or deposed. However mistaken and dangerous Zhou and his allies might have perceived Lin's policies to be, they were in no position to effectively oppose them.[2]

At the termination of the Great Proletarian Cultural Revolution in 1969, only the military still retained its effectiveness. Fifty-two percent of all members of the Politburo were military men, as were 72 percent of all Provincial Revolutionary Committee chairmen and 74 percent of all Provincial Party Committee first secretaries.[3] As the dominant force in the PRC's domestic politics, not only did their views on policy prevail, but they controlled state budgetary allocations. During the military's ascendency, between 1966 and 1971, the defense budget of the PRC increased significantly.[4]

This meant both a real and a relative decrement in the allocations for the civilian bureaucracy, as well as a reduction in its responsibilities and a corresponding diminution of welfare and power benefits. And of course, any funds disbursed to the military were withheld from economic modernization and development. To rectify the situation, the "moderate" bureaucrats sought to defuse the military crisis in the North without committing the nation to an aggressive policy against the United States. The interests of the civilian bureaucracy recommended a significant change in policy, a recommencement of economic development, and a curtailment of military procurement.

Throughout 1970, the PRC apparently made a frantic effort to reconstruct the civilian bureaucracy. There was increasing insistence that the military return to the barracks—that the party once again assume "control over the gun." At the same time, through a complex policy of firmness and compromise—influenced by Washington's suggestion that it would not be indifferent should the Soviet Union attack the PRC—tensions along the Sino-Soviet border were eased.[5]

This gradual reduction of tension, as well as the partial disengagement of the military from, and the reconstruction of, the civilian bureaucracy, increased the strength of the faction that had collected around Zhou Enlai. One immediate consequence was an erosion of the power of the military. By late 1970 it had become apparent that support for Minister of Defense Lin Biao and his policies had eroded. The effect was a decision, favored by the civilian bureaucracy, to seek rapprochement with the United States. Mao apparently acceded, for in October he informed Edgar Snow that Richard Nixon would be welcome to visit China. Rapprochement with the United States seemed imminent.

The United States had already made a move toward rapprochement. In his State of the World message in February 1970, Richard Nixon declared that it would be in the interests of the United States to improve relations with the People's Republic of China. In the following months, Washington reduced the restrictions against cultural exchanges, travel, and trade with the PRC that had been in effect for two decades. A presidential commission recommended that the United States no longer oppose the seating of the PRC as a member of the United Nations, and the president initiated a number of unilateral actions to convey to Beijing Washington's seriousness of purpose. On July 15, 1971, following the visit of Henry Kissinger to Beijing, Richard Nixon announced that Zhou Enlai had invited him to visit the PRC in order to explore the possibility of a normalization of relations between the two countries. On February 21, 1972, Nixon arrived in Beijing, and on the 27th the "Shanghai Communiqué," which foreshadowed the establishment of diplomatic relations between Communist China and the capitalist United States, was issued.[6]

The dramatic change in foreign policy represented by Nixon's visit to Beijing disoriented many Americans who had long been convinced of the irreducible hostility between communist nations and the nations of the "free world." Adjustment to the new policy was made easier, of course, by the fact that many Americans are regularly exposed to a variety of opinions on such issues—and for years academics and media professionals had proposed a change in Washington's "China policy."

In the People's Republic of China, however, where there is little public discussion of policy issues, and where all decisions are understood to be the deductive consequence of applying "Marxist-Leninist scientific principles" to a given situation, the visit to Beijing by the leader of "world imperialism" not only produced consternation but generated serious intellectual confusion. It became the task of the authorities in Beijing to provide the ideological rationale for the rapprochement with the capitalist West.

BEIJING'S RATIONALE FOR RAPPROCHEMENT

In December 1971, Zhou Enlai presented an internal report to the Chinese Communist Party that provided the first detailed rationale for Beijing's rapprochement with Washington. Zhou considered the major issues faced by the PRC's foreign policy establishment in the context of the philosophy of "Chairman Mao."

Convinced as they are that they can perceive "historic trends," government authorities in the PRC regularly speak of the "main trends" and the "subsidiary trends" governing contemporary events. For Mao and Zhou, in 1971, the main trend in the contemporary world was revolution. The obligation of revolutionaries was to foster that trend. Zhou believed that the competition between the USSR and the United States afforded Beijing an occasion to exploit the two nations' differences to further world revolution. Even though both the United States and the USSR remained Communist China's "main enemies," a qualified rapprochement with the United States would not only "bankrupt" the China policy pursued for two decades by the "imperialists" in Washington, it would preclude any "collusion" between U.S. imperialists and Soviet revisionists against "revolutionary China." In effect, the rapprochement with the United States was a tactical maneuver that was part of the program to achieve world revolution, which Beijing assumed would be a long process. Therefore, although Zhou advocated reaching some kind of accommodation with the United States, he insisted that the PRC would "never give up [its] principles and sell out [its] people and revolution."[7]

Once the decision was made to agree to rapprochement with the United States, the theoreticians in Beijing were quick to analyze its implications and to flesh out its rationale.[8] By 1973, the "declining" United States had been relegated to the rank of "secondary enemy"; the

Soviet Union was publicly identified as the "most important enemy" of revolutionary China.[9] Both the United States and the USSR were still villains, but Soviet revisionism was "expanding actively," whereas U.S. imperialism was undergoing "retrenchment."

In 1969, Beijing's objections to the Soviet Union, based on ideological differences, had found expression in armed resistance to what were considered violations of Chinese territory along the Sino-Soviet border. Beijing complained that the "Soviet revisionist renegade clique . . . [has] not only wantonly maligned and slandered China . . . but has also massed on the Sino-Mongolian and Sino-Soviet borders troops who repeatedly intruded into China's territory and air space."[10] These Soviet depredations were perceived not simply as a consequence of the malevolence of individual Soviet leaders, but as being representative of a fundamental transformation of the USSR's economic and social base. The argument was that the world was still in the "era of imperialism and the proletarian revolution," as Lenin and Mao had insisted it would be. Since the Soviet Union was no longer a force in the "proletarian-socialist world revolution," it could only be identified as imperialist. Its ideological differences with Beijing, and its violations of Chinese territory, were only symptomatic of the essential transformation taking place in the Soviet Union.

Although the bourgeoisie had been overthrown in the October Revolution of 1917, Beijing's theoreticians argued, the class struggle in the Soviet Union continued. As part of that struggle, after the death of Stalin, a small group of antiproletarian "renegades" had seized the state apparatus and had imposed a "fascist dictatorship" on the working people of the Soviet Union. They had re-created the bourgeois-dominated "state monopoly capitalism" that the revolution was supposed to have transcended.[11]

As a form of state monopoly capitalism, Beijing argued, the Soviet system took on all the attributes of an imperialist state as Lenin and Mao had defined it. The bourgeois renegades who had seized control of the Soviet system were driven to "export capital" and to exert "economic influence" throughout the world in order to compete with Western imperialists. The economic base of "capital-imperialism," like that of Soviet revisionist "social-imperialism" was understood to be "monopoly capitalism." In the Soviet Union, "socialist state ownership" had been changed to "ownership by the bureaucratic monopoly capitalist class," and the "state-owned economy" had been transformed into a "state monopoly capitalist economy." "In essence," the Maoists argued, "there is not much difference between the state monopoly capitalism in the Soviet Union and that in capitalist-imperialist countries. The only difference is that the former, transformed from socialist state ownership, is more intensified in the degree of concentration and monopolization." The result is a particularly virulent form of imperialism that has all the features of "the Hitlerite dictatorship of German fascism."[12]

The virulence of Soviet "social-imperialism" manifests itself in the "plunder" of less-developed countries and the militarization of Soviet society. The Soviet Union has become "one of the world's biggest arms merchants" in its search for market supplements to sustain its parasitic economy. It extracts inordinate interest payments in return for its "economic assistance" to developing countries. In order to satisfy its imperialist impulse, Moscow seeks to impose its "neo-colonialist yoke" on the nations of the Third World.[13]

By the mid-1970s, this analysis had matured into the conviction that Soviet social-imperialism was the "most dangerous source of war." Although social-imperialism was understood to be "entirely the same as capitalist-imperialism," the high degree of concentration of capital characteristic of state ownership made the Soviet Union "more rapacious and more truculent in its aggression and expansion abroad."[14]

This was the theoretical context within which the political leaders in Beijing contemplated closer association with the United States.[15] It was not that Beijing imagined that the "aggressive nature of U.S. imperialism" had changed. What Beijing argued was that the "counterrevolutionary global strategy" of the United States had met with grievous setbacks and that consequently, Washington's power had been greatly diminished. Whereas the Soviet Union was an imminent and adjacent threat, the United States was a weakened and relatively remote opponent.[16]

Because of the prevailing circumstances, the People's Republic of China was prepared to begin temporary and contingent diplomatic relations with the United States. It could then "exploit the contradictions" between Washington and Moscow. Initially it would take advantage of any opportunities to associate with any force capable of isolating and weakening the "principal enemy"; then it would crush the enemies of revolution "one by one." The strategy that was to govern the anticipated conflict was described as follows.

The two arch enemies facing us are U.S. imperialism and Soviet revisionism. We are to fight for the overthrow of these two enemies. This has already been written into the new Party constitution. Nevertheless, are we to fight these two enemies simultaneously, using the same might? No. Are we to ally ourselves with one against the other? Definitely not. We act in the light of changes in the situation, tipping the scale diversely at different times. But where is our main point of attack and how are we to exploit their contradictions? This involves a high level of tactics. Whether or not these tactics are applied properly is a question of paramount importance that determines the fate of the world.[17]

By 1977, this kind of analysis, and the policy prescriptions it contained, became standard fare in the Communist Chinese media.[18] This rationale had become part of the ideological convictions of Deng Xiaoping as early as 1974. In his speech to the Sixth Special Session of the United Nations General Assembly, Deng identified the "two superpowers, the United States and the Soviet Union," as "vainly seeking world hegemony." He characterized both nations as "the biggest international exploiters and oppressors of today. . . . They both keep subjecting other countries to their control, subversion, interference, or aggression. They both exploit other countries economically, plundering their wealth and grabbing their resources."[19] With regard to the issue of what Beijing's policy should be in light of these assessments, and given the configuration of forces in the contemporary world, Deng argued that "all American imperialistic leaders" were enemies of the Chinese revolution; the conflict between the USSR and the United States allowed the PRC to profit at their expense. Just as the United States sought to exploit the differences between Beijing and Moscow, Beijing must adroitly "take advantage of the prevailing contradictions."

Deng indicated that rapprochement with the United States would give the People's Republic of China access to the "scientific and technical knowledge and equipment" necessary for the nation's development. He was convinced that because of Washington's disadvantages in its contest with Moscow, "the American imperialists will defer to our wishes."[20]

At about the same time, Geng Biao (Keng Piao), chief of the Chinese Communist Party's Foreign Liaison Department, reiterated the same theses. Although both the Soviet Union and the United States were enemies of Communist China, it was essential to foreclose the possibility of their collusion. "If we forced these two mighty rulers to unite together as one," Geng maintained, "the result would be unthinkable. . . . From the viewpoint of overall strategy, if we reduce the 'Chinese-U.S.' dispute, we can concentrate fully on the USSR to gain the time needed to resolve our internal problems and construct our nation under relatively peaceful conditions. Therefore, we must do our best and build this friendship [with the U.S.] while working to eliminate the main enemy. This is a practical employment of 'Chairman Mao's revolutionary-diplomatic line,' and is based on the requirements of the current situation."[21]

Fascinated by the dramatic tactical shifts in Beijing's foreign policy, foreign observers often fail to note its doctrinal continuities.[22] The core of

Beijing's foreign policy has always been anti-imperialist. The temporary collaboration between the Chinese Communist Party and its Nationalist Chinese opponents during the Sino-Japanese War was predicated on Mao's conviction that the success of the revolution in China required a concentration of all forces (a "united front") against what was at that time China's "principal enemy." With the defeat of Japan in 1945, the temporary accommodation with the Nationalists could be abandoned and efforts could subsequently be focused on defeating them. Similarly, collaboration with the Western imperialists—Great Britain, France, and the United States—was recommended by the circumstances that prevailed during the "war against fascism."

In the Second World War, the fascist powers constituted the principal enemy and the Western imperialists were only "secondary enemies," with whom compromises could be made to further the cause of world revolution. With the defeat of the principal enemy, the United States took over that role. At that juncture, Beijing was prepared to welcome into its "broad united front" all nations opposed to the United States—even nations under "feudal fascist" and "military fascist" social and political systems. The Soviet Union's failure to assume responsibilities that would bring it into direct confrontation with the United States led to alienation and, ultimately, the conflict between Moscow and Beijing.

As the United States policy of containment in Vietnam proved increasingly ineffective, the Soviet Union emerged as Beijing's primary "imperialist" enemy. The United States was demoted to the rank of secondary enemy, with whom "united front" accommodation might be sought in order to isolate the new principal enemy.[23]

The vast intermediate zone between socialism and imperialism is now spoken of as composed of the "Second and Third Worlds." The Second World, made up of advanced industrial states that have ambivalent relations with both imperialist superpowers, constitutes a diplomatic resource to be used by Beijing to confound the hegemonic ambitions of Moscow and Washington. Beijing conceives the revolutionary potential of the Third World, composed of the "oppressed" and developing nations, to be determinate of the world's future.

Beijing has always conceived of its struggle—both its domestic revolution and its international initiatives—as anti-imperialist. It has always defined its "class enemies" on the basis of their support for imperialism. It has sought as allies, however temporary and expedient, those nations that could be of assistance in the anti-imperialist struggle. It has supported revolution in other nations only to the extent that such revolution would impair the strength, or obstruct the policies, of the imperialists.

To the leadership in Beijing, it was imperialism that had visited anguish on the people of China, warped its history, and denied China its rightful place. Imperialism was the cause of all the social ills of retrograde and "feudal" China. Imperialism is what oppresses millions in the modern world and condemns the bulk of mankind to the torment of poverty and the threat of nuclear destruction. There is very little in the vast literature of Communist China that does not provide evidence of imperialism's inhumanity.

China's communist leaders harbor a deep and abiding suspicion of imperialism and all of its works. Like the troubled leaders of dynastic China in the eighteenth century and at the beginning of the nineteenth century, the Maoists initially attempted to reconstruct their nation on the basis of "self-reliance." Even in the halcyon days of Sino-Soviet "eternal friendship," the Soviet Union was viewed with suspicion. When the effort to modernize the "new China" required an opening to the West, the Maoists (and the post-Maoists), like their Qing forebears, sought to incorporate Western science and technology to the exclusion of Western values. They sought to protect their unique "Chinese socialism," considering it to be of universal value—in the same way that their Qing antecedents had perceived their traditional ways as affording the moral ligaments that bound up the entire world.

The leadership of Communist China has had to abandon or modify many of these notions because of the reality of the modern world with which it must deal. China's security is constantly threatened by Soviet incursions along the Sino-Soviet border, and Soviet influence now stretches from Afghanistan, through India, into Indochina. China's flawed economic system requires extensive reform. And the rapid increase in its human numbers will leave China with a population of about 1.5 billion by the first decades of the twentieth century.

In attempting to come to grips with its population problem, Beijing has been compelled to abandon Marxist notions about the value of large families. To redress the failures of its economic policies, Beijing has been forced to experiment with manifestly "unsocialist" economic modalities. And to reduce the threats to its security, Beijing has sought to compromise with Moscow and to establish relations with the United States. (Before their deaths, both Mao and Zhou conceived the "revolutionary" possibility of exploiting the contradictions between Moscow and Washington to further Communist China's interests. They provided the guidelines followed by Deng and his supporters.)

Washington's decision to enter into diplomatic relations with Beijing was also perceived as serving U.S. interests and was accompanied by a collection of loosely framed arguments designed to lend some coherence to a major shift in foreign policy. Those arguments have never been carefully reviewed, nor have the benefits that have accrued to the United States as a result of rapprochement been carefully assessed.

THE UNITED STATES' RATIONALE FOR RAPPROCHEMENT

Many factors contributed to the U.S. decision to seek rapprochement with the People's Republic of China. Among the most important were the difficulties that surrounded the increasing popular resistance to the long and unconscionably costly war in Vietnam—a war in which the United States had become involved in order to "contain" communist expansion in Asia. These difficulties were compounded by the dollar crisis, accelerating inflation, and the singular lack of growth in the U.S. economy. As U.S. involvement in the war increased, the political costs escalated. Lyndon Johnson chose not to run for another term as president. Congress became increasingly restive concerning U.S. policy in East Asia, perceiving the policy of containment as too rigid, but most of all as too expensive and dangerous.

One of the items included in the implied policy review was a reconsideration of U.S. relations with Communist China. Since the Korean War, the United States had attempted to impose a total embargo on trade with the PRC. U.S. citizens had been proscribed from having any contact with the Maoist government and from purchasing mainland Chinese goods, even in Hong Kong. Washington regularly rejected any discussion in the United Nations of the proposal to seat the PRC.

By the mid-1960s, domestic and international circumstances had prompted a review and reassessment of prevailing policy. In Senate hearings on the war in Vietnam in January and February 1966, it became obvious that any discussion of the war would require an extensive inquiry into U.S. relations with the People's Republic of China. In March, the Senate held hearings on U.S. relations with mainland China, during which a number of sinologists commented on U.S. policy with respect to the PRC.[24] The majority of them favored an end to Beijing's "isolation" and recommended commencement of diplomatic relations with Maoist China. Their argument was that China's continued isolation from the international community would foster bitterness and fanaticism among the leaders of the most populous nation on earth. The PRC's involvement in international affairs would encourage Beijing to moderate its policies because it would have an investment in the world community. Such a policy would strengthen the position of the "pragmatic" and "moderate" Communist Chinese bureaucrats who were struggling to survive in an inauspicious domestic political environment.

Beijing would require technology transfers if it were to solve China's economic problems, according to this argument, and the United States could exploit that need in its effort to draw the PRC into bilateral and multilateral relations with Western nations. Increased contacts would serve the interests of the noncommunist nations because they would exacerbate Sino-Soviet differences, which were perceived as deeply rooted.

In 1967, Richard Nixon gave expression to precisely these notions in an article in *Foreign Affairs*. He spoke of ending the PRC's "angry isolation": "We simply cannot afford to leave China forever outside the family of nations, there to nurture its fantasies, cherish its hates and threaten its neighbors." The United States was counseled to "induce change" in the attitudes of Beijing's leaders and to "persuade" them that they could not satisfy their "ambitions" in "foreign adventures." If Communist China were drawn out of its isolation, its leadership would be induced to turn "inward," to devote their energies to "the solution of [their] own domestic problems."[25]

By the time Nixon acceded to the presidency in 1970, he had formulated the broad outlines of an altered "China policy." In his February State of the World message, he declared it would be in the interests of the United States to take practical steps toward improving relations with Beijing.

In the autumn of his first year in office, Nixon initiated a series of actions marking the liberalization of U.S. policy with regard to the PRC. Travel restrictions to mainland China were modified, and subsidiaries and affiliates of U.S. companies were permitted to sell nonstrategic materials to the PRC. In late 1970 a presidential commission recommended the seating of the PRC in the United Nations, and in 1971 a halt was called to patrols by U.S. naval vessels in the Taiwan Strait.

In 1969, the cumulative pressures of economic dislocation, domestic unrest, congressional resistance, and the seemingly intolerable burden of the policy of containment resulted in the Guam Doctrine, or the Nixon Doctrine—which prescribed a significant reduction in the forward deployment of U.S. forces in the West Pacific. Following this disengagement from Asia, Asian nations were expected to assume the burden of their own defense. The United States would provide only a "nuclear umbrella," that is, a fleet and air presence.

Although the new policy was advertised as allowing greater flexibility in meeting challenges, it was in fact predicated on the conviction that changed circumstances had allowed the United States to disencumber itself of some of the "preoccupations of the past quarter century."[26] The world was no longer bipolar, but multipolar—nations were now grouped in variable and sometimes complex regional and subregional arrangements that could best be preserved by satisfying current U.S. interests rather than by taking actions dictated by "cold war" commitments made a generation ago when the international situation was vastly different.

The reduction in U.S. troop strength along China's periphery served to allay Beijing's apprehensions at a time when its relations with Moscow were becoming increasingly strained. In 1968, the Soviet Union had invaded Czechoslovakia and was clearly prepared to use force to prevent the growth of any "deviant" form of socialism when the interests of the USSR so required. Massive Soviet troop deployments along the Sino-Soviet border suggested to the leadership in Beijing that the People's Republic of China might be subject to the same kind of "fraternal" intervention.

By 1970, both Washington and Beijing had reason to seek some kind of accommodation. It had become perfectly obvious to Washington that a policy of joint containment of the Soviet Union and the People's Republic of China taxed U.S. resources and required efforts that no longer had public or governmental support. Beijing's concerns, as we have seen, were no less troublesome. Thus, when Henry Kissinger made his first visit to Beijing, both Communist China and the United States were motivated to resolve their differences and commence the long process of rapprochement.

The U.S. reasons for seeking rapprochement were not dictated by a set of rationally ordered policy priorities. Rather, Washington sought to normalize relations because of the frustrations of military involvement in Vietnam, the apparent mismatch between U.S. obligations and its resources, the serious Sino-Soviet rift, and the perceived necessity to communicate with the world's most populous nation. All these reasons were essentially ad hoc responses. Washington anticipated that negotiations with Beijing would facilitate the withdrawal of U.S. ground troops from Indochina.[27]

Because the United States was unable or unwilling to match the Soviet arms buildup, which had required Moscow to allocate larger and larger portions of its gross national product to the attainment of conventional arms superiority and nuclear arms parity with the United States, the transformation of the PRC from a liability to an asset became a political

and strategic necessity. Both the Nixon and Ford administrations emphasized common U.S.-PRC strategic interests in opposing the Soviet Union.
The U.S. association with the PRC constituted something of a cost-free
strategic "quick fix."[28]

Any other reasons given for rapprochement were marginal ones.
Some analysts talked about "the great China market," but most of them
expected only a relatively modest growth in U.S.-PRC trade.[29] Thus trade
with mainland China was not one of the initial motives of "imperialist
America" in seeking rapprochement with Beijing, Marxist-Leninist-
Maoist convictions notwithstanding. By 1978 it was fairly obvious that
Maoist China, with or without Mao Zedong, would not enter into effortless cultural and trade relations with the capitalist West. In 1977, analysts
were prepared to admit that it would be "hard to make the case that trade
and cultural contacts with the PRC, in and of themselves, justify the
political costs of normalization. . . . [The] People's Republic will remain a
limited market and [will not be very] open to intellectual and social
interchange."[30]

The security concern was thus the primary motive for the Carter
administration's 1978 decision to proceed toward full normalization of
diplomatic relations between Washington and Beijing. By mid-1978 it had
become clear that the Soviet Union expected to fill the vacuum left in
Southeast and South Asia by the withdrawal of the United States and
Great Britain. Hanoi, for a variety of reasons, was being drawn closer to
Moscow. Soviet influence in Kabul, Afghanistan, had grown throughout
the 1960s. In the early 1960s, the Soviets constructed an all-weather road
system from the Oxus River at the Soviet-Afghan border to Kabul and to
most of Afghanistan's other urban centers. In the mid-1960s, the new
road system was integrated into that of the Soviet Union. By 1977,
Afghanistan's military was Soviet trained and equipped. It was evident
that the Soviet Union was prepared to remain permanently in the area.

In 1978, Soviet deployments along the Sino-Soviet border totaled
approximately 47 divisions consisting of as many as 500,000 troops.
Although these Soviet divisions were understrength, their number exceeded the number the Soviets were deploying along the borders of
central Europe by about 17 divisions. The 47 divisions were supported by
armored forces, conventional artillery, tactical nuclear rocket forces, and
multipurpose air combat units. About one-third of the Soviet Union's
entire nuclear inventory was deployed along the route of the Siberian and
the Baikal-Amur Main Line railways.

Both Nixon and Carter had expected that the "Chinese connection"
would not only restore some balance to the international distribution of

armed capabilities, but provide Washington greater leverage in its negotiations with Moscow.[31] The Soviet Union's ability to project its military
forces into East Asia was understood to be hostage to a U.S. "strategic
association" with Maoist China. As a consequence of the Washington-
Beijing rapprochement, Moscow would be compelled to assume more
conservative and defensive postures.

On the eve of formal normalization of diplomatic relations between
the United States and the People's Republic of China, one of the most
forthright statements of Washington's rationale for the rapprochement,
by an anonymous senior civilian specialist in the U.S. Department of
Defense, appeared in the *Armed Forces Journal International*. The main
reason given was that normalization of U.S.-PRC relations would constitute a "tough message" to the Soviet Union. The U.S. association with the
PRC would be a "counterweight to the Soviet and Warsaw Pact buildup."
By a stroke, the United States had altered the strategic environment in its
favor. "While it may be possible to postulate a Soviet conquest of NATO
and the strategic destruction of the United States in isolation," the author
argued, "it is infinitely harder to postulate a Soviet 'conquest' of both the
West and China in the 1980s or 1990s." Moreover, "the flow of Western
technology made possible by the shift in U.S.-Chinese relations may
strengthen PRC military capabilities to the point where the Soviet Union
is increasingly forced to pursue a conservative, defensive, and détente-
oriented strategy."

The new relationship with Beijing would be of "substantial benefit to
the free world in terms of the strategic balance, the NATO–Warsaw Pact
balance, and the balance in Asia." Furthermore, rapprochement with the
West would afford the mainland Chinese substantial security against
Soviet assault, thus allowing the more "pragmatic" leadership in Beijing,
which had come to power after Mao's death, to pursue the nation's
program of modernization. These circumstances—an increased sense of
security and an opportunity to concentrate on the demanding problems
of economic development—would domesticate the PRC and render it a
"responsible" member of the world community. The leadership in Beijing then would have little incentive to act aggressively against any of
China's neighbors.[32]

By the time of the establishment of formal diplomatic relations between Washington and Beijing in 1979, the public was familiar with the
rationale provided in its support. The popular and political response was
generally favorable; the image of fanatic Red Guards savaging China was
replaced by a conception of "pragmatic" Chinese who had become the
"new, great friends" of the United States in Asia.

THE IMMEDIATE CONSEQUENCES OF RAPPROCHEMENT

In the years between the Shanghai Communiqué in 1972 and the December 1978 announcement of the establishment of diplomatic relations (beginning on January 1, 1979), the behavior of the leadership in Beijing tended to confirm initial U.S. expectations of immediate security benefits from the growing rapprochement. In 1974, Mao Zedong had announced the dissolution of what had been the "socialist camp."[33] With the termination of the war in Vietnam, Communist Chinese support for insurrectionary movements in Southeast Asia rapidly declined. In effect, the United States no longer had to pursue a policy of containment of communist expansion in Europe and Asia. For the first time in a generation, the United States no longer faced strategic challenges on two major fronts.

Moreover, after the issuance of the Shanghai Communiqué, Beijing ceased its criticism of the U.S.-Japan Mutual Security Treaty. The Communist Chinese leadership not only actively encouraged the security relationship between Tokyo and Washington, but promoted the strengthening of the NATO alliance.[34] Beijing refrained from objecting to U.S. defense ties with and base arrangements in the Philippines and Thailand and the island of Diego Garcia in the Indian Ocean.

By early 1975 Beijing was displaying open hostility, duly reciprocated, toward Hanoi. In mid-1975 the communist Vietnamese reminded Beijing that "flowing in the veins of the people of Vietnam is the blood of their heroic ancestors who fought against the northern aggressors"—the Chinese.[35] At almost the same time, the government in Beijing announced its exclusive claim to the Spratly Islands in the South China Sea, then occupied by the armed forces of Hanoi.[36] It seemed evident that the Chinese were attempting to restrain the expansion of the Vietnamese Communists.

Beijing also seemed to support a number of Washington's foreign policy initiatives outside Asia. In the civil war that followed Angola's grant of independence by Portugal, the Popular Movement for the Liberation of Angola (MPLA) received Soviet (and Cuban) support, whereas the National Front for the Liberation of Angola (FNLA) and the National Union for the Total Independence of Angola (UNITA) were favored by the United States. In December 1975, Holden Roberto, leader of the FNLA, indicated that his troops had been trained by instructors from the People's Republic of China.[37] Jonas Savimbi, leader of UNITA, made essentially the same claim.

Reports from Africa lent some credence to these claims. There appear to have been Communist Chinese military advisers at FNLA bases in Zaire, and some FNLA combatants had apparently been trained by the Chinese in Dar es Salaam, Tanzania. Beijing is reported to have provided tanks and heavy artillery to both the FNLA and UNITA in 1975. In one account, Chinese pilots were said to be flying French-supplied Mirage fighters for the FNLA.[38]

Similar behavior by Beijing was reported in Latin America. In an interview with C. L. Sulzberger, General Augusto Pinochet, leader of the Chilean military junta that overthrew the Marxist government of Salvador Allende in 1973, reported that Beijing had offered his government a loan of $58 million. He contrasted that with the efforts being made by Russia and Cuba.

> Russia and Cuba are trying to recover their position, to make Chile the South American base it was under Allende. This country was then the center for all their activities throughout the continent—for guerrillas, for distribution of funds, and for sending terrorist arms throughout South America. But China, that is different. China has not participated in this. China has behaved well.[39]

In the Middle East, Beijing's initiatives were more restrained after 1971. In 1971, when President Anwar Sadat initiated negotiations with Washington in the hope of reaching an "interim settlement" with Israel, Beijing was silent and conveyed the clear impression that it welcomed Sadat's undertaking. Beijing fully approved of Sadat's expulsion of Soviet military advisers from Egypt in July 1972. And Beijing was equally supportive when, after the October 1973 war, the Egyptians abrogated their Friendship Treaty with the Soviet Union and denied naval facilities to the Soviet Mediterranean fleet.

Beijing's attitude toward each of the Middle Eastern governments with which it established diplomatic relations was determined by the government's degree of opposition to the Soviet Union. Beijing welcomed the U.S.-sponsored disengagement agreement between Israel and Syria in May 1974, perceiving it as a blow against the Soviet Union. After 1971, Beijing attempted to improve its relations with the shah of Iran— again with a view to obstructing Soviet designs in the Middle East and Southwest Asia. In 1973, the Foreign Ministry of the PRC declared that Iran "has to strengthen its defenses in view of the prevailing situation in the region." The PRC had, by 1975, become a champion of stability in the Persian Gulf region. It had gradually established diplomatic relations with the most conservative Arab governments and had disassociated itself from the national liberation movements in the region. Iran and

Kuwait were considered important obstacles to Soviet penetration into the Gulf region, and since the shah had helped suppress national liberation movements in the area, improved relations between Teheran and Beijing were deemed incompatible with Communist Chinese support for insurrection.[40]

By the mid-1970s, Communist Chinese foreign policy in major parts of the world was generally compatible with that of the United States. Most important, of course, was the fact that the large land army of the People's Republic of China had immobilized about 47 divisions of the Soviet Army along the Sino-Soviet border—a large, multipurpose force supported by strategic and tactical nuclear weapons, as well as armor and aircraft, and chemical warfare capabilities. This setback significantly complicated risk assessment by the strategists in Moscow.

The Soviet Union's attempt to extend its influence throughout the world at the expense of "the world capitalist system" is clearly a policy of risk-minimizing expansionism: Moscow will seek to expand into those areas where it will incur no serious military risks.[41] Moscow perceived the U.S. rapprochement with the People's Republic of China as increasing the risks of any Soviet military adventure in East Asia.

As a consequence of the U.S.-PRC relationship, Soviet strategists' planning presumably became more complex and uncertain. Washington anticipated that the consequence would be more cautious behavior on the part of the Soviet Union until planning complexity was reduced and (or) risks were minimized. One way Moscow might accomplish these aims would be to achieve overwhelming military superiority in every potential conflict region. There has been some suggestion that this is precisely what Moscow intends; however, the costs of developing and maintaining such superiority would be disabling. In effect, the anti-Soviet Western powers were not averse to seeing the Soviet Union attempt the task of achieving military superiority vis-à-vis both the West and the People's Republic of China.

In order to tax the capabilities of the Soviet Union, it was in the best interests of the anti-Soviet coalition that Sino-Soviet relations remain, at best, cool and cautious. Ideally, Moscow would like to have a deep buffer on its Asian border, similar to the one on its European flank. That would provide for a defense in depth and allow Moscow greater flexibility in deploying its armed forces. As long as the USSR and the PRC were allied powers, Soviet military planners enjoyed that advantage.

By the end of the 1970s, Washington defense planners seemed determined that any renewed Soviet–Communist Chinese entente be avoided. The costs to the United States, and to the entire anti-Soviet coalition, of such an eventuality, it was argued, would be oppressive.[42]

SUPPLEMENTARY BENEFITS OF RAPPROCHEMENT

Rather unexpectedly, trade between the United States and the People's Republic of China grew quite substantially between 1972 and the early 1980s. In 1972, U.S. trade with the PRC was a scant $96 million—with a $30 million favorable balance for the United States. By 1974, bilateral trade had escalated to about $934 million—with a balance in favor of the United States of approximately $700 million. After Washington accorded Beijing most-favored-nation status in 1979, tariffs on goods from the PRC were reduced to the level of tariffs on goods from the Western trading partners of the United States, and this reduction made Communist China eligible for Export-Import Bank financing.

With the reduction in tariff rates, trade between United States and the PRC doubled between 1978 and 1979, to $2.3 billion with a U.S. trade surplus of about $1.1 billion. By 1982, bilateral trade had increased to $5.1 billion, to fall to $4.4 billion in 1983.

In 1983 about 75 percent of U.S. sales to the PRC were sales of high-technology equipment, including computers, CAT scanners, and microcircuits. Such sales are expected to double in the near term as a consequence of an easing of export controls. In November 1983, the Commerce Department introduced new guidelines that would expedite licensing decisions required for high-technology exports.

In 1983, U.S. textile and apparel imports from the PRC increased by about 17 percent. Beijing also agreed to buy 6 million tons of wheat a year from the United States. In the same year, the United States negotiated treaty agreements with the PRC that facilitated U.S. joint-venture and full equity investments in mainland Chinese industry. Of the $800 million invested by foreigners in joint ventures in the PRC in 1983, the U.S. share was $406 million. At that time the McDonnell Douglas Aircraft Corporation was working out the final arrangements with the Shanghai Aircraft Corporation for coproduction of 25 MD-80 commercial airliners from knockdown kits. Occidental Petroleum was in the process of closing a coal mining venture that would involve a $600 million, 15 million metric ton-a-year mine in Pingshuo, Shanzi Province. About 30 U.S. firms were negotiating with Beijing concerning investment possibilities.

United States investment appears to be primarily in the energy-generating sector of mainland Chinese industry. Beijing has indicated an interest in the purchase of U.S. nuclear power technology and of whole plants involving approximately $20 billion in sales. Beijing's interest in the development of its offshore potential raises the possibility of substantial U.S. investment. The PRC expects to double its production of oil by exploiting offshore sites; by the early 1980s more than 25 foreign companies from nine countries were engaged in subsea exploration to identify oil-bearing geomorphological structures on the ocean floor of the mainland Chinese continental shelf.

Mainland China's most promising offshore sites are located in areas and at depths that require the highest level of technology to exploit[43]— and it is the United States that has most fully developed that technology. Drilling for oil at such depths requires sophisticated oil-drilling equipment: the drillship (especially the Catamaran), the jack-up rig, and the semisubmersible drill (which has floats that can be submerged to provide greater stability in the rough seas encountered in the mainland Chinese continental shelf).

In their effort to proceed independently, the mainland Chinese developed a modest barge-type offshore drillship in the early 1970s. Subsequent improvements in their technology enabled them to construct a prototype of a jack-up rig that they used at a location about 50 miles offshore. As recently as the mid-1970s, Beijing seemed committed to depending on its own resources for offshore oil exploitation. However, foreign experts judged that PRC technology had progressed to the point where drilling could be undertaken at depths of only about 250 feet in sheltered water—not sufficiently deep for the mainland Chinese to begin extracting from the more promising sites. The increased foreign interest in its offshore areas, the long lead times necessary, the high investment, and the sophisticated technology ultimately required have led Beijing to opt for service contracts or other joint arrangements with major foreign oil companies, from which U.S. industry expects to profit.

The United States anticipates the sale of fertilizers and pesticides and the export of the technology and machinery necessary for the manufacture of those by-products. If the PRC expects to achieve the agricultural goals it has set for itself, it will have to import substantial amounts of agricultural machinery. Moreover, the authorities in Beijing speak of increasing the consumption of meat in the PRC from the current (mid-1980s) annual rate of 10 kilograms per person to 25 or 30 kilograms by the year 2000. If that is to be accomplished, there will have to be a significant increase in inputs for livestock and poultry production, that is, millions of metric tons of feed corn and soybeans—a potentially huge market for U.S. agricultural suppliers.[44]

By the beginning of the 1980s, those who had worked for the normalization of relations between the United States and the PRC had considerable reason for satisfaction. The relationship seemed to have produced tangible benefits for U.S. foreign policy objectives and produced some material rewards. In the early 1980s, it was authoritatively decided that "communist China offers a unique opportunity both to counter Soviet expansionism and open up a vast export market for U.S. goods."[45]

In retrospect, it appears evident that Nixon's opening to the People's Republic of China represented an effort to restore equilibrium between the limited capabilities of the United States and its security commitments. By pursuing a relaxation of tensions with the Soviet Union and proceeding toward rapprochement with the People's Republic of China, Nixon attempted to restore a global balance of power without incurring unacceptable costs. Although not an advanced industrial state, the PRC did possess a limited nuclear weapons capability and the largest land army in the world. Communist China's military potential, central location, and massive size suggested that the nation might serve the West as a counterweight to the Soviet Union. Its military power would affect the military balance between the NATO forces and the Warsaw Pact countries. Beijing's ability to pin down about 25 percent of the Soviet Union's conventional land and air forces in Asia was a cardinal consideration in U.S. strategic calculations.

Détente between the Soviet Union and the United States did not produce the results anticipated, and domestic resistance to normalization of relations with the PRC, under the conditions insisted upon by Beijing, obstructed the process of U.S.-PRC rapprochement until Jimmy Carter's accession to the presidency in 1977. Carter's motivations for proceeding with the new relationship with Communist China remain unclear to this day. Prior to his election, Carter gave very little evidence of having an interest in the East Asian policies of the United States. Nonetheless, in 1977–1978, the major initiatives for normalization with the PRC emanated from the Oval Office.

Nixon had begun the process of normalization of relations with Beijing but "failed to leave behind a clearly defined, long-term agenda for bilateral and multilateral relations in Asian and global affairs."[46] Carter left little more. At the beginning of his administration, the United States was committed to a policy of "evenhandedness" toward both Beijing and Moscow. By the time Carter left office, however, he had decidedly "tilted toward Beijing." The Soviet invasion of Afghanistan had apparently taught Jimmy Carter something new about Moscow. The Carter administration subsequently regarded the PRC as a strategic asset in the competition with the Soviet Union.

The Reagan administration did not add any policy specifics to Washington's East Asia strategy. Candidate Reagan's remarks about "upgrading" U.S. relations with the Republic of China on Taiwan outraged Beijing, and Beijing officials expressed considerable misgivings about the future of U.S.-PRC relations. Only the subsequent tempering of

Reagan's views, the winnowing out of some of his pre-election advisers, and the increasing influence of the views of State Department professionals put U.S.-PRC relations back on track.

It is not difficult to understand why Reagan's views on U.S. policy in East Asia had to be modified. His administration had assumed an anti-Soviet posture reminiscent of the containment policy of John Foster Dulles, although the United States no longer enjoyed theater force military superiority in either Europe or Asia. Because of the evident shortfall in U.S. military capabilities, the hard-line position with regard to the Soviet Union lacked prima facie plausibility. Only if U.S. capabilities were supplemented by those of the PRC would Soviet forces appear disadvantaged. Alexander Haig's announcement that the PRC constituted a "major strategic asset" against the USSR reflected this kind of accounting.

Between the announcement of the Guam Doctrine in 1969 and Carter's 1977 announcement that the United States would initiate a gradual withdrawal of ground troops from South Korea, the United States conveyed the impression that it was no longer willing to maintain or capable of maintaining a military presence in East Asia. In an effort to offset that impression at minimum cost, the United States seized upon the idea of a "new relationship" with its "great and new friends" in Beijing as an inexpensive substitute for a U.S. military presence in the region.

Since normalization began in 1979, enthusiasm for the "China connection" has picked up its own momentum. There has been a "colossal shift . . . in Americans' views. . . . The new opening to China and . . . recognition of the authorities in Beijing have been . . . overwhelmingly approved by the population."[47] Various interest groups have a substantial investment in the new relationship. Academics, for example, have sought and received opportunities to study on the mainland of China; major U.S. institutions sponsor elaborate cultural and educational exchanges between the United States and the PRC. Exporters and investors[48] have been transfixed by the China market as an "outlet of great potential." Finally, some military leaders have argued that "only China [could] provide enough of an army to assure the sustained pressure upon, and attrition of, Soviet forces to make . . . strikes against vital Soviet interests [in East Asia] meaningful."[49]

As a consequence, it has become almost mandatory that any presidential candidate, or any president seeking re-election, be photographed standing on the Great Wall of China. Any major changes in the relationship between Washington and Beijing would entail obvious political costs; it is unlikely that any individual or group of individuals in the United States will ever want to face the charge of having "lost China." But for all that, U.S.-China policy demands review. What is still missing from that policy is a set of strategic principles that specifies what Washington realistically expects from its "China connection." Whatever general imperatives have determined U.S. policy in East Asia, it still remains a collection of ad hoc responses to the problems that have emerged as a consequence of strategic and political change in the region. Born of clandestine negotiations, it has given rise to numerous complicated dilemmas resulting from persistent and fundamental disagreements. Many of these problems have been buried in the ambiguities and vaguenesses of the bilateral communiqués periodically issued by Beijing and Washington. Moreover, the covert nature of U.S.-PRC policy deliberations has ensured that these problems would reappear with some regularity to further complicate and jeopardize relations between the two nations. Such a vaguely defined policy, which lacks strong consensus among policymakers, renders the relationship between Washington and Beijing subject to abrupt change. Since there are widely different views concerning what can be expected from the U.S. connection with Communist China, the future of the relationship remains uncertain. What seems to be required is a protracted, and public, policy review.

5

The People's
Republic of China
as a Security Asset

One of Washington's principal motives for entering into rapprochement with the People's Republic of China arose out of the conviction that such a connection would produce mutual security advantages. The United States Defense Department's *Fiscal Year 1984 Posture Statement* announced that one of Washington's national security objectives was "to build toward a durable strategic relationship with the People's Republic of China." The Pentagon, in its *Fiscal Year 1984–1985 Defense Guidance*, also anticipated that the PRC would serve as an ally of the United States should the Soviet Union plan any initiatives, particularly in the Persian Gulf region.

In February 1983, Secretary of State George Shultz had alluded to the strategic importance of the PRC in the deterrent policy of the United States with regard to the Soviet Union. On more than one occasion, Paul Wolfowitz, assistant secretary of state for Asia and the Pacific, has explained why the PRC is of strategic importance to the United States, citing as one reason the fact that military planners in Washington "no longer have to plan and spend to confront a Chinese threat." Moreover, he has reiterated that both the United States and the PRC had "repeatedly reaffirmed" their "parallel interests in containing the Soviet Union." Both Washington and Beijing opposed not only Vietnamese aggression in Southeast Asia, but Soviet aggression in Afghanistan. All of this, he concluded, was a consequence of the assumption by Beijing of "an increasingly responsible regional role" in East Asia.[1]

These were the reasons that made Defense Secretary James Schlesinger a partisan of improved U.S.-PRC relations during the Ford administration, and led Defense Secretary Harold Brown, in January 1980, to announce that the United States would provide the PRC with air surveillance ground stations and nonlethal military equipment, as well as civilian technology that might have both civilian and military uses.

In June 1981, Secretary of State Alexander Haig announced that the United States was prepared to make selected lethal military equipment available to Beijing. The Ford administration had already withdrawn its objection to such sales by its West European allies, and Beijing had contracted for the purchase of jet propulsion units from Great Britain and negotiated with France for the purchase of Crotale surface-to-air missiles.

The degree of conviction that supports the notion that the PRC would be a major military asset in East Asia and perhaps the Persian Gulf region varies, but there are few in Washington who simply reject it. The People's Republic of China maintains one of the largest military establishments, the largest land army, and the third largest navy and air force in the world. To suggest that the Soviet Union would not be concerned with the disposition of those forces and that the United States would not profit from their anti-Soviet deployment would be counterintuitive.

THE SOVIET PERCEPTION
OF THE GEOSTRATEGIC ENVIRONMENT

There is considerable evidence suggesting that the leaders of the Soviet Union have a more complex conception of war-fighting strategy than the United States. Not only does Moscow calculate the balance of military forces in potential regional engagements, but it regularly assesses the balance transregionally and in terms of nuclear conflict. A conflict that commenced in one locale could easily spread to other theaters. Not only could conflict spread horizontally; it might also escalate from the conventional to the nuclear level.

Ever since the Soviet acquisition of nuclear weapons, Moscow has considered global conflict in terms of the employment of such weapons.[2] Not only does it contemplate the use of such weapons, but it conceives such a conflict as one that would be potentially "protracted" and that, in some meaningful sense, could be "won."[3] Americans tend to think of nuclear conflict as resulting in the total destruction of mankind; therefore, their principal concern is the deterrence of nuclear conflict. The Soviets speculate on the kind of protracted conflict that would follow a nuclear exchange and how they might deal with surviving opponents.

This is not to suggest that the Soviets are disposed to precipitate such a conflict. There is substantial evidence indicating that Soviet strategists have little doubt that the United States possesses the capacity to inflict unacceptable damage on the Soviet Union.[4] Nonetheless, Soviet military writers are obligated to consider worst-case possibilities. The Soviets theorize that victory can be secured in a post–nuclear exchange environment only if ground troops seize strategically important regions of enemy territory, destroy the opponent's military potential, and suppress its capacity to resist.

Given this conception, Soviet strategists must consider the fate of a crippled Soviet Union that survives massive nuclear exchanges and might then have to resist follow-up nuclear or conventional attack. In this context, the People's Republic of China constitutes a major factor in Soviet calculations.

The Soviets conceive the PRC as possessed of certain survival advantages in a nuclear conflict. The backwardness of Communist China, its vast population, and its decentralized economy afford it significant advantages in the event of nuclear exchange. Although it is meaningful to talk of the "assured destruction" of the United States or the Soviet Union in a nuclear conflict, it is difficult to define what that might mean with regard to mainland China. Nuclear exchanges might destroy the PRC's population centers and much of its industrial base, but a considerable proportion of the ground forces of the People's Liberation Army (PLA) sustains itself through local procurement and is relatively self-sufficient. If appreciable numbers of Communist Chinese ground troops were still available for conventional assault on the Soviet Union following any conflicts, they could constitute a mortal threat to the USSR.[5]

If deterrence includes threatening a potential enemy with a credible counterthreat that it will find unacceptable, then the capacity of the People's Republic of China to survive a nuclear exchange possessed of war-fighting ability constitutes a deterrent threat to the Soviet Union.[6] But such a threat would become operative only in the event of a general nuclear conflict, and the credibility of the threat turns in large part on the probability of such a conflict. Insofar as all potential participants in such a conflict must consider such a possibility, the importance of the PRC in the global military balance seems evident. However, an equally substantial element in the credibility of the threat is a function of the capability of the People's Liberation Army to exploit the circumstances of any post–nuclear exchange environment. Only if the Communist Chinese military were able to penetrate and secure the Soviet Far Eastern regions would it serve as a deterrent in this sense.

The ability of the armed forces of Communist China to maintain themselves outside China's national boundaries is, in fact, problematic. One of the major deficiencies that beset the People's Liberation Army, despite three decades of effort at upgrading, is logistics—transport is still a "major weakness."[7] The national truck fleet, deployed in 42 motor transportation regiments, is estimated to consist of just over 1 million vehicles, and serviceable roads in all of the PRC total about 580,000 miles. This network is supplemented by only 32,000 miles of railroad track. (The United States, with about the same territory, had more track in the mid-nineteenth century.) As a consequence, many military units depend on animals for mobility and supply. Many ground units depend on local procurement and local storage facilities—and even air and naval commands sometimes rely on such a primitive support base despite their more centralized supply system.

In the Korean War, admittedly under particularly trying circumstances that compounded the difficulties, shortages and resupply problems not only constituted a hindrance to Communist Chinese military operations, but negatively affected troop morale as well.[8] In Beijing's month-long "punitive war" against Vietnam in 1979, because of the difficult terrain, the Communist Chinese military forces were compelled to rely on antiquated trucks, as well as horses, donkeys, and laborers to supply forward units that had penetrated no more than 30 miles into enemy territory.[9] Periodic lulls in the fighting were apparently the consequence of shortages that had hindered PLA operations. The transport facilities of the border provinces of the PRC were clearly overtaxed, and there is some evidence that the burden of providing supplies to the military caused Communist Chinese civilian production to all but cease in the local region during the fighting on the border.

The People's Liberation Army is essentially a foot-mobile defensive force.[10] The limited mobility of the civilian logistics base, the thinness of the transportation infrastructure, and the lack of transport vehicles and rolling stock[11] all suggest that the Communist Chinese military could not mount and sustain a major ground invasion of Soviet territory in Asia, even if the Soviet military had already been badly crippled in nuclear exchanges with another foe.

The logistical support available to Communist China's military could not sustain a major infantry, artillery, and armored force outside the confines of the PRC. The emphasis of Chinese military doctrine (a modified "people's war" doctrine) on the defensive role of the armed forces is dictated largely by the PRC's logistical disabilities. The notion that in the event of invasion, the defender should "draw the enemy deep" into its national territory in order to harass and degrade the enemy's forces is necessitated by the defenders' inability to bring the war to the enemy.[12] Such a defensive strategy would maximize the benefits resulting from the relative self-sufficiency of military units.[13]

The dispatch of substantial Communist Chinese forces into Soviet territory would almost immediately degrade their combat effectiveness. The logistical problems, which were serious in the Korean and Vietnamese campaigns of 1950–1953 and 1979, would be magnified by the necessity of sustaining an offensive force equipped with modern weapons and armored vehicles in a modern order of battle.[14] The military command in Beijing was capable of sustaining almost a million men under combat conditions in Korea, however, and the question of the effectiveness of the PLA in any hypothetical post–nuclear exchange invasion of Soviet East Asia would turn on the question of how impaired Soviet defensive forces might be. Should the remnants of the Soviet Far Eastern armies be supported by prepositioned supplies, and should a significant portion of their command and control facilities and hardened defense emplacements survive, any Communist Chinese assault could be very expensive and its outcome would be doubtful.

In effect, the decision by Beijing to attack Soviet territory after a nuclear exchange would depend on a number of imponderable factors. The utility of such an attack would be determined by the extent of the damage inflicted on Soviet forces and facilities in the targeted areas and the degree of radioactive contamination present in those areas (against which the PLA has only marginal defenses). Most of the Soviet facilities in the Far Eastern command are emplaced in hardened structures, designed to resist nuclear blast effects. It is unclear what margin of surplus the Soviet defense forces maintain in those hardened storage structures. Should substantial forces and supplies remain, it is doubtful that the Communist Chinese armed forces could launch an essentially foot-mobile offensive action to any depth in Soviet territory.[15] Before mainland China could contemplate a large-scale invasion of Soviet territory in a post–nuclear exchange environment, it would have to be assured of an elaborate logistical infrastructure that would enable it to store, distribute, maintain, and regenerate battlefield and support equipment rapidly through a combination of *in situ* repair, resupply from depot storage, and new production in the homeland. Battlefield conditions in the Soviet Far East territories would be arduous at best, and during the frigid winters they would be particularly demanding on supplies. The characteristic Communist Chinese battle plans include massive artillery bombardments followed by mass infantry assaults—both of which would tax the supply lines. Those lines of communication would rapidly degrade as the distance from homeland supply sources increased. It is doubtful whether the PLA has the modern vehicles, transport facilities, and communications and reconnaissance capabilities to sustain a mobile defense of Inner Mongolia or Xinjiang, much less an invasion of Soviet territory.[16]

Soviet strategists must have contingency plans for every situation ranging from peacetime to post–nuclear attack. Nevertheless, the possibility that the Communist Chinese armed forces might seek to exploit the circumstances of a post–nuclear exchange environment doubtlessly complicates Soviet military planning. But the influence of such a threat should not be exaggerated. So many unlikely contingencies would have to combine to make such a threat credible that it probably does not weigh heavily in Soviet calculations. Even if all those improbabilities should occur, it remains unlikely that Communist Chinese forces could successfully invade, secure, and occupy anything other than the border regions of the Soviet Far Eastern provinces. A more likely concern of Soviet planners is the deployment of large-scale Communist Chinese conventional forces along the Sino-Soviet border.

The Conventional Forces of the People's Republic of China

The People's Liberation Army is estimated to consist of approximately 3.9 million men under arms, serving in units organized in 7 Military Regions divided into 29 Military Districts. This mass is divided into Main and Local Forces. The Main Force divisions are the primary force constituents, are better armed and more mobile than the Local Forces, which are responsible for the defense of local areas, border protection, and internal security. There are about 190 Main Force divisions, consisting of about 40 army corps, including 121 foot infantry divisions, 12 armored divisions, and 3 airborne divisions. The rest of the manpower is divided into artillery, engineer, railway, production, and construction corps units. William Kennedy has referred to the fact that the PLA constitutes the largest land army in the world as "the most misleading military statistic in the world today."[17] Why that should be so is not difficult to understand.

The PLA is essentially a largely foot-mobile infantry force, lacking an adequate organic transportation system and armed with weapons that are in large part obsolete or obsolescent. The Main Force divisions are deficient in all types of modern weapons, except for light and medium arms and perhaps artillery. The PLA has about 20,000 field guns in inventory. Most of them, such as the widely employed Type 55 85-mm general-purpose weapon, are towed pieces. Given the lack of motor and tracked transport, artillery is frequently towed by mules. Most of the self-propelled weapons, such as the BM-13 and BM-14 rocket launchers, are obsolescent and are used as training weapons by the Warsaw Pact armies of Eastern Europe.

The PLA field forces generally lack precision-guided and antitank missiles, although a modified version of the Soviet-designed wire-guided Sagger antitank missile entered service with the PLA in 1979. Its performance is reported to be inferior to that of its Soviet prototype, and its distribution has been limited to the most vulnerable of the PRC's border regions. The PLA's gunnery control devices are relatively primitive, and modern communications equipment is in short supply throughout.

The PLA is also deficient in both tanks and armored fighting vehicles. Its armor is generally obsolescent. Its main battle tank is still the T-59 (introduced into the Communist Chinese armed forces in 1953), although there have been reports that a variant, the T-69, has entered service. The T-69 incorporates a weapon platform stabilizer that allows employment of its 105-mm smoothbore main weapon in uneven terrain, an automatic laser range finder for more adequate target acquisition and targeting, and an infrared night light, all calculated to improve its combat effectiveness.

Soviet armor outnumbers Communist Chinese armor by a ratio of 3 or 4 to 1. Moreover, Soviet tanks are modern, protected by special laminate armor, and armed with smoothbore 125-mm guns. The Soviet T-72 (in service since 1975), which fires armor-piercing, fin-stabilized rounds, could breach the shielding of PLA tanks from standoff positions outside the maximum range of Communist Chinese on-board weapons.

The 3,500 armored personnel carriers in service with the PLA are quantitatively and qualitatively outclassed by Soviet armor. The Soviet armed forces in the Soviet Far East—from Lake Baikal to the east—deploy about ten times more armored personnel carriers and armored fighting vehicles than does the opposing PLA. The ratio of personnel to armored personnel carriers in the Soviet Far East is about 20 to 1, compared with the PLA ratio of about 240 to 1.

Because Soviet units are motorized and therefore mobile, field commanders have the option of concentrating forces at chosen points to achieve overwhelming superiority over the enemy. The efficient communications system maintained by the Soviets allows them to rapidly concentrate superior forces in order to break through defenses and outflank opposing positions. Only in mountainous terrain, which precludes the massing of tank forces, might PLA defenders enjoy some advantages. In Xinjiang and Inner Mongolia, most of the terrain is open and flat and is thus a suitable surface for characteristic Soviet armored assault. At the close of the Second World War, the Soviet Union invaded Manchuria with a blitzkrieg armored attack in which daily advances averaging 35 miles were made against the Japanese Imperial Army.

In view of the Soviet forces' absolute air superiority, the availability of self-propelled fire support, the advanced state of their airborne target acquisition, and their superior fire control, in addition to their mobility, Soviet power could easily overwhelm PLA defenses. In fact, Communist Chinese conventional forces are inferior to those of the Soviet Union in everything but crude numbers, and numbers are hardly a useful indicator of war-fighting capabilities.[18] Since 1972, the Soviet Union has been implementing a program of infrastructural development east of the Urals that has radically altered the logistical and operational environment in which Soviet forces must operate. Spur lines and all-weather hard-surfaced roads now link Soviet divisional facilities to rear-based supplies. A network of prepositioned supplies and fortified repair stations facilitate sustained operations, and operations headquarters and communications centers have been hardened against conventional and nuclear blast effects. As a consequence of this effort, the Soviet deployment areas along the Sino-Soviet border constitute staging bases capable of accommodating combat formations. Collateral with these developments has been the establishment of air bases capable of supporting air combat, ground support, and bombing aircraft. Perhaps as many as 2,500 modern combat aircraft provide support for the Soviet ground forces. "By 1980 . . . the Soviet Union had acquired the capabilities needed to achieve decisive results in nonnuclear warfare and notably the ability to stage hightempo ground offensives to penetrate PRC territory up to depths of hundreds of kilometers."[19]

It is evident that the Soviet armed forces in the Far East provinces enjoy decisive advantages over the military forces of Communist China. They are vastly superior in military technology, communications, photo-intelligence, the availability of armor, troop mobility, firepower in the field, fire control, and air support. "Attacking at times and places of their choosing, there is little doubt that the Soviets could be advanced hundreds of miles into Chinese territory."[20] Should they choose to do so for whatever reason, the Soviets could probably break through into industrial Manchuria as far south as Harbin, reducing mainland China's capacity to generate electricity by one-half, destroying much of its truck and aircraft manufacturing plant, and depriving it of 70 percent of its iron ore production and 30 percent of its annual coal production.[21] "The notion that the Chinese at their present stage of development could stop or effectively threaten thereafter a Soviet occupation of Xinjiang and Northeast Manchuria by mass manpower is ingenuous. Climate, terrain, superior Soviet mobility, [and] Soviet air supremacy . . . preclude any such defense by China as long as the present military equation continues."[22]

The available evidence strongly suggests that there is very little that can be done to redress the Sino-Soviet military balance, which currently favors the USSR despite the PRC's advantage in raw manpower. Soviet technological advances in weaponry and related ancillaries mean that the existing gap will not be closed with any measures short of the modernization of Communist China's entire industrial base, which is two to three decades behind that of the USSR.[23]

There is no indication that the Soviet Union is planning any large-scale initiatives against the PRC. Soviet troop deployments along the border indicate that the force levels maintained by the Soviet high command in this theater are adequate to repel any PLA attack, but not sufficient to ensure success in a major invasion of mainland China's northern provinces.[24] But the fact that the Soviet Union is not particularly threatening to the PRC should not be taken to mean that Beijing's armed forces have rendered Moscow more compliant and conservative.

During the Communist Chinese punitive war against Vietnam, the Soviet Union not only undertook an air- and sealift of military supplies to Hanoi but increased its air and naval activity in the Tonkin Gulf. These actions forced Beijing to carefully calculate its operations in order not to precipitate an engagement with Soviet forces. Beijing failed to achieve its major objectives in its assault on Vietnam, and that failure provided the occasion for more aggressive Soviet penetration into Southeast Asia. The Soviet Union used the pretext to acquire basing rights for its air and naval units in Vietnam in Camranh Bay and Danang. Those units now reconnoiter the Southeast Asian region as far east as the Philippine Islands.[25]

Moreover, the putative Chinese threat did not inhibit the Soviet Union from embarking on one of its most aggressive military adventures in Asia: the 1980 invasion of Afghanistan—a complex, combined operation involving approximately 120,000 Soviet troops. East of the Wakhan corridor, Afghanistan shares a border with Communist China. So complacent were the Soviet authorities about any Communist Chinese reaction that the original invading force was composed of Category 3 units— those least trained and most poorly equipped.[26]

U.S. expectations that the armed forces of the PRC would induce the Soviet Union to behave in a less aggressive fashion in general, or less aggressively in Asia in particular, have not been borne out by events. The fact is that "the PRC . . . will remain a very much underdeveloped country for the next five to seven decades. . . . It is very doubtful that [it] could provide a viable counterbalancing force against Soviet hegemonic designs in the Far East for the next ten years."[27] The very existence of the People's Republic of China along the long Sino-Soviet border complicates the strategic planning of the Soviet high command. In that abstract sense, the armed forces of the PRC are a security asset for the West. But the central fact is that the PRC's service to the anti-Soviet alliance is a function of its geographic location. It complicates Soviet strategic planning simply because it is there. As we shall see, the PRC would continue to complicate that planning even if the relations between Moscow and Beijing were amicable. In fact, Beijing lacks the military capability and the freedom of maneuver either to increase or to reduce its threat to the Soviet Union or its security value to the West.[28] Most analysts have concluded that the Western nations would be ill-advised to hope for any increase in the deterrent capacity of the Communist Chinese in the years ahead.[29]

As the Carter administration moved closer to diplomatic recognition of the People's Republic of China, its representatives were sorely tempted to assume that Beijing would be a military counterweight to the Soviet Union. Although considerable information was then available on the primitive state of the Communist Chinese armed forces, the notion was that with technological assistance and weapons transfers from the West, the PLA (its nonconventional nuclear forces, if not its conventional forces) could be refashioned into a credible counterweight.

Beijing's Nuclear Deterrent

Since 1964, when the PRC detonated its first nuclear device, Communist China has been putting together a relatively small, but growing, nuclear deterrent. The PLA's Second Artillery, its nuclear forces component, deploys about 50 CSS-1 medium-range ballistic missiles with an estimated range of 1,800 kilometers and an explosive impact of 15 kilotons. These are augmented by about 85 CSS-2 intermediate-range missiles with an estimated range of 2,500 kilometers and an impact of 1 to 3 megatons. Four intercontinental missiles with a range of approximately 7,000 kilometers and an impact of 1 to 3 megatons are coupled with a few true intercontinental missiles with an estimated range of 13,000 kilometers and an impact of 5 to 10 megatons. The nuclear capabilities of the PRC are thus not negligible.

These strategic forces exist in a threatening counterforce environment. There is a grave suspicion that they would have little, if any, military value in a conflict situation. One reason for this suspicion is that in the mid-1980s the PRC's nuclear deterrent force was about two decades old, and all its known delivery systems were liquid-fueled. Although a space satellite launch in the early 1980s suggested that the PRC had developed solid-fuel technology for its rocket engines, its nuclear weapon delivery systems will probably continue to be liquid-fueled for a considerable time to come.

Liquid fuels are very unstable and difficult to store, and they degrade rapidly. Communist Chinese missiles have been in storage for so long that it is likely that a considerable number could not now be successfully launched. The history of such vehicles suggests that an indeterminate, but appreciable, number of the launches would abort. Moreover, the guidance systems on such vehicles are extremely sensitive and tend to deteriorate in the absence of constant and proper maintenance. Because of the shortfall in skilled PLA personnel, and the length of time such systems have been in storage, it is probable that errors and malfunctions would impair their effectiveness. Those considerations, coupled with the fact that the Communist Chinese have only limited operational photo-intelligence capability, suggest that questionable target acquisition and primitive guidance properties would significantly reduce the precision of PLA nuclear strikes. The "circular error probable" (cep) of PLA nuclear missiles is 4 kilometers (which means that only 50 percent of arriving warheads would be expected to fall within a target circle having a radius as large as 4 kilometers), indicating that nuclear strikes against Soviet targets hardened against nuclear blast effects would be largely in-effective.

Soviet hardening technology provides protection against 4,000 pounds per square inch (psi) overpressure—significant protection against all but direct hits. Communist Chinese hardened structures and silos provide protection against 600 pounds psi overpressure. Their hard-ened installations are consequently critically exposed to Soviet strikes. Given Soviet targeting precision (the cep of Soviet nuclear weapons is estimated to be 1,200 feet), it is likely that the Soviet Union could destroy most of the PRC's retaliatory nuclear capabilities with less than 10 percent of its current inventory of nuclear weapons.[30]

The long lead time necessary to prepare liquid-fueled nuclear weapons for launch, their exposure to blast effects, and the predictable failure of a significant number that do achieve launch all suggest that the PRC's relatively small nuclear deterrent does not at present pose a critical problem for Soviet planners. Given the advanced state of Soviet photoin-telligence capabilities, all of the PRC's nuclear sites have doubtless been targeted and are vulnerable to pre-emptive strikes. In 1982, Soviet spe-cialists, although concerned about the development of the PLA's nuclear weapons capability, advised that Beijing's nuclear missile potential "not be exaggerated."[31]

The fact that there are nuclear weapons in the inventory of the PRC is of some importance to the strategists of the West. At least some of the Soviet Union's strategic forces must be targeted on Communist Chinese sites if only to ensure the neutrality of the PLA in the event of an armed conflict between the USSR and the Western powers. But the possibility that the nuclear capabilities of the PRC could serve as a counterweight to the Soviet Union, deter it from pursuing its goals in East Asia, or render Moscow compliant is so unlikely as to be readily dismissed.

In the future, the two nations' strategic relationship will probably change. The PRC is experimenting with the submarine launch of ballistic missiles and is reported to have had some initial success. It will be a considerable time, however, before the navy of the People's Republic of China will have enough submarine platforms in service to provide Communist China with a survivable nuclear deterrent. One estimate is that the PRC would have to have at least six such platforms, with two on patrol, in order to enhance its strategic nuclear deterrent force.[32] But unless the nuclear forces of the Soviet Union had been previously destroyed, the threatened use of such PRC missiles would be extremely imprudent.

The very existence of Communist Chinese conventional and nuclear forces is of strategic significance. The benefits that the West derives from their existence are not dependent on the continuation of amicable relations with Beijing. Soviet planners have had to deal with the contingency of Sino-Soviet conflict and the possible U.S. responses thereto since the 1950s. By the mid-1960s, such calculations had become a standard component of the planning of the Soviet military command. The diplomatic recognition of the government in Beijing by the United States did not further complicate Soviet strategic planning, essentially change the Western-Soviet military balance of power, or make the Soviet Union less aggressive in Asia. Why this was so is fairly evident.

THE NATURE OF THE SINO-SOVIET DISPUTE

The Sino-Soviet dispute, which became public in the late 1950s and became something of a scandal in the communist world in the mid-1960s, was the culmination of a number of differences and conflicts. Mao and his entourage objected to Moscow's evident caution in dealing with the "imperialists" of the West. Aside from the arcane ideological differences between Moscow and Beijing, the two nations had different assessments of the "world configuration of forces" and the potential for an "upsurge in revolution."

Beyond that, by the early 1960s, the Soviet Union had increased its commitment to the long-term development of its energy resources in the Far East.[33] The largest untapped reservoir of natural resources in the USSR, in large part energy related, is found in the far reaches of the Asian provinces. This region thus constitutes the most valuable as well as the most vulnerable piece of real estate in the Soviet Union.[34] Approximately 80 percent of the energy consumed in the Soviet Union is employed in its heavily industrialized western provinces, but about 80 percent of its primary explored energy resources are located east of the Urals.

This Asian resource abundance, so critical to the future of the Soviet economy, exists in a region with one of the lowest population densities in the world. It is also a region that has been the center of territorial disputes since the cossack Yermak Timofeevich led his men into the domain of Tartar chieftain Khan Kuchum in 1579. The region was threatened by anticommunist intervention forces on the eve of the Bolshevik Revolution, by imperial Japan in the 1930s and 1940s, and by the PRC in the mid-1960s. Quite independently of any other consideration, the history of the area would have recommended that the authorities in Moscow provide for its adequate defense. Under almost any conceivable circumstances, the Soviet Union would eventually be obliged to commit substantial general-purpose and strategic forces to the region. Communist China's raising of the territorial issue in the 1960s simply accelerated a process that was inevitable.

By the 1970s, the situation in the region was rendered particularly complex by the conflicting territorial claims being made by Moscow and Beijing. Approximately half a million square miles of land was in dispute.[35] As a result of a series of treaties negotiated with the all but impotent Qing government of nineteenth-century China, imperial Russia gained vast territory north and east of the Amur and Ussuri rivers. After the Bolshevik Revolution, Lenin's acting commissar for foreign affairs, L. M. Karakhan, renounced all claims to territory that had been "ravenously taken from [China] by the Tsar's government and the Russian bourgeoisie."[36]

None of that territory, of course, was ever restored to China. In fact, in 1924, long after Lenin had abjured such acquisitions, the Soviet Union conspired to excise Outer Mongolia from Republican China, in order to create the satellite Mongolian People's Republic. This was the territory to which Mao alluded in the mid-1960s. The Soviet Union knows that the slightest change in the Sino-Soviet border might establish a precedent for other boundary revisions demanded by claimants who might have as strong a case as any made by Beijing. The Communist Chinese have not laid claim to all the disputed territory. Beijing has made plain that it is prepared to negotiate the territorial disputes on the basis of the "unequal treaties" signed by imperial Russia and the Qing government. Perhaps more than anything else, the Communist Chinese authorities want Moscow to acknowledge that the treaties that established the Sino-Soviet border were, in fact, unequal. The disputed territory consists only of several hundred small and uninhabited islands in the riverine system that separates mainland China from the Soviet Union, and some land in western Xinjiang.

That some resolution of the dispute is possible is evidenced by the fact that the People's Republic of China has resolved similar territorial disputes with Burma, the Mongolian People's Republic, Nepal, and Laos. Even if the Communist Chinese and the Soviets could find a satisfactory solution to their border problem and enjoy a period of détente and perhaps rapprochement, the Soviet high command would still be compelled to retain multipurpose forces in the Far East theater at something like current levels. In the mid-1980s, the bulk of those forces were deployed for a potential conflict with the West. The high-performance aircraft, the surveillance apparatus, the elaborate system of strategic and intermediate-range missiles armed with multiple warheads capable of being individually targeted (MIRVed), and the hardened launch sites, command posts, storage depots, and communications facilities all have an anti-Western, defensive and offensive potential. As many as 135 SS-20 MIRVed missiles have been emplaced in the Soviet Far East; about half of the Soviet Union's inventory of Tupelov Backfire bombers are also there, capable of reaching all of North America from Arctic staging areas. The submarine base at Petropavlovsk on the Kamchatka peninsula is one of the largest, if not the largest, in the world. A considerable component of the Soviet strategic nuclear deterrent is aboard the *Delta-* and *Yankee*-class nuclear submarines in the Sea of Okhotsk. Around that sea and the Sea of Japan, the Soviet Union has threaded together an impressive chain of military establishments. There are major naval bases at Vladivostok and Sovetskaya Gavan and military facilities at Possiet, Novgoradsky, Shkotovo, Korsakov, Nakhodka, Magadan, and Tynkin. A massive new air base has been constructed at Ussurisk. Smaller airfields, early warning stations, submarine pens, naval shipyards, and hardened storage depots dot the Soviet Maritime Province, Sakhalin Island, and the Kamchatka peninsula. Moreover, the troop buildup in the region was accomplished without degrading any of the Soviet forces committed to the Warsaw Pact armies. General DeWitt C. Smith, Jr., has pointed out that the Soviet forces in the Far East include "an army that has been built without any reduction of Soviet forces in the West," and is, nonetheless, "nearly as modern as [those] in the West."[37]

None of this has been assembled for any anticipated conflict with the PRC. The quality, inventory, and configuration of the military formations in the Soviet Far East indicate anti-Western missions. The capabilities of the Soviet military in East Asia far exceed the requirements for static defense or even for the kinds of missions required by the conflict with mainland China.

In order to protect the formidable military capabilities of the Far East provinces, the Soviet Union must ensure adequate air defenses and garrison enough troops to maintain munitions stores, communications, rails, roads, and rolling stock. By the early 1980s, Soviet forces were concentrated mostly in the Far East Military District, which faces the Sea of Okhotsk and the Sea of Japan, with lesser concentrations in the Trans-Baikal Military District, Mongolia, and the Siberian Military District. The logic of Soviet military strategy against the West required such deployment, and that deployment will not change substantially, irrespective of any change in the relations between Moscow and Beijing.

Should Sino-Soviet relations approximate the level of cautious normality, there could be some cosmetic Soviet troop redeployments; some Soviet forces might be withdrawn from the Mongolian People's Republic and from forward positions on the border. As long as the Soviet Union must provide a strategic defense against the Western powers, however, there can be no significant drawdown of Soviet forces in East Asia.

In the foreseeable future, Moscow can have nothing less than cautious suspicions about Beijing's policies. As a consequence, the USSR must maintain its force levels in the Far East if only to ensure PRC neutrality in any conflict between the USSR and the United States. Protection of the vast untapped resources of the region recommends such a course and prudence dictates it.

What is clear is that the People's Republic of China does not "tie down 500,000 Soviet troops" that would otherwise be deployed elsewhere. Soviet troops are in the Far East theater because the defense of the region requires their presence; they would be required even if relations between the Soviet Union and the People's Republic of China were amicable. Only a massive upgrading of the war-fighting ability of the PLA could have a significant impact on the Soviet military and alter the global strategic balance.

With deployments both in the Far East provinces and in Eastern Europe, the Soviet Union felt sufficiently confident of its strength, particularly in relation to the armed forces of the PRC, that it could launch an invasion of Afghanistan in 1980 by a force composed of 7 motorized rifle divisions and 5 air assault brigades, supported by airborne and ranger units, 240 helicopter gunships, 400 support helicopters, an undetermined number of squadrons of MiG-21s and MiG-23s, and at least one squadron of Su-25 ground attack aircraft, as well as tanks and armored personnel carriers. Moreover, the Soviet Union apparently maintains 40 divisions in ready reserve for any contingency that might develop—irrespective of its commitments in East Asia and Eastern Europe.[38]

WESTERN ARMS SALES TO THE PEOPLE'S REPUBLIC OF CHINA

A number of analysts have suggested that the backwardness of the PRC military might be readily offset by arms sales and weapon transfers from the West. Some have simply spoken of the "inappropriateness" of Washington's seeking a strategic connection with Beijing, yet refusing to allow arms sales to the Communist Chinese military.[39] The Carter administration's insistence that the United States sought to establish a "strong and secure China" was understood by the PRC to mean that Washington would aid in the modernization and upgrading of the Communist Chinese military by arms sales and weapons-related technology transfers.

In 1978 and 1979, PRC military officials seemed convinced that the People's Liberation Army would soon constitute a modern force capable of ensuring the nation's security. The leaders of the PRC pressed U.S. officials to sell weapons and weapons-related technology to their nation in order to ensure the usefulness of the PLA in any anti-Soviet containment policy. Military academies and defense research institutes were reopened after their long quiescence during the Great Proletarian Cultural Revolution. Training programs for the military were instituted in order to prepare for the incorporation of modern weapons systems and to teach new tactics.

At the same time, the PRC dispatched approximately 40 military procurement missions to all the major arms-producing countries of the world, ranging from Japan to Australia, to those in Western Europe and Latin America. Communist Chinese representatives showed a vital interest in every type of missile, computer control device, information ancillary, laser, electronic equipment, antitank weapon, armored fighting vehicle, transport truck, armor, helicopter, and high-performance fighting aircraft. PRC military delegations visited foreign military establishments to observe modern command and control systems in operation and to test the operation of modern weapon systems. By purchasing foreign military equipment in sufficient quantities to rapidly modernize the fighting forces of the PRC, the Communist Chinese conveyed the distinct impression that they were prepared to embark on a "Great Leap Forward." The impression was reinforced by a 20 to 30 percent annual increase in the PRC's defense budget between 1977 and 1979.[40]

By the end of 1979, however, it had become obvious that the hope of a Great Leap in military modernization was as illusory as the hope of a similar "leap" in economic modernization. When the Communist Chinese negotiated with the British for the purchase of Harrier "jump jets," they discovered that 70 such aircraft would cost approximately $1.2 billion. The most advanced fighter jets of the U.S. Air Force would cost about $25 million each. A modern battle tank would cost about $1 million. In 1980, the Pentagon was preparing a report on the estimated cost of modernizing the Communist Chinese defense forces to render them "credible" when they face the military might arrayed against them along the Sino-Soviet border. The estimates ranged from $41 billion to $63 billion.[41] Because of the escalating costs of the most advanced weapon systems, the same estimate in the mid-1980s would probably be closer to $200 billion.

By the beginning of 1980, it had become clear to the Communist Chinese that their military could not be modernized by massive procurements of foreign weapon systems. The immediate consequence was a sharp reduction in the defense budget of the PRC. It was evident that Beijing did not have the financial resources for such purchases; it was equally obvious that technologically advanced weapon systems could not be readily absorbed into a military establishment that was technologically primitive and that suffered grievous deficiencies in trained manpower. Communist Chinese inspection of the complex Harrier jet, for example, revealed to them some of the technical problems the PLA would face in trying to provide the maintenance and logistics for such aircraft. Unlike the Harrier, most of the in-service aircraft in the People's Liberation Army Air Force (PLAAF) are relatively simple platforms that date from the 1950s and 1960s. The on-board avionics are primitive and most of the fighters of the PLAAF are not armed with effective air-to-air missiles. Nonetheless, the MiGs in service with the PLAAF suffer more downtime than the more advanced aircraft of the U.S. Air Force. The propulsion systems of the PLAAF MiGs require overhaul after only 100 hours of flying time; the F-4s in inventory with Western air forces remain in operation without such major servicing for about ten times as long.

The PLA is handicapped not only by its technological backwardness and lack of adequately trained personnel, but by the difficulty some of the industries upon which the PLA depends have had in absorbing military-related foreign technology. In 1975, for example, the authorities in Beijing concluded negotiations with the British for Chinese production of the British Rolls-Royce RB168-25R Spey Mk 202M afterburning turbofan engine and procured 50 units to serve as engineering guides. The British assisted in the construction of the engine plant at Xian and provided technical assistance in testing and maintenance. Nonetheless, by the early 1980s, the plant had not yet produced fully serviceable engines.[42] In the mid-1980s, there was some evidence that a few of those engines were in service.

The Spey engine, although its design dates from the early 1960s, was far more advanced than any propulsion system in service with the PLAAF. Beijing had expected that Communist Chinese aircraft production could benefit by the foreign purchase of a more modern engine that would require a short gestation period and only a modest manpower investment. The ministry that was responsible, however, found that adopting and adapting the required technology to mainland Chinese conditions was a formidable task.[43]

The PRC cannot purchase sufficient quantities of foreign arms to alter the military balance along the Sino-Soviet border because of fiscal restraints. In order to purchase the arms necessary to provide "minimum effectiveness" against Soviet military initiatives, Beijing would have to abandon much of its developmental program. But even if such a decision were made and the purchases could be underwritten, the complex modern weapon systems could not be absorbed and maintained at combat readiness by the PLA. Any effort to coproduce such systems domestically would be limited by China's antiquated industrial technology, on which many Western observers have commented. Some of the equipment in use dates from the Japanese occupation and the rest was largely manufactured in the Soviet Union in the early and mid-1950s.

The difficulties that result from the PRC's technological backwardness are compounded by the dramatic shortages of trained scientific personnel in industry. Between the mid-1960s and the mid-1970s, virtually no scientific training was available in mainland China. Although the defense industries, in general, have enjoyed special status and have had a priority claim on the available talent, mainland Chinese research and development institutes have suffered from isolation and remain woefully understaffed and less than innovative. There is no evidence, for example, that much research has been conducted on the development of electronic countermeasures against antiship and antiaircraft missiles. Soviet naval vessels and aircraft have missiles with greater range and lethality than their Communist Chinese counterparts—and yet mainland Chinese defense industries have produced nothing that might serve as a defense against them.

Communist Chinese research and development has apparently produced few reliable sensor systems that might be used for antisubmarine warfare—and no essential components such as lookdown radar or long-range air-to-air missiles for combat aircraft. Most of China's available talent in the fields of research and development has apparently been concentrated on the development and modernization of the PRC's nuclear deterrent. A serious effort is being made to enhance the targeting capability of the PLA's ballistic missiles. The component miniaturization technology of PRC satellites is seemingly reasonably well advanced and should provide some of the photointelligence capability needed to upgrade the PRC's nuclear weapons potential.

It must be recognized, however, that irrespective of the Communist Chinese investment of both time and skilled manpower in the effort, the Soviet Union has succeeded in widening the gap between its nuclear weapons capability and that of the PLA. The Soviets markedly improved their ability to target and destroy small, time-sensitive, and elusive Communist Chinese targets by a factor of about ten between the mid-1960s and 1980. The Soviet Union continues to make steady and rapid progress and the PRC fails to keep pace.[44]

The current demands on the Communist Chinese national budget preclude the possibility that Beijing could allocate more for weapon systems or generic military modernization. "There is simply no such thing as a 'quick fix' for remedying current Chinese military inadequacies. . . . The Chinese are, at least for now, no more capable of absorbing massive doses of sophisticated military equipment or technology than they were before their . . . shopping (or window-shopping) spree. Their foreign exchange picture has not brightened; in fact, given their new interest in purchasing massive amounts of 'civilian' industrial technology, greater demands than ever are being placed on roughly constant resources, leaving relatively little for weapons and weapons-production technology."[45] Neither the United States nor its allies can significantly affect the military capabilities of the People's Republic of China, except in the very long term or in symbolic fashion.[46]

By the early 1980s, Soviet analysts were well aware of mainland China's circumstances. The PRC lacked a developed economic infrastructure, a sufficient quantity of skilled personnel, and the financial reserves to enable it to acquire or produce the technology and weapon systems necessary to make it more than a negligible factor in strategic calculations.

It has become transparent that the deficiencies of the PLA exceed the West's capacity to redress them.[47]

THE SITUATION IN THE MID-1980s

When diplomatic relations with Beijing were normalized in 1979, Washington felt that it had sufficient motives for pursuing military and quasi-military relations with the People's Republic of China. A number of influential studies prepared by U.S. government agencies and by foreign policy consultants since the early 1970s had recommended that the Sino-Soviet rift be exploited. The Sino-Soviet dispute had arisen fortuitously at a time of relative decline in Western military capabilities. The Soviet Union, which had enjoyed conventional arms superiority, was on the threshold of at least strategic weapons parity with the United States.

The *Rylander Report, Consolidated Guidance no. 8, Presidential Review Memorandum no. 24*, and the "L-32" study commissioned by the Department of Defense together constituted "a detailed plan for establishing a far-reaching military relationship with China in an incremental, step-by-step manner."[48] U.S. officials visited Beijing with some regularity in 1979, and gradually Washington made clear that it was prepared to sell weapons and military-related technology to the PRC. By the beginning of the 1980s, however, it had become obvious to the authorities in Beijing that the association with the West would provide no immediate solution to the PRC's security problems on the Sino-Soviet border. The Western powers could not supply the requisite quantities of arms, nor could the Communist Chinese military effectively absorb those weapons were they made available.

As an immediate consequence, Beijing began to scale down its military budget. Some small purchases were made, but otherwise Beijing's interests were restricted to "window shopping" in the West. When Washington communicated its readiness to provide arms for purchase, Beijing became increasingly coy.

By the end of 1979, it seems that Beijing had abandoned any notion of a "Great Leap" in the modernization of its armed forces. In the fall of 1979, Beijing's minister of national defense maintained that "blindly pursuing large-scale and high speed development in building national defense will invariably and seriously hinder the development of the national economy and harm the base of the defense industry. Subsequently, 'haste makes waste.' "[49] What was required was an incremental modernization of the industrial base of the nation and a correlative improvement in the technology necessary for military modernization. That would require a long period of peace and stability with a significant reduction in China's preoccupation with military affairs.

In order to create an environment conducive to implementation of its program, Beijing sought to reduce Sino-Soviet hostility while continuing to cultivate its Western contacts. In April 1979, at the same time that it notified the Soviet Union that it would allow the Sino-Soviet Treaty of Friendship, Alliance, and Mutual Aid to terminate in 1980, Beijing proposed that the two governments embark upon negotiations to improve bilateral relations.[50] It had become clear that whatever the extent of "strategic cooperation" between the United States and China, it would never mature into any kind of military alliance. Equally clear was the fact that no matter how amicable Sino-Soviet relations became, any change in the deployment of Soviet military forces along the Chinese border would only marginally influence the global military balance, for the bulk of these forces are configured for defense and offense against the United States and Japan. The major costs of the Soviet militarization of its easternmost provinces have been those of emplacement, construction of an adequate infrastructure, and hardening of facilities. Therefore, any cosmetic movement of Soviet troops along the Sino-Soviet border would require minimal expense, and they could be redeployed as conditions warranted.[51]

By the early 1980s, Beijing sought a limited relaxation of tension between itself and Moscow. It was clear that a Soviet attack was not imminent, and normal state-to-state relations recommended themselves. Some tentative moves were made to commence communications between the Soviet and Chinese communist parties with the visit of Georges Marchais, general secretary of the French Communist Party, to Beijing. The French Communist Party is the most pro-Moscow communist party in Western Europe, and the fact that Marchais attempted to re-establish his party's ties with the Chinese Communist Party after a seventeen-year suspension suggested that the possibility existed for improved relations between the communist parties of Beijing and Moscow.[52]

Since 1980, the intensity of the ideological conflict between Beijing and Moscow has been significantly reduced.[53] Beijing no longer refers to the Soviet Union as a "social imperialist" and "fascist" power. The USSR's "socialist" credentials have been restored. It remains "hegemonic," in Beijing's view, in terms of its foreign policy.[54] As far as Beijing is concerned, both the United States and the Soviet Union "meddle in the affairs of other countries and commit aggression everywhere." The difference between them is that the United States is in a state of relative decline; the Soviet Union achieved conventional military superiority in the early 1970s and "overtook and later outstripped the United States in the number of strategic nuclear arms." In the judgment of Beijing spokes-men, the Soviet Union will not be able to maintain overall military superiority into the 1990s. Beijing anticipates a virtual military balance, which would allow the PRC to exploit the differences between the two contending powers. Beijing also anticipates a relative growth in the "strength" of the Third World countries, an eventuality that will change the global strategic balance.[55] Given the evolving "configuration of forces," the People's Republic of China will be in a position to continue its drive toward industrial and agricultural modernization—and ultimately military security—with the revolutionary goal of "joining hands" with the "antihegemonic" Third World forces to "struggle against" the two superpowers and "frustrate their schemes."[56]

What this policy suggests is a limited accommodation with the Soviet Union, increasing "independence" of the United States, and a concentra-tion on Third World issues.[57] In 1982, the authorities in Beijing were "optimistic" about future Sino-Soviet relations and began to be publicly critical of an increasing number of U.S. policies.[58] The "parallel interests" that had sustained the initial U.S.-PRC rapprochement had rapidly eroded. Beijing made clear that it did not share Washington's concern about the suppression of independent labor unions in Poland. It began to put distance between itself and the anticommunist Central American policy of the Reagan administration, abstained from a condemnation of the downing of the Korean airliner by the Soviet air force in Asia, reas-serted its demand for the establishment of a Palestinian state, and voiced its objections to an "arrogant" Israel that "provokes" its peaceful neigh-bors with "armed assaults." Beijing also abandoned its effort to sustain the anti-Soviet and anti-Cuban guerrillas in Angola, and in January 1983 established formal diplomatic relations with the African nation that it had previously considered a Soviet satellite. It announced its opposition to U.S. policy on Namibia (South-west Africa). Finally, Beijing, for the first time in years, began to complain once again about the "revival of Japanese militarism."[59]

Thus, by the beginning of the 1980s, a good deal of the presumed benefits that resulted from the Sino-American rapprochement seemed to have evaporated. The People's Republic of China offered little that might qualify it as a military counterweight to the Soviet military buildup. Few of the "parallel interests" originally shared with Washington in the mid-1970s remained. Mainland China was clearly intent upon regaining "independence"—pursuing its interests as Beijing understood those interests.[60]

The deterioration of relations between Washington and Beijing has not been the consequence of some failure on the part of the United States.

Nor have disagreements on specific issues impaired bilateral relations. Rather, the intrinsic limitations of U.S.-PRC strategic cooperation have become evident.[61] What has changed since the heady days of the mid- and late-1970s is that Beijing has recognized that there is manifestly little to be gained from a close military relationship with the United States, and still less to be gained from supporting Washington's foreign policy in Africa, the Middle East, Latin America, and most of Asia.

However much the two nations' perceptions have changed, Washington's policies toward Beijing (specifically, U.S. arms sales policy) have gathered a momentum of their own. In the middle of 1984, Sikorsky Aircraft concluded an agreement with PRC military authorities concerning the sale of 24 Sikorsky S-70C helicopters (a "civilian" version of the Black Hawk) at a cost of about $140 million—admittedly for use by the People's Liberation Army.

The S-70 is one of the most modern helicopters developed for the U.S. military. Originally designed as a replacement for the UH-1 Iroquois, the U.S. Army version (the UH-60A) is capable of carrying either a fully equipped eleven-man infantry squad or a combination of external weapons and ordnance. It can carry antitank missiles, rapid-fire weapons, or mine-dispensing pods. With maximum internal fuel supply at take-off mission weight, the S-70 has a range of approximately 370 miles.

Such force enhancement will have no effect on the military balance along the Sino-Soviet border, but transport and weapons platforms might appreciably influence the military balance in the Taiwan Strait. Suitably equipped, such rotary-winged aircraft could perform minelaying duties in critical port areas. They could be used over the Taiwan Strait to interdict ship traffic when rough seas prohibit the use of surface vessels as missile launch pads. They could also be employed in missile and gun attacks against surface vessels of the navy of the Republic of China on Taiwan (ROC) or in air transport of invasion forces.

The reality is that the People's Republic of China has been engaged in a military conflict with the Republic of China on Taiwan since termination of the civil war on the mainland in 1949. There have been episodic clashes in the strait since 1950, and some of them (such as the major engagements in the late 1950s) have involved sea, ground, and air elements of both armed forces. Naval battles were fought in the mid-1960s, and a large-scale military mobilization in Fujian Province (directly across from Taiwan) in the mid-1970s appeared then to be preparation for a combined assault against the Nationalist Chinese. The authorities in Beijing have continually refused to renounce the use of force in the attempt to bring Nationalist Taiwan back to "the bosom of the motherland."

Although U.S. arms sales to the People's Republic of China can do nothing to alter the military balance along the Sino-Soviet border, they can appreciably affect the military balance between the PRC and some of its immediate neighbors—of whom the Republic of China on Taiwan is the most exposed. The military balance in the Taiwan Strait is at best precarious; little would be required to tip that balance and perhaps destabilize the region.

U.S. arms sales policy with regard to the People's Republic of China is not simply a matter affecting the triangular relationship between the United States, the Soviet Union, and the PRC. It can potentially affect the military balance between mainland China and its peripheral and insular neighbors. The military balance between the PRC and the Republic of China on Taiwan is one of the most important, affecting as it does the strategic, political, and economic interests of the United States.

6

The "Taiwan" Issue

Rapprochement between the United States and the People's Republic of China created problems in the relations between Washington and the Republic of China on Taiwan that are unique in the history of U.S. diplomacy. Yet many of the problems that have affected relations between the United States, the PRC and the ROC are symptomatic of the major difficulties that have attended Washington's East Asian policies since the mid-1970s.

As the United States moved closer to diplomatic recognition of the government in Beijing, the discussions in Washington became increasingly acrimonious, for it became obvious that the United States could not anticipate with any precision what the utility of such an association with the world's largest communist power would be.[1] Many critics of U.S. policy toward the PRC argued that it was unlikely that improved relations with Beijing would significantly influence the foreign policy or the strategic deployments of the USSR. They further argued that military assistance to the PRC would do little to further Western security interests and could improve Communist Chinese capabilities to the point where Beijing might "be inclined eventually to use its new power forcefully in areas sensitive to the United States—such as Taiwan, Korea and Japan."[2] There was concern that neither Beijing's new foreign policy nor its new leadership was sufficiently well established to preclude changes in either or both, to the detriment of the noncommunist states in the region in general and the Republic of China on Taiwan in particular.[3] Finally, there were those who lamented the fact that the ROC, the oldest ally the United States had in Asia, was being ill-served by Washington's decision to invest in a doubtful, if seemingly low-cost, solution to its strategic and political problems.[4]

The issue of whether arms transfers to the People's Republic of China would increase the threat to the PRC's noncommunist neighbors was only one of the policy problems generated by Washington's rapprochement with Beijing. But it certainly was potentially one of the most serious, for the Republic of China on Taiwan suffers the most immediate exposure to threats of military violence emanating from Communist China.

A review of the entire "Taiwan" issue in Sino-U.S. relations reveals some of the problems that immediately followed the establishment of diplomatic relations between Washington and Beijing and suggests some of the dilemmas inherent in that relationship. It also reveals the complexity of, and the actual costs resulting from, Washington's effort to establish and maintain relations with the communist government in Beijing.

THE ORIGIN OF THE TAIWAN ISSUE

The Taiwan issue was an unexpected by-product of the Second World War and the subsequent victory of the Communist Chinese forces on the mainland of China. The leaders of the antifascist alliance had decided that the island of Formosa (Taiwan) would retrocede to the Republic of China at the conclusion of the war. The island had come under imperial Japanese jurisdiction by the terms of the Treaty of Shimonoseki in 1895 (which concluded the Sino-Japanese War) and remained a Japanese colony until 1945. After mainland Chinese authorities accepted the Japanese surrender of Taiwan, they immediately began to reconstruct a Chinese administrative apparatus to govern what had once again become a province of China.[5]

Between 1945 and 1949, civil war ravaged the Chinese mainland. In early 1949, Generalissimo Chiang Kai-shek had decided to make the island of Taiwan a redoubt for the ultimate defense of the Republic of China. The remnants of the national government and the Nationalist armed forces were transported across the 100 miles of the Taiwan Strait, and the "temporary capital" of the Republic of China was established at Taipei. Communist Chinese armies began to mass along the shoreline in Fujian Province, across from Taiwan, in preparation for an amphibious assault on the last stronghold of the defeated Nationalist forces. An invasion of Taiwan by the forces of Mao Zedong seemed imminent.

Authorities in Washington advised U.S. foreign posts to prepare for the final extinction of the Nationalist Republic of China. However, the North Korean invasion of South Korea, which signaled the outbreak of the Korean War, dramatically changed the situation in East Asia. The United States government immediately responded to what it took to be an act of aggression orchestrated and directed by Kremlin leaders. The United States prepared to intervene in the conflict on the Korean peninsula and received the support of the United Nations. "Volunteers" from the PRC engaged the UN Forces—and the United States and its allies found themselves in armed conflict with the newly established Communist Chinese regime on the mainland. The island of Taiwan suddenly assumed strategic and logistical importance; it had become a critical link in the anticommunist archipelagic chain of defense that stretched from the northern Japanese islands to the Philippines.

By the end of the Korean War, U.S. defense policy required a string of bases strategically located on the periphery of mainland China. Consequently, mutual defense treaties were signed between the United States, Japan, the Republic of Korea, and the Republic of China on Taiwan. By 1955, the United States' "anticommunist containment policy" in East Asia was complete. An important element of this policy was the Mutual Defense Treaty with the Republic of China on Taiwan. That treaty, the U.S. refusal to recognize the communist regime in Beijing, and the establishment of diplomatic relations with Taipei would determine the pattern of Sino-U.S. relations for the next 25 years.

Prior to the establishment of this pattern, the Communist Chinese leadership had always considered Taiwan an area similar to Korea, inhabited by a "nationality" distinct from that of China's Han majority. Throughout the interwar years, the Chinese Communist Party considered the Taiwanese a "minority nationality" similar to the Mongols, the Mohammedans, and the Miao. Unlike the Mohammedans and the Miao, however, the Taiwanese were considered to have originated in a "separate homeland." As a consequence, in 1934 the Chinese Communist Party supported formation of a "Taiwanese Liberation Movement" whose goal was the establishment of an independent national state similar to that sought by the Koreans. At no time did the Chinese Communist Party suggest that Taiwan was an integral and inalienable part of the Chinese "motherland." Even in 1938, the party was still referring to Taiwan as an "oppressed nation," rather than as an alienated component of "sovereign Chinese territory."[6]

In 1943, the Nationalist government repudiated the Treaty of Shimonoseki and claimed that Taiwan was part of China. The United States government declared Taiwan a territory that had been "stolen" from China by the Japanese at the end of the Sino-Japanese War of 1894. When the Japanese surrendered in 1945, the Nationalist authorities assumed control over the island. Given the altered circumstances, the Chinese

Communist Party radically changed its position with regard to Taiwan and declared it an integral part of the "new China." In 1949 Mao Zedong prepared to restore the island to the "motherland" through the force of arms.

With the interposition of U.S. naval forces in the Taiwan Strait following the outbreak of hostilities in Korea, the issue of Taiwan's international status became one of Beijing's primary concerns. In 1943, the leadership of the Chinese Communist Party began to refer to Taiwan not as a potentially independent national state but as part of sovereign Chinese territory. In 1949, Beijing insisted that its sovereignty over the island had been established by right of succession. The PRC considered the communist government the successor of the defeated Nationalist government. In effect, after 1943, and particularly after 1949, the authorities in Beijing based their claim to Taiwan on the Nationalist policy of full integration of Taiwan into the unified Chinese nation.[7] They considered their failure to gain control over the island, as well as the Pescadores (P'eng-hu) and the offshore islands (Kinmen and Matsu), the consequence of U.S. "imperialist" intervention—the effort by Washington to make of Taiwan a "colony" of "parasitic capitalism." After 1955, Beijing characterized Taiwan as an alienated portion of Communist China "illegally occupied by American imperialist forces."[8]

When the first moves toward rapprochement between Washington and Beijing were initiated in 1971, the Communist Chinese authorities dropped their contention that Taiwan was "occupied" and that its reversion to the PRC had been prevented by U.S. imperialism. After issuance of the Shanghai Communique in 1972, Beijing simply insisted that the "government of the People's Republic of China" was the "sole legal government of China" and that Taiwan was "a province of China." The authorities in Beijing further insisted that they would "firmly oppose" any effort to create "one China, one Taiwan," "one China, two governments," "two Chinas," or an "independent Taiwan." Finally, Beijing objected to any suggestion that "the status of Taiwan remains to be determined."[9]

In the Shanghai Communiqué, the United States had simply affirmed what it considered to be a descriptive fact: "The United States acknowledges that all Chinese on either side of the Taiwan Strait maintain there is but one China and that Taiwan is part of China." Whether this allegation was true or not, the United States chose "not to challenge that position." It chose, instead, to urge the "peaceful settlement of the Taiwan question by the Chinese themselves."

The Shanghai Communiqué was only the first of what have been called "creatively ambiguous" U.S.-PRC joint statements of intention. In formulating such statements, the Communist Chinese state their position and Washington's diplomatic representatives state theirs in terms sufficiently vague and general to convey the impression of some sort of agreement, on the basis of which further negotiations proceed. The principal difficulty with this process is that the authorities in Beijing seem to think that when U.S. diplomats "acknowledge" a position taken by the PRC and choose not to challenge it, such behavior is tantamount to acceptance of the Communist Chinese position. Most of the problems that have adversely affected relations between the two countries have been a result of the studiously cultivated misunderstandings contained in the U.S.-PRC joint communiqués.

The official U.S. position on the international legal status of Taiwan and its associated territories is, in fact, very explicit. It has not been changed since it was first articulated in the early 1950s. The United States officially "takes no position on the status of Taiwan under international law, but does regard Taiwan as a country for purposes of U.S domestic law."[10] The U.S. position has been, and remains, that the international legal status of Taiwan "remains to be determined."[11] In effect, Washington does not officially accept the claim that the People's Republic of China enjoys legal sovereignty over Taiwan and its associated territories.

When the United States and the Republic of China on Taiwan signed the Mutual Defense Treaty in 1954, the United States maintained that Taipei "effectively controlled" Taiwan and the Pescadores (no mention was made of the offshore islands held by the armed forces of the ROC),[12] and therefore Taipei was possessed of the legal power to act as a signatory to legally binding international agreements. At a press conference held immediately after the signing of the treaty, the United States asserted that the issue of the "technical sovereignty" over Taiwan and its associated territories had not been settled—that is, neither the Japanese peace treaty nor the peace treaty concluded between Japan and the Republic of China had specifically transferred sovereign rights.

The authorities in Taipei have claimed sovereign rights over Taiwan and the associated territories by virtue of the abrogation of the Treaty of Shimonoseki, as a consequence of which sovereignty over Taiwan reverted to the ROC as the successor of imperial China.

Since the end of the Second World War, opinions concerning the validity of the claims made by the ROC have varied. Some legal authorities have insisted that the "undisturbed" control exercised by Taipei over the contested territories since 1945 constitutes a right by "prescription," and that "there can be no lawyer's doubts as to the legitimacy of Nationalist China's title to Formosa [Taiwan]."[13] Other authorities have held that the Nationalist government in Taipei has established its legal rights over the islands by subjugation, occupation, and establishment of effective control. Still others point to the fact that the Cairo Declaration of 1943 explicitly affirmed that Taiwan would be "restored to the Republic of China." That declaration was subsequently incorporated into the 1945 Potsdam Proclamation and was accepted by Japan as part of its instrument of surrender, a document legally binding on all signatories.[14]

What is clear is that the Shanghai Communiqué of 1972 did not establish the international legal status of Taiwan and the associated territories—nor did Washington accept Beijing's claims to sovereign jurisdiction over the disputed territories. The United States still maintains that the sovereign status of Taiwan remains undetermined. Moreover, irrespective of the interpretation given the Shanghai Communiqué (or any subsequent communiqué), bilateral communiqués are not considered legally binding in U.S. constitutional law. Such communiqués are neither executive agreements nor treaties and therefore do not give rise to obligations under law.

Beijing seems to have misunderstood both U.S. constitutional law and the nature of bilateral communiqués. Such a communiqué is nothing more than a political statement of intention. Although such a document is important as a statement of intended policy and international principle, it cannot be regarded as constituting a contractual obligation.[15] As a consequence, even if the Shanghai Communiqué, or any subsequent communiqué, were to convey the impression that the president of the United States was prepared to accede to Beijing's claim of sovereignty over Taiwan, that impression would be illusory. In 1954, the United States did not have it within its power to change the international legal status of Taiwan by entering into a treaty of mutual security with the Republic of China on Taiwan; it had still less power to do so by issuing a bilateral communiqué with the People's Republic of China in 1972.

The United States continues to maintain, in effect, that the international legal status of Taiwan and its associated territories has not been determined, and that for the purposes of U.S. domestic law, Taiwan can be dealt with as a nation. This position is compatible with the legislation that now establishes the legal basis of Washington's relations with Taipei.

THE TAIWAN RELATIONS ACT

When the first certain signs of U.S.-PRC rapprochement began to appear in 1971, the issue of Taiwan remained close to the surface in all deliberations. In the years between issuance of the Shanghai Communiqué in 1972 and the final negotiations that led to the normalization of diplomatic relations between the two countries in 1978, Beijing insisted that three conditions be met before the final step of formal mutual diplomatic recognition could be taken: (1) the United States was to break diplomatic relations with the Republic of China on Taiwan; (2) the United States was also to terminate its Mutual Defense Treaty with Taipei; and finally (3) all U.S. troops were to be withdrawn from the island and its associated territories.

Beijing did agree to continuation of U.S. trade and investment relations with the island, and it agreed that the United States could terminate its defense treaty in accordance with the terms of that treaty—which required its continuance for one year after formal announcement of a decision to terminate.

When the Carter administration announced its decision to proceed to full diplomatic relations with the People's Republic of China in December 1978, it clearly indicated that the United States would meet all the preconditions insisted upon by Beijing. The response was quite unprecedented.

Ever since 1969, the United States Congress had sought to exercise greater influence over the foreign policy prerogatives of the executive office. To that end it had established an ad hoc Subcommittee on United States Security Agreements and Commitments Abroad. In 1973 the War Powers Bill was introduced, and almost immediately Congress insisted on overseeing the foreign military sales of the United States government. By the mid-1970s, Congress was showing considerable assertiveness with regard to the executive's foreign policy prerogatives. When the decision concerning normalization of relations between the United States and the PRC was announced, the Senate Foreign Relations Committee had already emerged as a formidable potential obstacle to Carter's plans.[16]

For a variety of reasons—not excluding his interest in scoring a foreign policy "coup" that would aid in his bid for re-election—Carter had decided to proceed with normalization of relations with the PRC. A series of secret meetings were held between representatives of the Carter administration and Communist Chinese officials. At the end of 1978, President Carter communicated his desire to conclude those negotiations quickly and to begin formal diplomatic relations with the People's Republic of China on January 1, 1979.

When he acceded to the presidency in 1977, Jimmy Carter had faced the same problems with regard to the normalization of relations with the People's Republic of China that had obstructed the intentions of Richard Nixon. Beijing's preconditions for normalization clearly required the almost complete severance of Washington's ties with the Republic of China on Taiwan—a relationship that had served U.S. interests in East Asia for almost three decades. During that period, Washington had used almost every appropriate formal opportunity to emphasize its commitment to the security and stability of the ROC. As late as 1968, the undersecretary of state could insist that the U.S. commitment "to the defense of Taiwan . . . was not then and is not now open to negotiation" in any deliberations concerning the relaxation of tension between Washington and Beijing.[17] Presidents Nixon and Ford had regularly given similar assurances. During his campaign for the presidency, Jimmy Carter insisted that "I would like to improve our relationships with the PRC. . . . But I wouldn't go back on the commitment that we have had to assure that Taiwan is protected from military takeover."[18] Meeting the conditions set by Beijing could only appear to be an abandonment of just such commitments.

In a pre-emptive move to forestall just such an eventuality, Congress overwhelmingly approved a resolution (a rider to the Security Assistance Authorization Bill) requiring the administration to consult with the appropriate members of Congress before initiating any change with regard to the security relations between the United States and the Republic of China on Taiwan. At the same time that Congress was communicating its concerns, the Carter administration was engaged in secret negotiations with the leadership in Beijing. The Carter representatives apparently were convinced that the Communist Chinese conditions for diplomatic normalization were unalterable—and they made no effort to have them modified. When the normalization agreement was announced, it was evident that the United States had agreed to Beijing's conditions. The Republic of China on Taiwan would be "derecognized" by the United States; Washington would remove its troops from the island and its associated territories; and the mutual security treaty would be allowed to lapse. The United States had withdrawn its protection from Taiwan.

Congress was in recess when the normalization agreement with Beijing was announced. President Carter had agreed to conditions to which two previous administrations had been either unwilling or incapable of submitting. When Congress reconvened in January 1979, its first order of business was to deal with a poorly drafted piece of legislation (S. 245) that the administration offered as the legal basis for the continuance of "commercial, cultural and other relations with the people of Taiwan on an unofficial basis."[19]

This innocuous bill gave an assertive Congress the opportunity to participate in the ongoing process of normalization of relations with the

People's Republic of China. Perhaps more than anything else, the members of Congress were offended that they had not been consulted by the administration and that negotiations with Communist China had been conducted in secret. It was evident that the administration had sought to avoid public discussion of its decision to normalize relations with Beijing on Beijing's terms. The administration was aware of congressional concern about the security of the Republic of China on Taiwan. The Republic of China was faced with the termination of the security arrangements that had afforded the 18 million Chinese on the islands the protection of the United States.

The administration had been unable to obtain a binding assurance from the authorities in Beijing that force would not be used against the ROC. They had insisted that the return of Taiwan to the "motherland" was an "internal affair"—a concern of the Communist Chinese government alone.[20] To Beijing, this was a case of violated sovereignty. Taiwan was a province of the People's Republic of China, and the government of the "rebellious" Republic of China was thus "illegal." Whether force was to be used to restore Beijing's sovereignty was a matter that must be left to its discretion. In substance, the United States was being asked to leave the Republic of China on Taiwan to its fate.

In the legislation proposed by the administration to serve as the legal basis for continued relations with the "people of Taiwan," virtually nothing was said about the security of the islands or their population. The "other relations" alluded to in S.245 (in addition to commercial and cultural ties) presumably included the "continued arms sales of defensive character on a restrained basis"—to which Beijing objected. At his press conference announcing the normalization of relations with the United States, then Chairman Hua Guofeng stated: "During the negotiations the U.S. side mentioned that after normalization it would continue to sell a limited amount of arms to Taiwan for defensive purposes. We made it clear that we absolutely would not agree to this . . . [since it] would not conform to the principles of . . . normalization."[21] The bill sponsored by the administration discreetly avoided any mention of arms sales to the ROC after its "derecognition."

The agreement on diplomatic normalization between the United States and the People's Republic of China gave every appearance of being a calculated abandonment of the security obligations the United States had assumed 25 years earlier, when Washington needed the Republic of China on Taiwan to service its needs in East Asia. In his commentary on the normalization arrangement, John B. Oakes, then senior editor of the *New York Times*, maintained that as a consequence of Washington's apparent indifference to Taiwan's fate, "President Carter has seriously undermined American pretensions to be the moral leader of the world and an exemplar of constancy and faithfulness to our friends." The majority sentiment of Congress was expressed by Senate minority leader Howard Baker when he complained, "The Taiwanese have been a good and faithful ally, and we certainly owe them more than this."[22]

In Congress, there was a sense of moral outrage at the betrayal of an allied nation and a conviction that the Carter administration could at least have required Beijing's renunciation of the use of force against Taiwan. The administration's sponsorship of a vague and half-articulated piece of legislation as the domestic legal foundation for continued relations with the Chinese on Taiwan prompted the members of Congress to entirely reformulate bill S.245 into an effective vehicle for substantial and specific, if unofficial, relations with the government of the Republic of China on Taiwan.

The legislative history of the Taiwan Relations Act (Public Law 96-8, 1979) confirms that its primary purpose was to ensure the security and continued economic prosperity of the Republic of China on Taiwan. The Senate, in its report on the bill, affirmed that the bill was "intended to enable the United States to maintain close and friendly relations with the people on Taiwan on an unofficial basis and to do so in a manner that contributes to the peace, stability and well-being of the Western Pacific area." These same sentiments were expressed in the House report: "The establishment of full diplomatic relations between the United States and the People's Republic of China . . . has been accompanied by concern that this action not affect adversely the future well-being of the people on Taiwan."[23]

The policy and the implementation procedures of the Taiwan Relations Act are described in sections 2a and b and 3a, b, and c.[24] The act was said to be necessary to "help maintain peace, security and stability in the Western Pacific"; its purpose was to "declare that peace and stability in the area are in the political, security, and economic interests of the United States." The act was further intended "to make clear that the United States' decision to establish diplomatic relations with the People's Republic of China rests upon the expectation that the future of Taiwan will be determined by peaceful means," and that "any effort to determine the future of Taiwan by other than peaceful means, including by boycotts and embargoes, [will be considered] a threat to the peace and security of the Western Pacific area and [will be] of grave concern to the United States." The threats to U.S. interests were to be offset by providing "Taiwan with arms of a defensive character"; the United States would also maintain its capacity "to resist any resort to force or other forms of coercion that would jeopardize the security, or the social or economic system, of the people of Taiwan."

The stated policy was to be effected by making available "to Taiwan such defense articles and defense service in such quantity as may be necessary to enable Taiwan to maintain a sufficient self-defense capacity." Section 3b of the act establishes that the nature and quantity of the defense articles to be provided to Taiwan would be determined solely by the president and Congress—in effect, without the intercession of, and without the necessity of consultations with, the authorities in Beijing. Finally, section 3c of the act provides that the president will notify Congress of any threat to the security of Taiwan in order that "appropriate action" might be undertaken "in accordance with constitutional practices."

The Taiwan Relations Act is, in fact, the equivalent in domestic law of an international security arrangement. The Congress of the United States announced that any threat to the security of the Republic of China on Taiwan would be a matter of "grave concern," for it would affect U.S security, economic, and political interests. Congress also stated that any threat to the "people of Taiwan" would elicit a response "in accordance with constitutional practices." Few security treaties between the United States and foreign states promise much more. Only the security treaty between the United States and its NATO allies contains an automatic engagement clause that applies in the event of enemy attack on any of the signatories. All the rest make response conditional on prevailing "constitutional practices" (as does the Taiwan Relations Act).

As duly enacted domestic legislation, the Taiwan Relations Act takes constitutional precedence over presidential communiqués. In fact, it can be argued that anything said in such communiqués is legally binding on the United States only when it is operationalized in such legislation. The Taiwan Relations Act establishes the meaning of commitments made by the United States in the Shanghai Communiqué and the Joint Communiqué on the Establishment of Diplomatic Relations between the United States and the People's Republic of China (released on December 15, 1978).

Although presidential communiqués, in and of themselves, do not constitute binding obligations, and for legal purposes congressional enactments take precedence over them, the executive branch of the U.S. government nonetheless exercises significant initiative in foreign affairs. A presidential communiqué is an expression of serious intention. Because the president is empowered to make foreign policy, policy initiative rests with him. Only the executive branch, for example, can initiate arms sales; Congress can only oversee such transfers. The Taiwan Relations Act requires the sale of sufficient weapons to the Republic of China on Taiwan to ensure its capacity for self-defense, but only the president can initiate such sales. Although the Taiwan Relations Act prescribes the continuance of all treaties (save that of mutual security) between the United States and the ROC, the Congress can realistically employ few sanctions against a president who chooses to abrogate them.

The history of the implementation of the Taiwan Relations Act has been one of conflict between the president and the Congress. Not long after enactment of the Taiwan Relations Act, which permitted the "continuation in force of all treaties and other international agreements" (sec. 4c), President Carter reduced the formal Air Transport Agreement between the United States and the ROC to an "informal" arrangement. Congress could do little more than remonstrate.[25]

Although the Taiwan Relations Act stated that "nothing in this Act may be construed as a basis for supporting the exclusion or expulsion of Taiwan from continued membership in any international financial institution or any other international organization" (sec. 4d), the Department of State agreed to, and may have assisted in, the expulsion of the ROC from the International Monetary Fund and the International Olympic Organization. Again, Congress could do little more than remonstrate.[25]

The Republic of China on Taiwan has had particular difficulty in purchasing specific arms and weapon systems from the United States since the commencement of the rapprochement between Washington and Beijing. The Taiwan Relations Act requires the United States provide the ROC with a deterrent capability. Nonetheless, Washington has denied necessary arms sales and transfers to the Republic of China on Taiwan. Given the gross asymmetry in the military force levels of the ROC and the PRC, the Chinese on Taiwan require significant force enhancements if they are to attain and maintain a capacity for self-defense.

The ROC requires precision-guided munitions, longer-range anti-ship missiles, enhanced antisubmarine warfare capabilities, more advanced surface-to-air missiles, electronic countermeasures against incoming missiles, over-the-horizon early warning systems for defense against surprise attacks by quantitatively superior forces, and more sophisticated air-to-air missiles to give its air combat forces greater survival potential against the large numbers of aircraft that can be deployed by the air force of the communist air command. Perhaps Taiwan's single most serious deficiency is the absence of a high-thrust, heavier interceptor aircraft, with greater ordnance-carrying capacity and endurance than those currently in inventory. In order to defend itself against attack, the nation's air command must have qualitatively superior machines—since the ROC's potential adversary on the mainland of China can easily station 1,500 combat aircraft on airfields within 250 nautical miles of Taiwan. Against that force, the ROC air command could dispatch no more than about 350 aircraft. In order to serve as a credible deterrent against PRC air attack, the aircraft of the ROC would have to be able to exact a "loss exchange ratio" (a "kill-ratio") of about 6 to 1—that is, the potential enemy would have to anticipate a loss of at least six of its aircraft for every one lost by the air command of the ROC. To inflict such losses, the aircraft of the ROC would have to have combat properties and weapon systems that were qualitatively superior to those of the opponent.

Without tactical control of the air over the Taiwan Strait, the ROC would be exposed to naval blockade, conventional air attacks, and possible combined amphibious assault. If the Republic of China on Taiwan is to attain a deterrent capacity for self-defense, the availability of high-performance combat aircraft is a necessity.

As the United States and the People's Republic of China moved closer to mutual diplomatic recognition, Beijing turned up the decibel level of its objections to U.S. arms sales to the ROC. The Carter administration, under considerable prodding from Congress, had contemplated the sale of a more advanced aircraft to Taiwan; however, the Reagan administration, under still stronger pressure from Beijing, rejected the request. In an effort to foreclose a predictable deterioration of U.S.-PRC relations, the Reagan administration issued a joint communiqué with Beijing on August 17, 1982. That communiqué reiterated Beijing's position that "the question of Taiwan is China's internal affair." The United States affirmed that it attached "great importance to its relations with China" and insisted that it had "no intention of infringing on Chinese sovereignty and territorial integrity, or interfering in China's internal affairs." The United States further maintained that "it does not seek to carry out a long-term policy of arms sales to Taiwan, that its arms sales to Taiwan will not exceed, either in qualitative or in quantitative terms, the level of those supplied in recent years . . . and that it intends to reduce gradually its sales of arms to Taiwan, leading over a period of time to a final resolution."[26]

The communiqué of August 1982 seems to contravene some of the central commitments made in the Taiwan Relations Act. The communiqué appears to commit the United States to a quantitative and qualitative limit on arms sales to Taipei. The Taiwan Relations Act specifies that arms sales to the ROC should be governed solely by the concern that the Republic of China on Taiwan "maintain a sufficient self-defense capability." The Taiwan Relations Act makes those sales contingent only on the needs of the Republic of China on Taiwan and suggests nothing about phasing out those sales at any particular time.

Both the presidential statement that accompanied the communiqué of August 1982 and the statement made by John H. Holdridge, assistant secretary for East Asian and Pacific Affairs, however, maintained that the policy intentions expressed in the communiqué were fully "compatible" with the Taiwan Relations Act.

Section 3b of the act provides that the "nature and quantity" of such defense articles and services made available to the ROC be determined by "the President and Congress" based "solely upon their judgment of the needs of Taiwan." In the judgment of President Reagan, Beijing's affirmation of peaceful intentions with respect to the "reunification" of Taiwan with the "motherland," as expressed in the joint communiqué, had relaxed tensions in the Taiwan Strait and had correspondingly reduced the defense needs of the Republic of China. This allowed the United States to impose a quantitative and qualitative ceiling on any future arms sales to Taipei without violating what was understood to be the firm commitment "embodied in the Taiwan Relations Act . . . to sell to Taiwan arms necessary to maintain a sufficient self-defense capability."[27]

The communiqué of August 1982 thus made the measure of the ROC's "sufficient self-defense capability" a function of the declarative behavior of the leadership in Beijing. As long as Beijing does not overtly threaten the peace of the Taiwan Strait region, the United States will not sell Taipei arms or weapon systems that exceed in quantity or quality those that were sold to the ROC in the immediate past. A "sufficient self-defense capability" is no longer measured against a potential threat, but against Beijing's assurances of peaceful intent.

The difficulty with this interpretation of the commitments contained in the Taiwan Relations Act is that it makes the Republic of China on Taiwan a passive agent in its own defense. As long as the defense needs of the ROC were being measured against a real or potential threat, some reasonable judgment about those needs could be formulated. If those needs are judged on the basis of some announcement emanating from Beijing, it will be impossible for Taipei to predict U.S. arms sales behavior. Since the ROC military cannot anticipate Beijing's diplomatic pronouncements, or the U.S. response, it cannot pursue a rational procurement policy.

The procurement agencies of any military system are concerned with measurable threat assessments and not with diplomatic pronouncements made by potential adversaries. Pronouncements can change with unanticipated rapidity; military capabilities do not. High-performance weapon systems, such as modern combat aircraft, require from three to five years to be effectively incorporated into a contemporary fighting force. Should Beijing take initiatives that might threaten the security of Taiwan and its associated territories, the armed forces of the ROC could only respond with the forces available in inventory. The only alternative in such an eventuality would be to hope that the United States was prepared to assume the responsibility of armed response—a responsibility there is reason to believe Washington would be incapable or reluctant to assume. Should the United States be unable or unwilling to intervene in such circumstances, for whatever reason, the authorities in Taipei would have no other option but to surrender or to face overwhelming military odds.

As will be suggested later in this chapter, the situation in the Taiwan Strait is even more complicated than has been indicated. The Taiwan issue has greatly complicated Washington's relations with Beijing. The Reagan administration has insisted that the relationship with the PRC serves "vital" functions in the "long-term national security interests and contributes stability in East Asia." The administration has also stated its "firm resolve" that the "security of Taiwan . . . not be compromised."[28] A brief review of the U.S. economic and political investment in the ROC and that nation's importance to the security of East Asia will make clear why the United States has continuously asserted its "firm resolve" to protect the Republic of China on Taiwan, irrespective of its differences with Beijing regarding the Taiwan issue.

THE U.S. ECONOMIC AND POLITICAL INVESTMENT IN THE REPUBLIC OF CHINA ON TAIWAN

In the early 1950s, having established its policy toward the two Chinas, the United States began to become intimately involved in the economic development and modernization of the Republic of China on Taiwan. Following the program for economic development that had been prescribed 30 years earlier by Sun Yat-sen, the founder of the Kuomintang, the leadership in Taipei began a program of agricultural and industrial development that has been one of the most successful in the modern world.[29] Almost immediately, U.S. agencies began to collaborate with the Chinese on Taiwan, who displayed a "competence, energy, development-mindedness, and cooperative spirit" that distinguished them from most other U.S. aid and assistance recipients.[30]

Although the Republic of China on Taiwan has a population density that is among the highest in the world and a high reproductive rate (the population of Taiwan doubled in about fifteen years), the ROC sustained a stable cumulative yearly real economic growth rate of 8.08 percent from 1952 through 1977. Gross saving as a percentage of the gross domestic product escalated from 9.2 percent in 1952 to 30.1 percent in 1977. Industrial output as a percentage of net domestic product increased from a mere 17.9 percent in 1952 to 38.8 percent in 1977. During the same period, the average annual increase in overall crop yield was 4.2 percent, and the annual rate of real growth of total multilateral trade was 13.4 percent. Bilateral trade with the United States reached a level of almost $10 billion dollars in 1979.[31]

This spectacular economic growth was accompanied by stable prices, effective labor absorption, and improved income distribution. The real income of the poorest segments of the population rose much more rapidly than that of the wealthiest, and by the end of the 1960s unemployment had virtually been eliminated.[32] Between 1952 and 1981, the level of personal consumption in the ROC more than tripled (1952 = 100, 1981 = 373). In 1952, 55.6 percent of the average family's expenditures was allocated to food consumption; in 1981 the percentage had declined to 34.9 percent. In 1984, per capita income on Taiwan was over $3,000, and 99.7 percent of all children of school age were attending school. Labor productivity averaged a 6 percent increase per annum, and average annual income rose by about 18 percent per year. Between 1953 and 1975 real earnings doubled, and disparities between rural and urban incomes declined significantly. Whereas the lowest quintile of all households earned only 3.0 percent of total income in 1953, by 1980 the lowest quintile of all households was earning 8.8 percent. The ratio of income earned by the highest and lowest quintiles of all households declined from 20.5 to 1 in 1953 to 4.2 to 1 in 1980.[33] By 1980, the Republic of China on Taiwan had one of the lowest "inequality indexes" of all developing economies; income was distributed more equitably in the ROC than in many developing socialist economies—including that of the People's Republic of China.[34]

The part played by the United States in the dramatic performance of the ROC's economy was substantial. Between 1951 and 1964, the United States provided about $1.5 billion in economic aid and concessional grants. By 1964, the ROC had graduated from the ranks of developing economies that required concessional loans and direct aid. Thereafter, capital inflow took the form of foreign investment, the bulk of it originating in the United States. In 1977, $1.19 billion in private foreign investment contributed to the growth of the ROC's economy, and 43.3 percent of that amount was provided by Americans. Thereafter, even though the domestic economy of the ROC generated enough capital (in savings, both public and private) to meet the nation's requirements, foreign investment in Taiwan increased. By 1980, U.S. investors owned about $2.0 billion in equity in the islands. Major multinationals, including many based in the United States, had made significant investments in the economy of the ROC. Such companies as Ford, ITT, RCA, IBM, Union Carbide, Minnesota Mining & Manufacturing, General Instrument, Zenith, Admiral, Goodyear, Singer, Gulf Oil, Pfizer, Parke Davis, Sylvania, Du Pont, and Phillips Petroleum embarked on joint ventures in the ROC, making Taiwan one of the largest producers and exporters of nontraditional commodities in Southeast Asia. Of the more than 800 firms in the ROC whose export volume exceeded $1 million in 1974, 210 were either joint-venture enterprises or were owned by foreign nationals. The exports of these 210 firms constituted about 40 percent of all ROC exports.

All of this foreign activity, however, did not alienate local control over industry. The inflow of foreign capital, in the form of both loans and equity, must be approved by the Foreign Exchange Bureau of the central bank of the ROC. All outflow of foreign exchange, whether in payment of interest, principal, or royalty, or for the importation of machinery, equipment, or merchandise, is approved on a case-by-case basis. Remittance of capital on foreign investments is made only two years after the completion of an approved investment program. In effect, foreign investors, no matter how important, are controlled in order to ensure that they do not invest simply to reap a windfall profit without contributing to the real growth of the domestic economy.

The ROC welcomed foreign investment largely because it was generally accompanied by the technological knowledge and skills essential to a more sophisticated economy. The 837 technical cooperation projects approved by the government of the Republic of China on Taiwan between 1952 and 1974 contributed to the deepening and forward and backward linkages in the economy. By the early 1980s, the ROC had the twelfth largest shipbuilding industry in the world; it was the sixth largest trading partner of the United States; its aircraft industry had produced two locally designed and manufactured aircraft; and its steel industry, capable of producing nuclear-grade steel, was among the most rapidly growing in the world. The Republic of China on Taiwan thus ranked as a "newly industrialized country" and was rapidly achieving full industrialization. It was making the transition from a labor-intensive to a "skill-intensive" economy.[35]

The sum of U.S. investments in the Republic of China on Taiwan and the $20 billion in bilateral trade exchanged in 1983 does not capture the measure of importance to U.S. policy represented by the developmental history of the island and associated territories. The economic history of Taiwan in itself, is politically important to the United States simply because it has been such a dramatic success. In a world in which U.S. economic aid programs have not been particularly successful, the modernization and industrialization of Taiwan stands out as a singular exception. The success of the collaboration between the United States and the ROC in the development of Taiwan belies the contentions of critics, both foreign and domestic, that the United States has been and is incapable of assisting in the economic growth and modernization of the less-developed countries—those on the "periphery" of the world economic system. The argument (asserted ever since the mid-1960s) was that U.S. involvement in the process only created conditions leading to "dependency"—stagnant growth, high unemployment, political repression, and inequitable distribution of the community's welfare benefits. Bilateral aid was perceived as a device to reduce the economic and political independence of the less-developed country. Foreign loans were contrivances to entrap the unwary. The capitalist overlords of the United States, in concert with self-selected elites in the less-developed country, were charged with exploiting the masses of the Third World.[36]

The ROC initially suffered the disabilities of backwardness and dependency, but with U.S. aid and cooperation, it achieved agricultural modernization and increasing industrialization with absolutely no unemployment and with an equitable distribution of family income.[37] The economic development of Taiwan, as well as the impressive development of Japan and the Republic of Korea, suggest the less-developed countries involved in the international market system, supported by the economic aid and technological assistance of the advanced capitalist democracies, can achieve self-sustained growth with equitable income distribution and stability. Moreover, nations with such rapidly developing, market-based economies have revealed a tendency to adopt a democratic form of government. Japan is a functional parliamentary democracy, and although the political development of South Korea has been impaired by military threats from the North and subversion from within, the government in Seoul offers more standard political and civil rights and more creature comforts than does the communist regime in the North. Similarly, the Republic of China on Taiwan has undertaken a gradual, but evident, development of pluralistic political institutions. The ROC has extended more economic benefits and gradually made available more political and civil rights to its citizens and those in its associated territories than has the communist regime on the mainland of China.[38]

The experience of the Republic of China on Taiwan is a model instance of what can be accomplished when foreign aid and assistance are combined with a rational program of rapid economic growth and development, and a commitment to essentially democratic principles. U.S. concessional and grant aid was welcomed by the leadership in Taipei in accordance with the overall program of development left as an intellectual heritage of Sun Yat-sen. Sun, unlike Mao Zedong, conceived international capital inflows as essential to China's economic development. His conception of "imperialism" was subtle and complex. He understood that foreign powers would seek economic and political advantage wherever and whenever they could. But China's leadership should welcome economic assistance whenever it served the national purpose, allowing foreigners to reap whatever profit was to be legitimately gained from such capital transfer, without compromising the program's growth and equity goals.[39]

The program left as an intellectual heritage to the leadership in Taipei by Sun also focused on the development of parliamentary democracy. Along with the commitment to nationalism and rapid economic development, the ideology of Sun recommended the adoption of Western political institutions. As early as the turn of the twentieth century, Sun conceived modern China as a democratic China, with a political system overtly similar to that of the United States. Although the protracted crisis in which the Republic of China on Taiwan has been involved since 1949 has delayed its political development, the leadership in Taipei remains committed to political democracy as an ideal.

Since 1949 the Republic of China on Taiwan has been a repsonsible member of the international community and an effective participant in the nonsocialist world market. It has empirically demonstrated the possible benefits to be gained from a program of rapid economic whose implementation is facilitated by international collaboration; market-based resource allocation and pricing; and private initiative. Neither the Soviet Union nor Communist China provides such an impressive model of economic or political development. The erratic and suboptimal economic growth pattern of the People's Republic of China, the PRC's political instability, and the suffering of its citizens make clear the inadvisability of the "Marxist-Leninist-Maoist" strategy for economic growth and for the establishment of an effective political system.

By the 1990s, the Republic of China on Taiwan will have made the transition from a traditional agricultural economy to a fully developed industrial economy.[40] That accomplishment will be the consequence of pursuing a program based on the political ideals and economic modalities advocated by the United States since the end of the Second World War. In the competition between the socialist and "capitalist" methods for achieving political and economic development, the experience of the Republic of China serves as empirical proof that the democratic ideals of the United States might well serve the ultimate interests of the majority of the world's population. The presidential statement released simultaneously with the communiqué of August 1982 alluded to the sense of pride experienced by Americans at the "great progress that has been made by the people of Taiwan . . . and of the American contribution to that process."[41] More than that, however, is the fact that the developments on Taiwan have invalidated all the arguments concerning "capitalist imperialism" so favored by the "Marxist-Leninist-Maoists" of our time.

The United States has a considerable investment in the success of the Republic of China on Taiwan. Its credibility as the leader of the noncommunist world will depend in large part on the outcome of the economic and political experiment the island of Taiwan and its associated territories. To allow that nation to be returned to the embrace of the communist "mother" would be considered a defeat for U.S. normative and practical ideals.

For at least that reason, the members of Congress have sought to defend the integrity, stability, and security of the Republic of China on Taiwan since the first moves were made toward rapprochement with the People's Republic of China in the early 1970s. Beyond that, the economic, political, and moral concerns that were the basis of U.S. preoccupation with the future of the ROC were part of a larger concern: the security of East Asia.

THE REPUBLIC OF CHINA ON TAIWAN AND THE SECURITY OF EAST ASIA

Most of the discussions of the security of the ROC are one-dimensional, for they center on the military threat arising from Communist China's insistence on "reunification." Clearly that is the most immediate security concern for the political leadership in Taipei. But since the U.S. military withdrawal from Southeast Asia and the acquisition of Vietnamese bases by the Soviet Union, the Southeast Asian littoral has become the scene of U.S.-Soviet military confrontation. The Soviet Union now utilizes Camranh Bay and Danang in Vietnam to service about 30 surface combatants of its Far East navy. The air bases in the vicinity provided logistical support for reconnaissance and antisubmarine Tupelov 95 Bear bombers and at least 9 Tupelov 16 Badger intermediate-range turbojet aircraft with a range of about 3,000 miles. Armed with 20,000 pounds of explosives in its internal weapons bay, the naval version of the Badger can carry air-to-surface standoff missiles for use against ship targets.

In March 1984, the Soviet Far East fleet, then composed of 785 ships, displacing a total of about 1.52 million tons, was supplemented by a Soviet flotilla led by the 38,000-ton aircraft carrier *Novorossiisk*, supported by an 8,200-ton missile cruiser, a 3,000-ton *Krivak*-class destroyer, and a replenishment vessel. During the Iran and Afghanistan crises, the Soviet Union deployed a minimum of 10 vessels in the South China Sea and 30 vessels in the Indian Ocean, and dispatched the carrier *Minsk* to the Pacific. The United States was able to sustain only one carrier battle group in the Indian Ocean, due to budgeting problems and the limited resources of the Seventh Fleet based in the Philippines.

In the early 1980s, the Soviet Pacific Fleet outnumbered the U.S. Seventh Fleet by a factor of about four to one. This Soviet force consisted of at least 2 aircraft carriers, 11 cruisers (including the most modern *Kresta II*- and *Kara*-class missile-capable vessels), 27 destroyers, and 50 frigates, some of which were missile capable. The Soviet submarine fleet in the Pacific consisted of about 125 submarines, including about 30 ballistic missile boats. The U.S. Seventh Fleet deployed 2 aircraft carriers, 8 submarines, and a total of 21 surface combatants. Even if the Third Fleet, based on the West Coast, were combined with the Seventh Fleet, the joint force would consist of only 6 aircraft carriers, 39 submarines, and 87 surface combatants.

More important, perhaps, than the development of Soviet naval power in the Pacific has been the collateral growth of Soviet air power capabilities. The number of Soviet aircraft has increased dramatically, and Soviet bombers, with their extended ranges, can wage attacks against Asian land and sea targets at significantly greater distances from their bases in the Soviet Far East than ever before. Perhaps as many as 80 Tupelov 22M, Backfire B bombers are now based on airfields east of the Urals. Armed with from one to three Kitchen or Kingfish air-to-surface standoff missiles with a range of about 500 miles, the Backfire B constitutes a major threat to surface vessels. The Backfire has a high-altitude maximum speed of about Mach 2, and the most modern electronic equipment affords it protection against air-to-air and surface-to-air missile attacks.

The annual report of the U.S. Department of Defense in 1979 suggested that Soviet aircraft might soon replace the Soviet submarine force as a threat to the U.S. surface fleet. In the West Pacific that possibility has, to a significant extent, become a reality. In any conflict in East Asia, the United States and its regional allies, with their limited naval resources, would be hard put to contain the Soviet fleet in order to protect the long sea-lanes of communication. With the increase in Soviet strike capabilities resulting from the transfer of Backfire bombers to East Asia, U.S. and allied surface combatants and merchant vessels are increasingly at risk.

The anticipated attack mode used by Soviet forces in the Pacific against U.S. and allied vessels is submarine-, surface-, and air-launched multiple-missile strikes. Backfire air-launched missile attacks are among the most difficult to counter, and adequate defense requires early warning and early interception by the most modern weapon platforms in the U.S. Air Force inventory, as well as complex electronic countermeasures to blind Soviet airborne radar and missile-homing devices.

Because so few aircraft carriers are available to the anti-Soviet forces in the Pacific, land-based staging areas have become increasingly important to the improvement of both deterrence and war-fighting capabilities. Since 1979, Soviet aircraft have been flying greater and greater distances from their bases in the Soviet Far East provinces. Military supplies and hardware—including components for fighter aircraft provided Vietnam for its invasion of Kampuchea—were flown from the industrial sector of the Soviet Union to Tashkent and Bombay over Thailand to Hanoi. The violation of Thai airspace by Soviet military aircraft has become increasingly commonplace and is of increasing concern to defense planners in Southeast Asia. In Northeast Asia, Soviet military aircraft regularly violate the airspace of Japan; scrambles of the Japanese Air Self-Defense Force have increased from an average of 360 to an average of 600 per year since 1976. It is apparent that an adequate perimeter defense of this entire region requires the reconstruction of a chain of air bases along the East Asian archipelagic barrier that stretches from the Japanese home islands to the Philippines. Increasingly, local air forces are being equipped with the most modern U.S. interceptors and air combat machines. The Japanese have begun procurement of the McDonnell Douglas F-15, and the South Koreans have begun to incorporate the General Dynamics F-16 into their inventory. The United States Tactical Air Command is prepared to deploy F-15s as a quick-reaction force, rotating this high-performance aircraft between the United States Air Forces Europe and the Pacific Air Forces. The F-15s and F-16s that are part of the domestic forces of Japan and South Korea are the permanent first-contact units in a defense against the threat of Soviet air strikes in the Pacific region. Two squadrons of United States Air Force F-15s are stationed in Okinawa but are slated for redeployment in the event of crises in the Indian Ocean or the Middle East.[42]

If Japan attains its announced procurement goals, it will have about

155 F-15s in inventory by the late 1980s, and they could provide critical initial defense against Backfire bombers crossing Japanese airspace to attack targets in the Pacific or the major East Asian sea-lanes of
communication. Soviet attack aircraft could follow an alternative route
over the territories of the PRC and the Ryukyus chain. To cover that
route, the PRC would have to develop its antiaircraft capabilities and
(or) its air interception forces. The alternatives would be to permanently station U.S. forces in Okinawa or to station an adequate force on
Taiwan.

For the armed forces of the PRC to act as a first-contact force against
Soviet bombers would require the modernization of the entire People's
Liberation Army. Beijing could not be expected to become involved in an
armed defense against the Soviet Union unless its forces were capable of
resisting collateral Soviet initiatives along the extensive Sino-Soviet border. The PRC would not commit itself in the air unless it were reasonably
sure of containing Soviet forces on the ground. That the Communist
Chinese armed forces can be brought up to that standard of capability in
the foreseeable future, at manageable expense, is very unlikely.

A more reasonable alternative would be to allow the armed forces of
the ROC to modernize and upgrade their air capabilities with the introduction of aircraft of the quality of the F-16. The F-16A is one of the most
modern combat aircraft developed by the United States. Originally designed for inclusion in a lightweight fighter program, it is cheaper to
purchase and easier to maintain than the air superiority F-15. This flexible
aircraft is capable of performing beyond-visual-range interception missions. Armed with the General Electric M61A1 20-mm multibarreled
cannon with a rapid rate of fire and mounting three air-to-air Sidewinder,
Sparrow, or Sky Flash missiles, the F-16 is a formidable aircraft capable of
achieving Mach 2 speeds at about the same service ceiling as that of
Backfire bomber. With a combat radius of about 575 miles and the possible enhancement of some all-weather capabilities, the F-16 provides a
major air defense asset against Soviet bombers that would have to range
over the sea-lanes without fighter escort.

By 1985, the government of the ROC, holding over $30 billion in
surplus foreign services, could purchase a sufficient number of F-16s to
constitute a significant defense supplement to anti-Soviet air defenses in
East Asia. The ROC was negotiating for such purchases when the Reagan
administration refused permission in January 1982. That decision for-
closed, at least temporarily, the possibility of adding the improved air
combat forces of the ROC to the anti-Soviet combat forces in the West
Pacific.

Addition of the F-16s to the inventory of the ROC air command would provide air cover for a considerable length of two critical water passages—the Taiwan Strait and the Bashi Channel. Moreover, incorporation of such advanced fighter aircraft would ensure that maintenance and servicing facilities were available on the island of Taiwan for use as needed by units of the United States Air Force. Taiwan's location makes it important to the air and naval defense of the sea-lanes that are critical to the survival of Japan and South Korea—and much of the Chinese mainland as well. In view of the balance of forces in the Far East, the U.S. decision concerning military sales to the ROC should turn not on what weapons Taipei needs to deter an attack from the communist mainland, but on those weapons required to play a role in a coordinated defense of the West Pacific sea-lanes of communication against a potential Soviet attack[43]—especially since the Republic of China on Taiwan already is, in fact, a passive and unofficial link in the offshore defense chain by virtue of the substantial air and naval bases it has developed. The Japanese have never abandoned their concern with the security of their vital and extended sea-lanes around Taiwan.[44] An enhanced ROC air command would supplement the scant forces of the Japanese Air Self-Defense Force, and the naval bases on Taiwan would reduce the amount of time necessary to get U.S. naval vessels on station along the threatened sea-lanes. Bases in the immediate vicinity would allow those vessels to remain on station without the replenishment ships otherwise necessary. Moreover, air bases on Taiwan could provide the aircraft necessary for aircover—releasing the few aircraft carriers available to the West Pacific naval forces for other missions.

If the strategic aim of the United States is to deter Soviet aggression in East and Southeast Asia, a credible defense must be mounted to counter growing Soviet capabilities. Taiwan is a strategic component of that defense.[45] Unlike the People's Republic of China, which would be unlikely to extend support in the event of conflict (exposed as it is to a repertoire of Soviet threats along its extensive border), the Republic of China has every political, ideological, economic, and moral reason to support the anti-Soviet defense strategy of the United States. The Republic of China long ago committed itself to a general anticommunist defense. Should the United States withdraw from the West Pacific entirely, the ROC would hardly survive. It would be subject to Beijing's threats and would have no hope of any intervention by Washington. Since Moscow recently reaffirmed its acceptance of Beijing's claims of sovereignty over Taiwan, Taipei could not expect to profit from Sino-Soviet hostility. The security of the ROC, for the foreseeable future, will depend on the United States and its continued military presence in the West Pacific.

The major requirement for an adequate defense of Taiwan and its associated territories is the procurement of advanced fighter aircraft to afford tactical air control over the Taiwan Strait.[46] Although Taipei has established "unofficial" ties with many nations in the international community and enjoys substantive relations with about 140 countries, only the United States has a security commitment to the ROC, embodied in the Taiwan Relations Act. Thus, Taipei's expression of its readiness to "unofficially" become part of a coordinate anti-Soviet defense system could bring it the quality aircraft so necessary for its credible defense against any military threats emanating from the People's Republic of China.

Since 1949, the authorities in Taipei have indicated their readiness to provide facilities for use by the U.S. military in times of crisis.[47] Upgrading Taiwan's military response capabilities would provide the ROC with a credible defense against the PRC and allow its armed forces to serve as part of an anti-Soviet deterrence policy. The ROC would thus contribute to the stability and security of the region. It should be remembered as well that anything that complicates Soviet military planning in the Far East contributes to the security of the People's Republic of China. Thus, if Beijing seeks a stable external environment that will enable it to pursue its domestic programs of economic development and modernization, the enhancement of the military potential of the Republic of China will ultimately be in its best interests. Beijing is neither disposed to nor capable of assuming first-contact responsibilities vis-à-vis any Soviet conventional military threats. Taipei has little choice other than to do so. Moscow has every reason to believe that the PRC would not become involved in any anti-Soviet coalition unless the territorial integrity of Communist China were directly threatened. Moscow can be equally certain that the ROC would make its bases and its capabilities available to the United States for implementation of any anti-Soviet defense strategy. With U.S. bases stretching from the Japanese home islands to South Korea, the Ryukyus, Taiwan, and the Philippines, Soviet forces would suffer serious disadvantages. Should complementary permanent local response capabilities be available at least in Japan, South Korea, and Taiwan, there would be additional disincentive for Soviet military adventures.

The importance of the ROC to the implementation of any deterrence policy recommends the upgrading of both its air defense and its naval capabilities. The provision of longer-range antiship missiles and antisubmarine warfare capabilities to the relatively small fast-attack craft currently stationed at Taiwan's naval bases would disrupt the Soviet Union's lines of communication throughout the various choke points in the region. The logistical lines from Europe to the Soviet Far East military district are essential to the survival of the armed forces stationed there. Small, fast missile and antisubmarine warfare platforms could be effectively used by the anti-Soviet naval forces in the narrow and cluttered waters of the Taiwan Strait and the Bashi Channel. Should ROC naval vessels develop antiship missile and antisubmarine warfare capabilities, and should the air command provide suitable air cover, the Soviet Union would have to anticipate attacks on its supply lines and naval shipping by local forces based not only in South Korea and Japan, but on Taiwan as well.

What all this suggests is that the United States has more to gain from the defense of the Republic of China on Taiwan than has been suggested in much of the policy debate. The ROC has the potential for playing a significant role in an anti-Soviet regional defense strategy. Therefore, upgrading the capabilities of the military forces on Taiwan will serve U.S. strategic interests.

By 1979, the U.S. rapprochement with Beijing could be expected to provide no further strategic benefits for the anti-Soviet alliance. The PRC could do little thereafter that would increase its value as a deterrent to Soviet initiatives in East Asia. Moreover, any rapprochement between Moscow and Beijing constitutes little real threat to the West. The Soviet Union will always maintain sufficient forces along the Sino-Soviet border to ensure Beijing's neutrality in any conflict, whatever the degree of rapprochement between the PRC and the USSR. Should the United States or its allies attempt to enhance the military capabilities of the PRC in an effort to increase its value as an anti-Soviet deterrent, those enhancements would have little effect (as we have seen), given Soviet potential. What such force enhancements would do would be to increase the threat to which the littoral and insular noncommunist states in East Asia would be subject. The PRC is an ally of the Democratic People's Republic of Korea, the enemy of South Korea. The PRC continues to insist that it must resolve the "Taiwan issue" in this century—perhaps with force. Moreover, with increased military capabilities, Beijing could complicate the situation in Southeast Asia by undertaking further initiatives against Vietnam—initiatives that have, in the past, worked only to the benefit of the Soviet Union.

In this context, military sales and arms-related technology transfers to the People's Republic of China make little strategic sense. Such sales to Taipei, on the other hand, could very well be critical to the success of a policy of anti-Soviet deterrence and to the effort to maintain peace and stability in the Taiwan Strait. Although Beijing has obvious reason to resist the logic of such an assessment, there does not seem to be any reason why Washington should not see its merit.

THE CIRCUMSTANCES IN THE MID-1980S

If the United States were to obey the mandate of the Taiwan Relations Act and provide the Republic of China on Taiwan with a credible defense capability, it would not only be furthering the interests of the anti-Soviet coalition in the West Pacific, but it would help to ensure the People's Republic of China a stable external environment so that it could pursue its domestic modernization program. Not only would the Soviet Union be constrained, but Beijing would have little temptation to attempt to resolve the Taiwan issue militarily. Beijing's restraint would reduce the possibility of straining its relations with the industrialized democracies upon which it increasingly depends for capital transfers, management skills, and advanced nonmilitary technology. Nonetheless, Beijing remains steadfast in its refusal to countenance continued arms sales to the military on Taiwan.

In making public its case against such sales in 1982, Beijing maintained that Washington cannot honor the commitments made in its various communiqués and, at the same time, satisfy its obligations under the Taiwan Relations Act. Beijing holds that the United States' "acknowledgement" that there is but "one China" and that "Taiwan is part of China" constitutes an acceptance of Beijing's claim to sovereignty over Taiwan.[48] As previously mentioned, Washington's official position remains the same as it was in the early 1950s: the status of Taiwan in international law remains undetermined. In his statement accompanying the joint communiqué of August 17, 1982, Assistant Secretary for East Asian and Pacific Affairs John H. Holdridge affirmed that "there has been no change in our longstanding position on the issue of sovereignty over Taiwan."[49] In its official statements, the United States has said that it "takes no position on the status of Taiwan under international law."[50] When queried by the Senate, a Department of State representative insisted that "U.S. arms sales to Taiwan [do not] constitute a violation of Chinese sovereignty. . . . The United States takes no position on the question of Taiwan's sovereignty."[51]

Beijing is convinced that the joint communiqués issued by the United States and the People's Republic of China constitute the equivalent of an international treaty (which for some reason does not require ratification by the U.S. Senate). It argues that the Taiwan Relations Act, which is a domestic law, cannot take precedence over a treaty[52]—and that, of course, is true in international law. The fact remains, however, that a joint communiqué, no matter how celebrated, is not a treaty and does not amount to a contractual obligation between signatories. The U.S. position is quite clear. In response to queries, the Department of State unequivocally characterized "joint communiqués" as something other than an "international agreement between the United States and the People's Republic of China."[53] Assistant Secretary Holdridge, in his statement accompanying the issuance of the joint communiqué of August 17, 1982, stated explicitly: "We should keep in mind that what we have here is not a treaty or agreement but a statement of future U.S. policy."[54]

Because of its interpretation of the Taiwan issue, Beijing has allowed its public media to insist that the behavior of the United States, with respect to arms sales to the Republic of China on Taiwan, is "perfidious"—for if Taiwan is "a province of China," it cannot "enter into external relations with regard to rights and obligations without the authorization" of the communist authorities in Beijing.[55] Even though the Chinese Communist Party discovered that Taiwan was a province of China only after the Nationalist government of Chiang Kai-shek had made the claim, the claim has become a permanent element of Beijing's policies.

As a consequence, the Taiwan issue will remain an important bone of contention between Washington and Beijing for the indeterminate future. The United States must decide if protecting the security of the Republic of China on Taiwan contributes to its own deterrent strength, serves its own economic interests, and satisfies its legal and moral obligations. Pursuing those interests and satisfying those obligations will predictably bring Washington into conflict with Beijing. No matter how creatively ambiguous the joint communiqués of the past and future, the fact remains that the issue will have to be resolved—it is hoped without further sacrifice of U.S. strategic, economic, and political interests.

As has been suggested, the United States can probably expect no further benefits from its association with the People's Republic of China. Barring the most unforeseen circumstances, those benefits will not change even if Beijing should move toward a rapprochement with the Soviet Union. Most analysts no longer consider the security relationship with the PRC an important issue but rather place the emphasis elsewhere. In 1982, to mark the tenth anniversary of his trip to Beijing, Richard Nixon articulated a theme that has been heard with greater frequency in the United States: "China today seems to be making some progress in becoming more Chinese and less Marxist, embracing capitalist-style incentives rather than continuing to wear an ideological straitjacket."[56] According to this thesis, the People's Republic of China is enduring a "quiet revolution." It is undergoing an ideological and economic transformation.[57]

Nixon's belief is that "it would be the height of folly to try to 'save' Taiwan at the cost of losing China. If China slipped back into the Soviet orbit, the balance of power in the world would be overwhelmingly shifted against us." This assertion is less than convincing to most Americans. But the conviction that the People's Republic of China has abandoned the cardinal tenets of Maoism and has become increasingly "capitalist" seems to have captured the U.S. imagination. If the Republic of China on Taiwan is not to be abandoned for security benefits that have become increasingly less certain, there might be some justification for accommodating Beijing if Communist China is in fact undergoing a transformation—particularly if that transformation promises political rewards to the antisocialist nations as well as substantial trade and investment profits for U.S. business.

In 1984 Beijing was expected to renew its 1983 agreement to purchase 6 million tons of wheat a year from the United States. Twenty-three U.S. firms were then operating joint-venture enterprises in Communist China, and approximately half of the $800 million in foreign investment in the PRC was that of U.S. businessmen. By the fall of that year, 30 U.S. firms were negotiating investment opportunities in Beijing; oil companies were competing for drilling and recovery rights on the continental shelf of the PRC; and there was talk in the ministries of the PRC of a $20 billion investment in nuclear power technology.

If the PRC were no longer a particularly important security asset to the United States, it perhaps held forth the promise of transforming itself from a communist state to one that was "authoritarian-capitalist," and in the process, provide a market and investment supplement for U.S. capitalism. Once again the United States appeared dazzled by the prospect of achieving multiple cost-free gains by accommodating Beijing. The People's Republic of China might become a more "open" society as a result of its modernization program. Moreover, that program appeared to offer substantial material benefits to U.S. industry and commerce. The security advantages may not be as great as had first been imagined, but the political and economic benefits that appeared to be forthcoming might warrant the suppression of undue concern with the future of the Republic of China on Taiwan, as well as that of the noncommunist states on the periphery of the PRC. However "independent" Beijing became, the prospect of its transformation through a "quiet revolution" seemed exciting enough to justify Washington's tireless effort to ensure its "China connection."

7

The "Transformation" of the People's Republic of China

The foreign policy notion that engaged the U.S. imagination in the mid-1980s was the idea that the People's Republic of China was being "transformed" by a "new breed" of "moderate and pragmatic" leaders whose intention (perhaps more covert than overt) was to "restore capitalism" to their economy and to "liberalize" their political system. Ever since the first contacts with China, Americans, like almost all Westerners, have sought its "transformation." Missionaries attempted to make China Christian. Educators tried to make it Western. Politicians and philosophers tried to democratize it, and businessmen tried to make it capitalist. In seeking to work these changes, Westerners have used blandishments and preachments; attempted to educate and to set an example; resorted to intimidation, blockade, and subversion; and incited episodic violence and even war. Many Americans interpreted the announcement made at the Third Plenary Session of the Eleventh Central Committee of the Chinese Communist Party (December 1978), that the intention of the leadership in Beijing was to correct the "ultra-left errors" of the Great Proletarian Cultural Revolution, shift the nation's concern to "socialist modernization," and "readjust the national economy and restructure the economic managerial and distributive system," to mean that the PRC was beginning to follow the "capitalist road," which would ultimately lead to a more open economic system and ultimately, a more democratic political system.

In 1967, Richard Nixon anticipated that the result of the U.S. rapprochement with Communist China would be a "dynamic detoxification" of the regime—drawing "off the poison from the Thoughts of

Mao."[1] In fact, with the developing U.S.-PRC rapprochement, the revolutionary credentials of the leadership in Beijing began to be discounted by the international community. An extreme example was the outrage expressed by Enver Hoxha, first secretary of the Central Committee of the Albanian Workers' Party, one of the few "proletarian" parties in the world to support the PRC through the most trying period of the Great Proletarian Cultural Revolution. Hoxha vehemently denounced Beijing's rapprochement with the United States as a compromise of its revolutionary obligations.

Some of Beijing's behaviors lent credence to Hoxha's complaints. After 1972, Communist Chinese support for the Third World revolutions diminished rapidly, whereas the PRC's pursuit of normal diplomatic relations between governments increased significantly. In 1978, the "pragmatic" leadership in Beijing also began to allude to the introduction of a "market-socialist" development strategy for Communist China—which included opening the PRC to direct foreign investment and joint-venture projects. At the same time, thousands of Chinese students and scholars were sent abroad to study in capitalist countries. The PRC joined the International Monetary Fund and the World Bank, the two major multilateral institutions that linked the capitalist world with the developing countries of the Third World. Beijing sought out long-term foreign loans and embarked on the establishment of a foreign tourist industry in a search for foreign exchange. Foreign goods were imported for use in the PRC, and domestic companies were organized to market the labor of Chinese workers and technicians to multinational corporations and foreign governments for use in projects abroad.

In January 1984, Communist Chinese Premier Zhao Ziyang (Chao Tzu-yang) reported that in the five years between 1979 and 1984, the PRC had absorbed $12 billion in foreign funds and had become involved in 2,000 projects utilizing direct foreign investment.[2] By that time, loans totaling approximately $2.5 billion had been made available to the PRC or were the object of negotiation. In 1979, the authorities in Beijing established the first special economic zones in the PRC, which were designed to encourage foreign investment and joint-venture projects. Four such zones were established in the provinces of Guangdong and Fujian. Adjustments were instituted to reduce bureaucratic red tape, and laws and regulations were promulgated to regulate both investment and enterprise operations; an effort was also made to improve infrastructural facilities in these zones. By 1981, total foreign investment in the zones amounted to $1.7 billion—about 60 percent of all direct foreign equity commitment in the mainland at that time.

Beijing also announced that by 1984, the 42 corporations established to contract engineering projects and to market labor services abroad had signed agreements with approximately 40 countries. The PRC had initiated a series of contacts with capitalist countries that had become increasingly complex and significant. By the mid-1980s, trade had been established with a variety of capitalist states; loans had been negotiated with international banking institutions; investment opportunities had been made available to many nonsocialist partners; and licensing arrangements, offshore exploration and recovery contracts, communications technology transfers, intelligence-sharing agreements, and arms purchases had been undertaken with "imperialist" governments.

Between 1979 and 1984, the domestic economy of mainland China was made the object of equally dramatic "rehabilitation." Communist Chinese economists began to speak candidly of giving domestic "enterprises economic independence and responsibility." Enterprises were given greater discretion in the use of their profits and depreciation funds—and profit was being employed more frequently as a success indicator. Enterprises were increasingly free to purchase their own inputs directly from other enterprises and to sell their output directly to other firms, domestic and foreign. Furthermore, some enterprise managers were allowed to choose potential employees; they no longer had to simply accept those assigned them by the state labor bureaus. More and more frequently, one heard that "the role of the market [is to be] brought into full play." Finally, there was an explicit abandonment of "egalitarianism" as a social and economic ideal. "For many years," it was lamented, "under the 'left' influences, egalitarianism was considered to be socialist and payment according to work done was regarded as capitalist. . . . This led to people getting equal payment regardless of whether they worked or not and regardless of the quality [of their work] and amount of work they performed. In such a situation, there was no way of improving work attitudes and labor productivity."[3]

In agriculture, the large production units created by Mao Zedong as "people's communes"—understood to be integral industrial, agricultural, military, educational, and commercial organizations that were transitional to an "all-embracing" communist society[4]—were decentralized, and peasant household plots were restored and protected.[5] Spokesmen for the Beijing regime decried the "errors" that had resulted from the frenetic pursuit of "socialism" and the attempt to establish "public ownership" following the Maoists' seizure of power, "without regard for the level of economic development or the state of the productive forces."[6] In the rural areas, the "errors" were rectified by restoring productive responsibilities to the family group or the small production team. The most radical departure from past practices has been that the production team now enters into contracts with individual peasant households for the delivery of fixed quantities of produce at state-determined prices. Under the contracts, households receive allocations of land for specified periods to allow them to meet their contractual obligations. Anything produced on that land in excess of the quantity contracted for with the state can be disposed of at the discretion of the producer household—even at individually negotiated sales in the reopened agricultural bazaars. The household units are permitted to hire a limited number of agricultural laborers and also to engage in sideline nonagricultural occupations to supplement their incomes. They are allowed to diversify their crops, establish their own production schedules, and dispose of their income freely (after prevailing fees are paid and contributions are made to collective capital and social funds). By the middle of 1982, approximately 65 percent of all production teams in rural Communist China were implementing the new "responsibility system."[7] By 1983, that figure had risen to about 94 percent.

By the middle of 1984, peasants were allowed to contract for parcels of land that varied in size in accordance with the number of family members in their households. Originally the new output-related system of contracted responsibilities was set at from 1 to 3 years, but by 1982 it had been extended to 15 years. In some regions where farming is particularly difficult, the duration of the contracts has been extended to 30–50 years. Another change is that any plants and trees on the land contracted for may be passed on to heirs or to others.

These developments have been accompanied by structural reforms that are expected to separate the basic political administrative organizations from the modified "people's communes." The communes, presumably, will become purely economic units—and when the proposed local governments are established, even the name "people's communes" will be abandoned. The new local governments will be responsible for civil, judicial, financial, cultural, and educational matters, as well as for sanitation, family planning, and construction. The new economic units will have specifically economic functions, however they are identified.

In the judgment of Communist Chinese theorists, all these changes amount to nothing less than a "far-reaching and thoroughgoing transformation" of the Chinese economy.[8] Some foreign observers, having analyzed that "transformation," harbor the conviction that the present leadership in Beijing, freed from the influence of Mao Zedong, has decided that "communism is a total failure." Others perceive "de-Maoification" as the prelude to "de-Marxification"—and are convinced that the ultimate result will be an ideological commitment to some vaguely formulated non-Marxist combination of "nationalism, Confucianism, and the Four Modernizations" as official state doctrine.[9] China will finally be "detoxified," and the dream of four generations of Americans will be realized. China will be free, modernized, democratized, secure, and responsible—and will provide a market for Western commodities and an outlet for Western investment.

The Imperatives Behind The "Transformation"

By the early 1980s, sufficient reliable data were available to permit a quantitative assessment of the performance of the Communist Chinese economic system for the period beginning with the rehabilitation of the war-ravaged economy in 1952, through 1980. Measured against the performance of other developing nations, that of the People's Republic of China seems to have been quite satisfactory. In this period of almost 30 years, net domestic material product increased at an average annual rate of 6.1 percent. Disaggregated, the average annual increase was as follows: gross value of industrial output, 10.9 percent; gross value of heavy industrial output, 13.0 percent; gross value of light industrial output, 9.5 percent; gross value of agricultural output, 3.4 percent; and production of unprocessed food grains, 2.4 percent. The per capita national income increased by 4.1 percent in this period.[10] Such a performance could only be envied by many developing countries.

All that notwithstanding, the authorities in Beijing undertook to "transform" the economy of the PRC. An analysis of why that should have been necessary is instructive.

Without focusing on the question of the reliability of the PRC's economic data, it is clear that something was seriously wrong. Economists on the mainland have been candid in identifying a clutch of complex problems that have afflicted the national economy since the Communist Party came to power in 1949. They have acknowledged that "China's industrial and technical level lags about 20 years behind the developed capitalist countries and its agricultural production level is about 40–50 years behind."[11] Poverty has been one of the most persistent problems. Per capita income in the PRC was about $183 in 1978, making it one of the world's poorest countries. In 1981 the per capita income of the agrarian sector was only $127.

That the lives of the vast majority of the citizens of the PRC have improved only "insignificantly" between 1952 and 1980, despite respectable rates of real economic growth,[12] is the consequence of a number of problems. Perhaps the most intractable problem is that the available cultivated land is not adequate for the PRC's rapidly growing population. The population of the People's Republic of China grew at an average annual rate of 2.0 percent in this period. In the mid-1980s, there were about 16 million births per annum.

Between 1957 and 1977, 33.3 million hectares of prime arable land (almost 30 percent of the prime arable land available) were lost to urban and rural construction and to natural disasters. In addition to the construction of houses, roads, canals, reservoirs, and storage facilities, there was an uncontrolled and hasty expansion of small rural industries in an (unsuccessful) attempt to satisfy local needs. That loss was only partially offset by the reclamation of 21 million hectares of relatively poor quality land. As a consequence, the per capita availability of farmland in the PRC declined from 0.172 hectares in 1957 to 0.104 hectares in 1977.[13]

The loss of land, combined with low rates of investment in the rural sector, have contributed to sluggish agricultural development. The economists of the PRC have indicated that "China's agriculture never gained momentum after the people's communes were established in 1958."[14] Between that year and 1979, gross agricultural output increased only 84 percent, while the population grew by at least 300 million. Between 1957 and 1978, per capita grain yield increased by only 1.2 kilograms, per capita cotton yield decreased by 0.2 kilogram, and the yield of oil seed crops decreased by 1.2 kilograms. Official statistics indicate that in those years there was a decline in consumption; average per capita peasant income from commune labor in 1978 was only $47. In that year, about one-fourth of the rural population earned less than $30 per person.[15] At times agricultural production fell below the "consumption threshold," and there was a radical decline in the birth rate and a rapid increase in the death rate. During the Great Leap Forward, perhaps as many as 20 million to 30 million persons perished as a direct or indirect consequence of the shutdown of production.[16] In the judgment of Beijing's economists, "this situation could not be allowed to continue. . . . [It] was imperative to formulate a new agricultural policy."[17]

The industrial sector of the PRC has also faced problems, although not as serious as those of agriculture. After the initial period of rehabilitation, the productivity of both labor and capital steadily declined. Between 1957 and 1978, labor productivity in industry increased at an average annual rate of only 0.7 percent.[18] Although the fixed assets of industry increased more than 2,500 percent, industrial productivity declined dramatically in that period. In the 1970s, productivity of capital was only one-half to one-third the level of that during the First Five-Year Plan

(1953–1957). Productive fixed assets remained largely idle or were wasted, and current inputs as a percentage of gross industrial output increased steadily over the period.

Beijing's official explanation includes the admission that "from 1958 onwards, we repeatedly attempted to achieve a rate of economic development that was too fast. We increased accumulation at the expense of the people's level of consumption." The rate of capital accumulation as a percentage of national income increased from 24.9 percent in 1957 to 36.5 percent in 1978. "The rate of accumulation far exceeded the capacity of the economy. Vast amounts of the means of production were tied up in large-scale capital construction, while a great number of factories could not operate at full capacity due to their lack of raw materials and equipment. . . . [Many] construction projects failed to progress according to schedule and the investment cycle was immensely prolonged. . . . Contrary to expectations, the excessive rate of accumulation did not result in high speed of economic growth. . . . [Moreover,] the abrupt rise in the rate of accumulation . . . brought great hardship to consumers."[19]

In order to sustain the high rates of capital accumulation, a policy of chronic consumption postponement was instituted. "Rational low wages" were imposed, rendered tolerable by rationed and equitably shared poverty. Industrial monetary wages increased only marginally between 1957 and 1976, but the cost of living index for urban worker households increased about 30 percent.[20] The result was a rapid decline in worker well-being and motivation—and a predictable decrement in per capita productivity.

Imbalances became evident throughout the industrial sector. Heavy industry expanded more rapidly than light industry, and "productive" output (material-factory) outstripped "nonproductive" output (housing, education, consumer services, and construction of infrastructural facilities). In the heavy industry sector, there was a lack of balance between the various subsectors as well as between the growth rates of industry and the energy needed to operate machines.

Because Communist China initially adopted Soviet economic priorities, the development of its economy has been heavily biased in favor of heavy industry. The economists of the PRC now view that decision as "irrational," for it has resulted in serious imbalances in the growth rates of light and heavy industry. "Because of the overgrowth of heavy industry, the use of too much of its output for the purpose of its own expansion, and the insufficiency of farm produce and goods from light industry, people's consumption has been kept at a low level."[21] Moreover, there is a general recognition that the preoccupation with the growth of heavy industry led to serious neglect of investment in "nonproductive" production. Investment in housing and consumer services declined from 40.2 percent of the national total in 1957 to a low of 2.8 percent in 1960, and increased to only 17.1 percent in 1976. One result has been that the housing needs of the PRC's growing population have not been met. In 1978, there were only 3.6 square meters of living space per person—down from 4.5 square meters in 1952. "Investment in heavy industry was too high—thereby distorting the industrial infrastructure and depressing the people's livelihood."[22]

Beijing's economists have also acknowledged the existence of imbalances within heavy industry: "Huge quantities of steel rods were stockpiled in warehouses [even though] there was an acute shortage of certain types of steel to manufacture farm tools, build facilities and produce chemical fertilizers, insecticides and synthetic fibers. . . . [The] machine-tool industry . . . either turned out too many general-type lathes or too little agricultural machinery."[23] Furthermore, they have identified the diminishing "energy supply" as a "pressing problem . . . [that has arisen] in part because of our . . . inconsistent energy policy . . . [and] the huge waste of energy due to inefficient old equipment . . . and to poor management. Energy shortage had idled something like 20 percent of the industrial capacity [of the PRC] in the last few years [1979–1982]."[24]

All of this, coupled with systemic inefficiencies and other policy failures, has led to relatively rapid rates of real growth in material output, without a significant improvement in living standards or an increase in the technological sophistication of machinery or management. Throughout the economy, growth has been achieved through excessive capitalization rather than the improvement of factor productivity via technological innovation. In industry, the infusion of new technology has been very slow. Increased output is a function of massive investment in fixed capital. By 1979, there was a considerable amount of fixed capital, but most of it was obsolete. In agriculture, the improvement in gross output between 1958 and 1979 was the consequence of the application of more and more labor to the land available. During those years there was a 70 percent increase in the number of agricultural laborers. The doubling of gross grain output during that period was the result of more workers working longer hours, thus infusing more capital of the traditional kind (the construction of irrigation and drainage conduits, reservoirs, terracing, and so forth) into the agricultural areas.

The entire economy is highly bureaucratized (more than 20 million bureaucrats attempt to perform the functions of the market) with the exception of the State Statistical Bureau, which is notoriously under-staffed. Information on the economy has been faulty, fragmentary, and often consciously misreported. Attempting to plan with such distorted and erroneous information had led to allocative imbalances, enormous wastage, inventory stockpiling, inordinate delays in the investment cycle, and a chronic failure to regulate production to meet the needs of end-users.

As important as the shortfall in planning information for the economy, the sheer mass of the bureaucracy is a serious drain on the system. In the rural areas, for example, there are 30 cadres per 1,000 peasants (but only one technician), as well as about 40 million Chinese Communist Party members (who are sometimes employed as state bureaucrats as well), all of whom must be directly or indirectly supported by increased agrarian yields.

If the rural bureaucracy contributed to production, its presence might be justified. The difficulty is that considerable evidence is available that suggests that the rural cadres, although politically essential, have not been particularly helpful in increasing mainland China's agricultural productivity. There are documented cases of massive interference in the farm economy by the rural bureaucracy and political cadres to the ulti- mate detriment of production. In the effort to meet immediate quotas, for example, the rural cadres have often imposed policies on the peasants that have resulted in tragic and expensive ecological damage and eventually a decline in yield.

The economy of the PRC consists of about 49 central ministries and commissions and about 500 departments and bureaus (employing, as mentioned, about 20 million bureaucrats at various levels). Most of the personnel staffing these agencies are (in the judgment of many PRC analysts) poorly equipped for their assignments, risk-averse, compliant, and conservative. Many Communist Chinese economists have recognized that failures of policy and personnel incompetence have hindered the nation's economic and social development. Yet those responsible for such failures, irrespective of their seemingly modest wages, enjoy important job-related perquisites. A bureaucrat has access to more and better food and other consumer commodities, medical care, education, entertainment, and transportation facilities than his nonbureaucratic counterpart[25]—all of which must be paid for out of current production.

Ultimately, the entire bureaucracy of the state is controlled by the highly centralized Chinese Communist Party. The party leadership has dominated the economy since 1949. Economic rationality is hostage to political decisions, made at the center by the principal functionaries of the party. The "transformation" of the economy of the PRC, as a case in point, was not initiated by the beleaguered economists of Communist China, but the small entourage around Deng Xiaoping.

In 1979, the leaders of the Chinese Communist Party were compelled to acknowledge that the economic system of the PRC involved "excessive command planning from above" and was "too rigid."[26] It had been inspired by a "foreign model" (the Soviet system), and however modified it had been by "leftist" revisions, it was "generally not a success and [was] unsuited to China's specific condition and the development level of the productive forces." In effect, they had decided that the "situation [cried] out for reform."[27]

At the same time that Beijing and Washington were commencing diplomatic relations, the leadership of the PRC was launching the "transformation" of the domestic economy that has inspired so much enthusiasm in the United States and has aroused expectations that only massive changes in the Communist Chinese economic and political systems can fulfill. Those expectations are based on the faith that the People's Republic of China is now headed down the road to "capitalist restoration" and political democratization.

THE ECONOMIC
"TRANSFORMATION" OF AGRICULTURE

Since 1949, mainland China's economic and political systems have been characterized by marked instability. Beijing's official statistics reveal massive economic fluctuations; national income, for example, increased at an average annual rate of 8.9 percent during the First Five-Year Plan (1953–1957) and then fell to a negative average annual rate of −3.1 percent during the Second Five-Year Plan (1958–1962). Gross agricultural output increased at an average annual rate of 4.5 percent during the first five-year period, but fell to a negative average annual rate of −4.3 percent during the second five-year period. In the readjustment period (1963–1965), national income increased at an average annual rate of 14.5 percent, but the rate fell to 5.6 percent during the Fourth Five-Year Plan (1971–1975).

A similar pattern of inconstancy is revealed in the regime's political policies. In the initial period of "new democracy," the communist leaders insisted that "the national bourgeoisie" and "national capitalism" would be protected and their rights enhanced. In 1952, irrespective of all prior protestations, restrictions began to be imposed on "private" enterprises. Between 1954 and 1957, notwithstanding the party's commitments to moderation and to the "gradual evolution" of socialist "property relations," the entire private sector of mainland China's economy was nationalized. From 1957 until the beginning of the "transformation" in 1979, frequent political upheavals dislocated the economy. In the intervals between those upheavals, there were periods of "readjustment," when ideological purity was sacrified in an attempt to restore lost productivity to both agriculture and industry.

These periods of readjustment regularly included economic reform. For example, a system by which fixed levies were imposed on individual peasant households for the usufructuary right to collective land was experimented with at least four times before its spread in 1979. In 1954, when Mao decided to collectivize agriculture, he sought to telescope a scheduled "socialist evolution" of fifteen years into two. By 1958, 120 million independent peasant households had been incorporated into 750,000 cadre-managed cooperatives and collectives; peasant indifference had led to high mortality rates of draft animals and a significant decline in production. At that point, a form of the current "responsibility system" was introduced. It had been provided as an alternative to peasant households in 1956–1957 and again in 1959. In 1961, after the catastrophic decline in rural production that was a direct consequence of the Great Leap Forward, a different form of the current responsibility system was introduced in an effort to restore farm yields. In 1964, it was introduced once again.

Each time the system of allowing individual peasant households the use of collective land in exchange for quota sales to the state at fixed prices was introduced, the innovation was castigated as "a most backward, perverse and reactionary" policy and was suppressed.[28] When Liu Shaoqi advocated increasing the number of plots assigned for private household use in the late 1950s, making individual peasant households responsible for fixed output quotas, and giving them access to relatively free rural bazaars for the marketing of any surplus, that policy was attacked as representative of an "out and out counterrevolutionary revisionist line" and was subsequently suppressed.

In 1979, approximately 100 million peasants in rural areas were living at the threshold of subsistence. Conditions were so life-threatening that the responsibility system was once again introduced in an attempt to revive production. Since then, the system has been instituted throughout the agricultural sector. The process was not conducted without resistance. In 1979 there was still official resistance. In 1980, the system was made applicable only to the 5 percent of the production teams that were having "difficulty." Shortly thereafter, the proportion was increased to 15 percent, then 20 percent, of all production teams. By the end of 1982, it was clear that the process could not be stopped, and by 1983, all restrictions on contracted household production were lifted.

Since 1978, if official PRC statistics are accepted, there has been a remarkable increase in agricultural yield, as follows: cotton, 45 percent; sugarcane, 70 percent; sugar beet, 160 percent; oil seed crops, 155 percent; and meat, 62 percent. Peasant incomes have substantially improved and rural consumption has generally increased.

None of this is particularly surprising. One of the best attested empirical generalizations about agricultural policy is that as centralized interference in agrarian productive enterprises decreases, productivity increases. All East European nations with collectivized , nonmarket economies have experimented with some form of "responsibility system" whenever low agricultural yields have threatened their economic stability. The state expresses a more liberal attitude toward "private plot" farming; pays higher procurement prices to farmers who meet and exceed their quotas; supplies farm inputs at lower rates; extends more credit to farmers, and increases its investment in agriculture. Agrarian surpluses are allowed to be sold on the free market; and fewer output and input requirements are specified, allowing more initiative and diversification. In Poland, private farmers sell their output to the state at negotiated prices. In Hungary, there are no quotas at all; collective farmers sell their output to the state at negotiated prices.

That such modifications of what might be considered the "classical Stalinist model of socialist development" do not constitute a "restoration of capitalism" is evident in the fact that no matter how extensive the reform, there is no private ownership or market sale of land. Land remains public property and the state is the landlord. The new responsibility system of mainland China is simply a form of tenancy; the peasant household pays rent to the state in the form of forced quota sales. The peasant household must contract with the state to provide a quota that is determined by the state's produce target, then sell that quota to state purchasing agencies at state-fixed prices that average about 50 percent below open-market prices. Each household must also satisfy tax obligations and make a contribution to state-controlled capital and welfare funds.

These obligations differ little from those that were assigned to the socialist collectives in the past. The major difference between the two forms of socialism is that in the responsibility system, there is a direct relationship between work and output, and the rewards enjoyed. The household responsibility system focuses not on the issue of capitalism as opposed to socialism, but on the issue of peasant motivation. In all socialist plans that have been contrived by the central authorities, peasant households are required to deliver specified quantities of output, in major product categories, to the state at below-market prices.

The revised agricultural policy has created many problems for China's socialist economy. It has revealed the redundancy of many of the lower party and state bureaucratic functionaries in the agricultural sector. As peasant households have assumed more responsibilities in such areas as input procurement, work scheduling, productive allocation, crop selection, and marketing, the rural cadres have experienced a diminution of their functions.

As the cadres' functions diminished, so did their status and privileges. As the peasant farmers became more autonomous, they perceived any intervention by the cadres in the productive process as interference. The press in the PRC has frequently carried reports of the cadres' "confusion" with regard to their function and status as a result of the rapidly changing circumstances. The party and the government have admonished the rural cadres to "rectify their behavior" and to cooperate in implementation of the agricultural reforms. It is clear that both the function and the status of the rural cadres have become uncertain. For at least those reasons, there has been cadre resistance and more can be expected in the future.

The military has also had reason to find the agrarian reforms objectionable. It is no longer easy to recruit farm youths for the massive People's Liberation Army. When able-bodied young men can contribute directly to family income with their labor, they do not willingly accept low-paying military responsibilities.

Urban dwellers have been equally skeptical about the changes effected in the agricultural sector. Increases in farm income, and the corresponding increases in the cost of farm products, tend to inflate the urban cost-of-living index. Moreover, increases in the amount of discretionary income in the rural areas increase the cost of scarce commodities. Unless the state insulates the urban population from such cost pressures, urban workers can anticipate at least a short-term increase in the cost of living.

Government authorities charged with controlling population growth and increasing the nation's economic potential through improvements in education have also had reason for concern. Because increased family farm yields translate directly into improved income and a higher standard of living, there is every incentive to increase the number of family members to add to the available labor force. Even if "above-quota" children are not duly registered or provided state rationing coupons, their contribution to farm output might be sufficient to justify their birth in the eyes of their parents. In the rural environment, where there are long-standing incentives for producing large families, the economic incentives explicit in the new "responsibility system" may very well work at cross-purposes with the present antinatalist policies of the government.

In 1980, the authorities in Beijing announced the official "one-child per family planning policy." Compliance was to be rewarded and violators were to be penalized. Nonetheless, the 1982 census revealed that of the total number of births (20,444,000) in Communist China in 1981, 53 percent were births to families that already had one or more children: 26 percent of the births were to families with one child, and 27 percent were to families with two children or more. If reproduction continues at this rate, the population of the PRC in the year 2002 will be approximately 1.33 billion—considerably above the planned population targets. Any incentives to accelerate the rural birth rate that are implicit in the new agrarian policies can only be viewed with grave misgivings by those charged with administering the birth-control policies of the Communist Chinese government.

Moreover, since the introduction of the new responsibility system in the countryside, there have been reports of a decline in rural school enrollment and attendance, apparently traceable to the need for more family labor to increase farm yields. Such a reduction in school attendance could have disabling implications for the economy of a nation already beset by a shortfall in trained and semiskilled personnel.

It is likely that resistance to the new agrarian policies from all these quarters will increase, rather than diminish, in the years to come. Party and bureaucratic officials have a corporate interest in opposing such reforms. Some of them have policy, as well as more general ideological, objections to the entire program. The influential urban constituencies have real or anticipated objections. Should there be any disruptions of the rural economy, it is likely that concerted pressure will be brought to bear on the authorities to once again reverse policy. That dislocations are likely to occur seems evident, given the magnitude of the problems in the agrarian sector.

It is unlikely that the rapid increase in agricultural yields (for example, that achieved between 1979 and 1984) can be sustained. Most of the increase is attributable to abandonment of the irrational cropping practices that had been dictated by the government as part of its emphasis on grain production. Peasant farmers were compelled to plant grain crops on unsuitable land that produced low yields. As a result of the permission to diversify crops, areas previously used for growing low-yield grain crops are being used for growing valuable oil seed crops, such as rapeseed, peanuts, sesame seed, and sunflowers, as well as soybeans and sugarcane. Significantly, the sharp increase in noncereal crops has not been accomplished at the expense of large grain harvests, because staple grain crops are once again being cultivated on soils and in locations that are most suitable for their growth. That, combined with the reduction in the constraints imposed by command farming, explains much of the recent improvements in the rural sector.

The increase in agricultural yields will probably plateau in a few years, and further increases will require a steadily increasing investment of both capital and labor. Land reclamation would seem advisable (there are probably 33 million hectares of wasteland that could be rendered suitable for farming), but it would require massive capital expenditure, necessitating once again an increased rate of capital accumulation, more state intervention, and increased cadre involvement.

Mainland Chinese economists calculate that in order to provide an adequate diet for a low population estimate of 1.2 billion inhabitants in the year 2000, Chinese farmers would have to harvest 480 million tons of grain (400 kilograms per capita)—a yield almost 50 percent higher than crops in the mid-1980s. In 1956, the grain yield was 307 kilograms per capita, and twenty years later, production remained at approximately the same per capita level.[29] Achieving a level of production that will yield 400 kilograms per capita will be very difficult and will probably require the reimposition of socialist controls to ensure compliance and to achieve a rate of capital accumulation sufficient for the construction of a more elaborate (and more expensive) infrastructure and for the purchase of larger quantities of expensive fertilizers (because of the increasing unavailability of the traditionally employed natural fertilizers). Moreover, massed labor will be needed to restore and expand the intricate waterworks system and the large and small water storage reservoirs upon which future agricultural yield depends.

The capital and labor required to achieve Communist China's agricultural goals suggests an early return to a Maoist policy of controlled consumption and mass mobilization projects—a swing once again from "pragmatic" to "leftist" solutions.

How fragile the current policies may be is suggested by the fact that the experiments in increasing the income of peasant families had already run into difficulties by the early 1980s. Between 1978 and 1980, the state increased its farm procurement prices by about 30 percent. As a consequence, gross farm income, in constant prices, rose slightly over 20 percent. In order to offset the possibility of an increase in the urban cost of living, the state subsidized urban prices. The cost of this subsidy produced deficits that amounted to about 7 percent of state revenue, or 2 percent of the national income. Since 1980, the state response has been to stop increasing its farm procurement prices and to reduce the amount of agricultural output purchased at higher above-quota and negotiated prices. Furthermore, in order to eliminate some of the competition for available farm products, it has assigned surveillance and control responsibilities to rural cadres, apparently in an effort to limit rural marketing opportunities.

In the short term, the agrarian reforms in Communist China will probably fail because of party and bureaucratic self-interest and budgetary constraints. In the long term, mainland China's failure to solve its dual problem of a growing population and declining or static domestic resources will probably cause it to return to the policies of the past. The reforms of the 1980s, like the reforms of the past, may be only temporary expedients. That suggests that "capitalism" will not be restored to the countryside and that Communist China's agriculture will probably remain "socialist."

THE ECONOMIC "TRANSFORMATION" OF INDUSTRY

By the late 1970s it had become evident to the authorities in Beijing that although Communist China's output of goods and services had increased over three decades, there had been little technological development and almost no improvements in efficiency. In addition, total factor productivity in both agriculture and industry had markedly declined, a large amount of industrial output had been wasted, and the living standard of the population had increased only marginally over the level attained in the early 1950s.

In the early 1980s, Beijing's leaders decided that one of the reasons for the system's failures was "excessive centralization." They argued that the "central authorities" had issued "arbitrary directions . . . [and] set excessively high targets for production and construction." All of which led to work habits that lacked "initiative and flexibility [and produced] workers and staff [devoid of] dedication and a sense of responsibility."[30] This situation led to the constraints on consumption, excessive capitalization, and serious sectoral and subsectoral imbalances previously referred to.

The "excessively centralized" system to which Communist Chinese economists allude has been modeled after that of the Soviet Union. Having ordered nationalization of the means of production, the state accumulates profits as revenue and allocates that revenue in the form of grants to firms for investment in industry. Decisions, both microeconomic and macroeconomic, are made at the highest level of the party-controlled bureaucracy and are based almost exclusively on administrative, rather than economic, criteria. Those decisions are transmitted downward to firms in the form of annual and quarterly physical and financial norms for inputs and outputs. Inputs and outputs are theoretically "balanced" by rationed allocations and mandated outputs. Consumers are rationed goods, at fixed prices, in state-determined assortments and in quantities deemed sufficient to ensure capital accumulation at state-determined rates. All these activities are undertaken without the influence of the market. Prices in such a system are conceived to be allocatively neutral, reflecting only the decisions made by the planners at the center. Labor placement and mobility are made subject to state control. The state sets enterprise output goals, and their achievement is compulsory. There is every bureaucratic incentive to do so; consequently, the state can expect a surplus of goods. What the state seems unable to provide under such a system are incentives for technological innovation, increased labor productivity, quality control, and coordination of output and input between and within sectors and subsectors of the economy.

The deficiencies of the modified Soviet system seem to have become abundantly clear to the authorities in Beijing by the end of the 1970s and led to the readjustments that have been cumulatively introduced since 1978, which have included efforts to make the industrial economy more sensitive to the needs of enterprise, ensure more rational allocation of resources, and increase efficiency. What those efforts involved was a modest decentralization of decision making. Firms have been allowed to retain a small proportion (about 10 percent) of profits generated and of depreciation funds and to use them for expansion, technology acquisition, or bonus payments to workers and staff. Over-quota production may be marketed in lateral transactions with other firms without the approval of state bureaucrats. In theory, firm managers are permitted to directly recruit and "discipline" their work force; they can fire those guilty of the "most serious offenses" that interfere with plant production and work performance.

These readjustments of the established economic system have been intended to reduce resource misallocation, draw off some of the inventory of firms, satisfy needs overlooked by the State Bureau of Supplies in using the centralized and hierarchical "balances," and provide material incentives for firms to utilize both state resources and the labor force more efficiently. Some of these modifications had been made in the Soviet economic system as early as Lenin's New Economic Policy in the 1920s. Whenever the inefficiencies of a controlled economy become politically threatening, communist authorities resort to "liberalization," "decentralization," and "material incentives." Sometimes there is even talk of "worker participation" in enterprise management. Some Westerners pretend that these readjustments indicate a failure of the communist economic system and an increasing convergence with the West.

Whether any of these readjustments should be interpreted as permanent or fundamental alterations in the controlled economic system is difficult to determine. What seems reasonably certain is that the innovations were intended to increase efficiency and to reduce or eliminate the most serious anomalies of the system while maintaining effective centralized control of the productive processes. This was nowhere more clearly expressed than in a speech by Communist Chinese Premier Zhao Ziyang in March 1982:

> Efforts to expand decision-making powers and activate the economy are . . . apt to foster the trend toward departmentalism, decentralism, and liberalism, to weaken and depart from the state's unified plan, to interfere with and break up the unified market of socialism and to affect our efforts to take the whole country and overall situation into consideration. . . . Ours is a unified socialist nation. We must have a unified plan and a unified domestic market. . . . In order to strengthen centralization and unification in economic work, we must adhere to the overall plan on major issues while allowing freedom on minor issues. We must advocate centralism on major issues while allowing decentralism on minor issues. . . . The products to be transferred according to state plans, including farm and sideline products, must be transferred strictly according to such plans. The commodity price and revenue system must be centralized and unified. . . . No matter what reform is to be carried out, the general guideline is to combine the strengthening of centralization and unification with the activation of the economy.[31]

The delegation of decision-making power to the local enterprises does not represent a basic alteration of the original system of centrally planned output. Even the right to market over-quota production is limited by the requirement that all such products first be offered for sale to the state's supply distribution system. Only then can their sale be negotiated among enterprises. Sales negotiated at that stage must be made at state-determined (or lower) prices. Prices are not set by market mechanisms, as those mechanisms are understood in the West.[32]

The effect of the decision to reduce the high rates of capital accumulation that had caused the serious imbalances in the system was to release funds for the improvement of the industrial wage structure. This had become expedient because, according to the available evidence, the average real wage of staff and workers in industry declined by about 5 percent between 1957 and 1977. The 1978 wage adjustment also represented an effort to forestall political unrest. Similar ad hoc wage adjustments have been employed in almost all command economies when it has become painfully obvious that protracted periods of low wages cause a radical decline in labor productivity and an increase in political instability.[33]

As effective demand increased, however, the inadequacies of the socialist distribution system in urban areas became increasingly manifest. In order to offset the inadequacies of the service industries, the Communist Chinese authorities allowed the formation of urban cooperatives and the establishment of small private businesses—such as tailor shops, restaurants, and repair facilities—to augment the thin consumer service infrastructure of the cities. The establishment of such enterprises (at no expense to the state) also eliminated some of the urban unemployment that had contributed to the general unrest before 1978.

This kind of "penny capitalism" is not new to Soviet-type economic systems. An unplanned service sector has regularly been allowed in such systems to compensate for the allocative inefficiencies of state planning. A similar (but larger) unplanned private sector flourished in Communist China during the 1950s until it was suppressed by officials who termed it "antisocialist." In 1982, the new private urban service sector was composed of 1.47 million individuals—about 23 percent of the number so employed in 1955, and about 65 percent of the average number so employed between 1962 and 1964 (an earlier period of readjustment).

The magnitude of these renascent private economic activities indicates their marginality. In 1984, only 3 percent of total retail sales originated in this private sector. This hardly heralds the rebirth of capitalism on the mainland of China. What the new private service industries accomplish is to supplement the poorly articulated commercial network for trade and exchange that is part of the command economy of the PRC.

Under the "classic" socialist planned system, the state provides to enterprises, free of cost, all fixed assets and working capital. Firms are not held responsible for the efficient utilization of these state-supplied assets and funds. Under such conditions there is no incentive to meet end-users' demands by reducing costs, improving quality, and increasing assortment. In the PRC, this has been particularly true in the consumer goods and the services industries.[34] Penny capitalist enterprises present no threat to Beijing's central planning and control and satisfy some urgent urban needs. When they enter into direct competition with state industries, they provide a standard of efficiency, otherwise absent, against which the performance of such firms can be measured. In sum, they introduce some measure of rationality into an otherwise irrational economic system.

The incorporation of some elements of a market system into a planned economic system (the establishment of private enterprise in the urban areas, the negotiation of sales of over-quota production among industries, and the marketing of agrarian products in the rural bazaars) has led some Westerners to anticipate an unraveling of the socialist system in the People's Republic of China. In fact, there is little that might sustain such an expectation.

If all the sales negotiated among the penny capitalists of the urban areas in 1983 are added to those negotiated by over-quota producers in the industrial sector, and to those negotiated among peasant households in the "free markets" of the countryside in the same year, it is clear that in no more than 25 percent of sales in Communist China were prices allowed to exceed administratively fixed price levels. Included in that percentage are sales in which prices were allowed to fluctuate only within certain prescribed limits. Enterprises that sell over-quota production at negotiated prices are frequently not permitted to sell above administratively fixed price levels. Therefore, the suggestion that 25 percent of mainland China's prices were established by the open market in 1983 is an upwardly biased estimate.

At least until 1984, the bulk of the prices at which goods were exchanged in the People's Republic of China were determined by the standard "prime cost plus profit" formula of the Soviet economic system—that is, the prices simply reflected administrative decisions concerning output goals and distributive preferences rather than relative scarcities and utilities. Communist Chinese economists acknowledged that evident fact by indicating that "planned prices" did not correspond to any "objective criteria" that might identify the "value of a product." They granted that "planned prices of many products [deviated] from their values by a wide margin."[35]

Given the irrational pricing policy, it was impossible to determine whether or when an enterprise was efficient or inefficient. If state-fixed prices for inputs were too high and state-fixed sale prices were too low, even the most efficient firms would consistently show book losses. If sale prices were set too high, even inefficient firms would show a profit. Moreover, inefficient firms would tend not only to overproduce, but to overproduce products of inferior quality. For example, in 1977, the target for the quantity of machines to be produced in machine shops was set at 60,000 units. In fact, those shops produced 190,000 units. Because the sale price had been set high, each extra unit increased the shops' book profits. In 1978, the output of machines exceeded planned goals by 100,000 units—units that were then warehoused at great expense. However efficient or inefficient the firm, and to whatever extent it overproduced, the enterprise was still "profitable."

By 1979, even the most obtuse economist in the PRC was compelled to recognize that "prices in China [were] very much out of joint with reality."[36] The entire pricing system required major reform. One of the first reforms, implemented in the early 1980s, was to use price as a "lever" to influence output. Output could be reduced or increased by raising or lowering state-fixed prices. Thus, the first reforms of the pricing system were intended not to have prices reflect the true scarcity values of commodities, but rather to have prices serve as levers to guide enterprise to the attainment of some planned outcome. Resource, commodity, and credit prices are now used to "guide" and adjust the economy. Together with new profit and wage incentives, the new pricing policies of the PRC are a means of attaining the goals set by the state economic plan. Prices in such an environment are not determined by market influences but are set within variable ranges determined by the state to satisfy state, rather than market, demands. The new pricing policies, Chinese Communist economists warn us, should not be construed as "condoning anarchy. . . . Price variations should not be allowed to deviate beyond the planned range." Chinese economists oppose "the exaggeration of the functions of the market at the expense of planning."[37]

Even when the Beijing authorities, in 1984–1985, allowed households and collective enterprises more freedom to expand services, produce intermediate and consumer goods, and supply those services and goods at prices determined, to a large extent, by the market, the effects were marginal. Although there had been an expansion in the "private" sector of the economy, the authorities appeared confident that market-determined prices would not significantly change the controlled nature of the economy.

In adopting a decision on industrial reform on October 20, 1984, the Central Committee of the Chinese Communist Party anticipated changes in the pricing system that were designed to render the industrial sector more efficient. But those changes were not intended to fundamentally transform the economic system. The pricing system was no longer to be allocatively neutral. Prices were to become levers that would be used to more efficiently accomplish the goals of the state plan.[38]

The only prices that are actually determined by market forces in the PRC are those in the underground economy, the rural free bazaars, and the privately run portions of the service economy. Early in the implementation of the most recent reform, Chen Yun (Ch'en Yun), one of the most influential economists in the PRC, described the reformed system as follows:

> The bulk of the nation's industrial and agricultural production is carried out according to state plans. At the same time, some products are turned out in conformity with the market conditions but within limits permitted by the state plan. . . . Stimulating the economy is to be done within the framework of the state plan. The relationship between the two is like a bird and the cage. A bird should be allowed to fly, but within the framework of a cage. Otherwise, it will fly away.[39]

Although it is impossible to tell where the current rage for reform will lead the People's Republic of China, it is evident that the present leadership is not contemplating the abandonment of socialism. Like the leaders of the Soviet Union, PRC leaders are prepared to introduce a number of substantial modifications of the state-controlled economy to achieve greater efficiency, in what appears to be a genuine effort to improve the standard of living of a population that has endured considerable privation. It is conceivable that the reforms being introduced will result in an economic system much like that of communist Hungary.

However modified, the system will retain many features of the old dispensation. Since 1978, the leaders of the PRC have been attempting to reduce the overall rate of investment and the growth rate of heavy industry—something that is apparently very difficult to do. The attempt to moderate the rate of investment in heavy industry seems to have proven especially difficult. In 1982, for example, the rate of growth of heavy industry was 9.9 percent, far in excess of the target of 1 percent. That growth was at the expense of light industry, whose growth was supposed to be emphasized. The growth rate of light industry in 1982 was 5.7 percent, significantly less than the targeted 7 percent. Not only had investment accumulated in heavy industry, but the rate of investment had exceeded the level set under the state plan.[40]

The partial "marketization" of the Communist Chinese economy since 1979 has had some impressive results. There has been a marked improvement in the performance of the agricultural sector, as well as some spectacular improvements in the industrial sector (if we can believe the official statistics). A number of serious problems have accompanied those improvements, however. They include major budget deficits resulting from an attempt to stabilize the prices of staples in the cities, a significant increase in urban unemployment, foreign-exchange imbalances, and substantial inflation.

When central control over public finance at the local level was relaxed and firms were allowed some measure of decision-making power, some enterprises attempted to increase their market shares by penetrating geographical regions that the state had closed to them in the past. In response, some local governments, in an effort to reduce competition from neighboring regions, denied those firms access. Local production brigades were compelled to purchase raw materials and producer goods from local sources. Duplicate facilities were constructed, overlapping investments were made, and some regions withheld the shipment of needed supplies to other regions.[41]

Because of the problem of unemployment, the authorities have not allowed inefficient and noncompetitive firms to fail. As a consequence, workers have not lost their jobs. The price paid, however, has been the perpetuation of inefficiencies. Moreover, job security has been purchased by a denial of the right to change one's place of employment. Whatever "freedom" the economic reforms were supposed to provide, it was "by no means [to be] construed as [freedom of] . . . movement from one enterprise to another, from one department to another, or between rural and urban areas without any control."[42] The authorities in Beijing have qualified their commitment to both enterprise efficiency and the relaxation of controls over the labor market.

Since 1982, the degree of central control over the economy has varied widely. That the reform of the Communist Chinese economy will result in a system that resembles nonsocialist systems is most unlikely. Such fundamental changes would threaten the stability of the political system and the power of the Chinese Communist Party.[43] That the party and the bureaucracy are prepared to surrender that power is disconfirmed by everything we know about the established political system in the People's Republic of China.

THE "DEMOCRATIZATION" OF THE PEOPLE'S REPUBLIC OF CHINA

Foreign commentators have sometimes pretended to see a potential "democratization" of the Communist Chinese polity accompanying the "liberalization" and "marketization" of its economy. They anticipated that changes would be made in the political system for much the same reason that the economy was being "reformed." The Maoist political system cried out for institutional reform. During Mao's final years, an intolerable burden had been imposed on both the people and the leadership. It was only after the death of Mao (1976) that the extent of that burden, and the horror of the Great Proletarian Cultural Revolution, in particular, became public knowledge—and only slowly was the extent of the devastation, the terror and suffering, revealed. Hundreds of thousands, perhaps millions, were senselessly butchered during the Cultural Revolution. Millions more were tortured and humiliated in a paroxism of sadism that has had few parallels in a century of bloodletting and violence.[44] More important because of its political consequences was that many in the highest echelons of the Chinese Communist Party were subjected to the brutality and many, including Deng Xiaoping, were divested of their authority and driven from power—at a time when personal worth, status, and well-being were determined by the position held. With the conclusion of the Cultural Revolution and the death of Mao, it became obvious that the political system would have to be restructured in order to prevent a recurrence of the upheaval that had all but destroyed the results of two decades of economic effort, as well as the political careers of countless party functionaries.

What recommended itself in such circumstances was some extensive restructuring of the system in order to preclude the arbitrary exercise of power at the expense of functionaries. Before that task could be accomplished, however, the unregenerate heirs of Mao had to be suppressed. The first group to be purged was the "Gang of Four," led by Mao's widow, Jiang Qing (Chiang Ch'ing). Between 1976 and 1978, Deng Xiaoping jockeyed for position against Hua Guofeng, who had inherited Mao's mantle and was nominally in control. Until well into 1977, Hua could continue to speak of the Great Proletarian Cultural Revolution as a "signal victory" for Chinese communism and to praise its "unprecedented" value to the party and the people of Communist China.[45]

Only in December 1978 (at the Third Plenum of the Eleventh Central Committee) was Hua defeated by the political forces marshaled by Deng,[46] and only then did the process of ideological "deradicalization" begin. Hua had attempted to maintain an ideological continuity that would have legitimized his succession. If Mao had indeed been the "greatest Marxist of our time," and if his "Thought" had been infallible, his choice of Hua as a successor could hardly have been questioned. But Deng, who had been divested of his position no less than twice during the last decade of Mao's tenure, could only have doubted the infallibility of the "Great Chairman." Deng, as a consequence, advocated making "practice," rather than devotion to Mao, the "test of truth."

Hua had had every incentive to foster and protect Mao's reputation for infallibility. Deng, on the other hand, had every reason to emphasize Mao's fallibility. At his urging, the charges against the Gang of Four were gradually extended to include increasing criticism of the Great Proletarian Cultural Revolution itself. Ultimately, the Cultural Revolution was identified as an unmitigated disaster for all of Communist China. References to the glories of Chairman Mao gradually decreased in frequency and many of the "capitalist roaders," who had been defamed during the Cultural Revolution, were restored to favor.

In doing so, Deng exploited the genuine desire of Communist China's intellectuals, educated youths, and the new generation of urban workers, for increased political freedom. Deng spoke of "liberating the mind" in an effort to enlist the support of a vocal "anti-leftist" opposition against the unregenerate Maoist forces that had resisted political change. The so-called Democracy Movement was formed in 1978, and for the first time in almost three decades, there was a proliferation of "unofficial" publications in Communist China.[47] The demands made in those publications were fairly simple and straightforward. The "most pressing priority" was "to regain freedom of thought, speech and publication." "Unity and stability," it was argued, "are not a stagnant pond, thay are not excuses to deny the people freedom of speech, and above all they do not deny people the freedom to speak the truth. True people's democracy can come about only if everybody dares to say what they have to say; in this way corruption has nowhere to hide itself and the will of the people determines society's course." Soon, however, the demands were broadened to include the "release of all those imprisoned for acts of free speech and free thought" and a change in the Constitution so that it would "really guarantee the right to criticize and comment upon Party and national leaders." There was also an insistence that "citizens elect directly their national and local leaders at every level." Ultimately, a "gradual elimination of the system [was recommended] whereby the government controls the means and material of production."[48] "Democratization" had begun to threaten the integrity of the system.[49]

Throughout 1979, the behavior of intellectuals, artists, and educated youths followed a similar pattern. At first there was euphoria. Artists began to paint nudes and rendered abstract, rather than "socialist realist," likenesses. Soon there was barbed criticism of the party and of life under China's version of communism. Cartoonists satirized the political system. Novelists focused on life's inadequacies.[50]

The government's response was a tightening of controls. By that time Hua and his faction had been defeated. A retrenchment was begun. Agents of the Public Security Bureau arrested the most notable of the leaders of the Democracy Movement (the most celebrated of whom was

Wei Jingsheng [Wei Ching-sheng], now serving a fifteen-year sentence as a "counterrevolutionary element"[51]). In the beginning of 1980, the brief period of "liberalization" came to an end. The "unofficial" publications that would "liberate the mind," and the contested elections at the local level, were either abruptly abolished or so regulated as to make them innocuous.

Deng Xiaoping himself made the official position eminently clear. In a speech to a cadre conference in the Great Hall of the People in Beijing on January 16, 1980, Deng reminded the party functionaries that what the People's Republic of China required was "a stable and unified political situation. . . . The last twenty years are proof of this." He referred to the prevalence of "currents of social thought"—particularly among Chinese youths—that threatened that stability and unity. Such thoughts, which found expression among those identified with the Democracy Movement, threatened to create "disorder" within the system.

To forestall any such eventuality, Deng attempted to mobilize the party cadres against "those who publicly oppose the socialist system and the leadership of the Communist Party, the so-called 'democratic factions'." He went on to affirm, "When did we ever say that we would tolerate the activities of counterrevolutionaries and destructive elements? When did we ever say we would abandon the dictatorship of the proletariat?" Then he counseled them: "In fact, we should be more strict, not more lenient, about these problems, or there will be terrible disorder. . . . We must loudly proclaim the superiority of socialism, and the correctness of Marxism-Leninism–Mao Zedong Thought. We must proclaim the leadership of the Party."[52]

At the end of 1982, a new Constitution was promulgated that superseded that of 1978. Just as the Constitution of 1978 reflected the concerns of Hua Guofeng and his faction, the Constitution of 1982 gives legal expression to the views of Deng and his victorious allies. The Preamble includes the "Four Basic Principles" that are to govern post-Maoist China. In the Preamble, it is affirmed that Communist China will "concentrate its effort on socialist modernization" under "the leadership of the Communist Party of China and the guidance of Marxism-Leninism and Mao Zedong Thought." The people of the PRC are admonished to "adhere to the people's democratic dictatorship and follow the socialist road."[53] Thus, whatever reforms are introduced, Deng's post-Maoist China fully intends to emphasize "socialism," the "democratic dictatorship," the rule of the Chinese Communist Party, and "Marxism-Leninism–Mao Zedong Thought." Moreover, Article 1 of the Constitution of 1982 states that "sabotage of the socialist system by any organization or individual is prohibited." In effect, any rights extended in the

Constitution are qualified by the blanket proscription that "the exercise by citizens of the People's Republic of China of their freedoms and rights may not infringe upon the interests of the state." (Article 51).

The "liberalizing" aspects of the Constitution of 1982 are clearly intended not to foster "democracy" but to serve the interests of the dominant faction—in the mid-1980s, that supporting Deng Xiaoping. An effort has been made to diffuse power throughout the system so that no one leader can violate the personal or corporate interests of those who now make up the ruling elite. Deng, and those around him, suffered directly as a consequence of the arbitrary use of power by Mao, whose long tenure and simultaneous occupation of the posts of chairman of the Central Committee of the Chinese Communist Party and chairman of the Central Military Affairs Commission made the lives and careers of his subordinates hazardous and unpredictable. In the Constitution of 1982, limits are imposed on the tenure of officials (with the notable exception of Deng's tenure as chairman of the Central Military Affairs Commission), and responsibilities are divided. With regard to the recognition of "capitalist property," the Constitution simply permits continuation of the foreign equity investments that the Deng leadership has been attempting to attract to help resolve Communist China's economic problems.

In a speech before the Second Plenary Session of the Twelfth Central Committee of the Chinese Communist Party in October 1983, Deng made the goals of the party and of the Communist Chinese state very clear.[54] The obligation of the leadership of Communist China, he said, was to "reestablish the ideological line, the political line, and the organizational line of Marxism." The Chinese Communist Party must be a party "full of combat effectiveness . . . that . . . will become a strong core to lead the people throughout the country." It must also serve as an "engineer of man's soul" and resist "bourgeois liberalization and . . . flabbiness and laxness in leadership." Communist China can prevail only if individuals assiduously defend the "socialist system and the Party's leadership." (This is the core of the Four Basic Principles and the essence of the Constitution of 1982.) Deng recommended that his audience reread Mao's injunctions, contained in his article "Combat Liberalism." "All loyal, honest, active and upright Communists must unite to oppose . . . liberal tendencies."[55]

The developments since 1979 do not suggest that Communist China is undertaking anything more than the "reforms" and "revisions" that most communist states initiate when they emerge from particularly trying institutional and political crises. The post-Stalinist Soviet Union, for example, displayed some of the same features. There was an effort to build safeguards into the system in order to preclude the damaging employment of personal power. There was an insistence that "freedom of thought" was fostered, and an appeal was made to "socialist legality" to protect both the functionaries and the general population from the unpredictable violence of arbitrary personal rule. The "rule of socialist law" was introduced in an effort to stabilize the system.

In 1978, after a similar period of tyrannical constraint, the leadership of Communist China agreed that the disorder and uncertainty that the People's Republic of China had endured for almost three decades had not only prejudiced economic development but had bred widespread cynicism and caused a general lack of initiative among party and state functionaries. Since 1949, the PRC had been governed essentially without a body of law.[56] A "Common Program" had served as a provisional Constitution between 1949 and 1954, when a formal Constitution was adopted. Except for the Code of Criminal Law and Criminal Procedures, passed in January 1980, the Communist leadership has not enacted supplementary substantive and procedural civil and criminal laws to replace those that obtained during the pre-communist period. The Act for the Punishment of Counterrevolutionaries, one of the few important criminal laws to have been promulgated in that period, was passed in 1951 and is still part of the law of the PRC. Article 16 is of considerable importance, for it sets forth the principle of culpability by analogy: persons who have undertaken acts with "counterrevolutionary intent that are not specified in the law" shall be prosecuted and punished as though those acts were crimes.[57]

In 1979, the National Peoples' Congress decided that this act, as well as the Labor Reform Statute, passed in August 1957, should remain in force. These two laws, coupled with the Four Basic Principles embodied in the Constitution of 1982, ensure Chinese Communist Party dominance over the political system in mainland China. Whatever rights and protections are extended by the Constitution of 1982—for example, the provisions for the protection of the judiciary from interference—it is evident that any acts that result in "sabotage of the social system" or that "infringe upon the interests of the state" are culpable offenses. The clear purposes of criminal law in the PRC (as stated in Article 2 of the Criminal Law) are "to use punishment to struggle against all counterrevolutionary and other criminal acts [and to] defend the dictatorship of the proletariat."[58] The Act for the Punishment of Counterrevolutionaries and the Labor Reform Statute are to be employed to those specific ends.

The Act for the Punishment of Counterrevolutionaries allows for the extension of law to cover by "analogy" acts that are not proscribed by law but that, in the judgment of the leadership, constitute instances of "counterrevolutionary intent." The Labor Reform Statute allows the security police to impose administrative (nonjudicial) sanctions against those "without legitimate employment, hoodlums or irresponsible characters . . . , those opposing security control and those who have been unsuccessfully reeducated," as well as "counterrevolutionary elements . . . , anti-socialist reactionary elements . . . , those who impede social order [and] those who constantly make trouble or impede official matters."[59]

Even if the authorities in the PRC were to faithfully grant all the rights to citizens and to observe all the restrictions imposed on themselves in the Constitution of 1982, there is sufficient latitude in the law as it presently obtains to permit the Chinese Communist Party to control all political activity in the People's Republic of China. The Labor Reform Statute allows the security police to incarcerate individuals for up to four years by following administrative procedures against which those involved have no recourse. The Labor Reform Statute was invoked to suppress most of the activists in the Democracy Movement. The rest were criminally charged under the provisions of the Constitution that make it obligatory for individuals to defend the socialist system and the state.[60] Failure to do so was deemed a criminal act.

Thousands, perhaps hundreds of thousands, of citizens of the PRC are still undergoing "rehabilitation through labor" in hundreds, if not thousands, of camps throughout mainland China. Severe restrictions are placed on voluntary association, freedom of movement, access to information, and communication. All of this is carefully controlled by agencies dominated by the Chinese Communist Party. Because "sabotage of the socialist system" is proscribed, no direct criticism of the Chinese Communist Party, the government, or the socialist system is allowed. All mass organizations are controlled by the party.

Whenever the political leadership decides to do so, it can rapidly revamp the prevailing laws. The PRC's anticrime campaign of 1983–1984 was fostered by a revision of the criminal procedure codes promulgated but a short time before—allowing an increase in the number of offenses to be punished by the death sentence, as well as more rapid prosecution, sentencing, and execution. Provincial agencies were apparently assigned arrest quotas, and in a few months over 100,000 "criminals" were arrested and prosecuted. Between 5,000 and 10,000 were reported executed, including several "spies from Taiwan" and other "counterrevolutionary elements."[61]

In substance, there has been an effort by the leadership in Beijing to introduce some measure of security and predictability into the political system inherited from Mao Zedong. It is clear that the reforms introduced have mitigated some of the more outrageous caprices and inequities of the Maoist period. Equally clear is that the reforms have resulted in a carefully controlled system that serves the interests of the Chinese Communist Party and its current leadership. The Constitution of 1975 reflected the interests of the political faction that engineered the savagery of the Cultural Revolution; the Constitution of 1978 reflected the concerns of Hua Guofeng; and the Constitution of 1982 reflects the preoccupations and political interests of Deng Xiaoping and those around him. Those preoccupations and interests do not include introducing "democracy" into the People's Republic of China. Deng has specifically expressed an intolerance of ideas that "lead people to criticize, to doubt, and to . . . lose faith in socialism and communism." He has specifically denounced any propagation of "abstract democracy" that might juxtapose "democracy in opposition to the Party's leadership."[62]

Deng, and those around him, have made it eminently clear that they wish to maintain an "open door" to Western technology. They desire access to Western markets to obtain the foreign exchange necessary to pay for Western producer goods. They wish to obtain from the "highly developed capitalist countries only advanced science, technology, management methods and all other aspects of Western civilization that [would be] beneficial" to Communist China. What they do not want are the "pernicious things in . . . capitalist culture," including "humanism," "liberalism," and "abstract democracy."[63]

THE PROBABLE FUTURE

Many of the economic reforms instituted by the People's Republic of China beginning in the late 1970s were dictated by stark necessity. The system inherited from Mao was afflicted by massive problems of static misallocation of resources, structural imbalances, pervasive inefficiency and waste, and persistent, and frequently grinding, poverty. The party was split into many factions, and its members were demoralized and disillusioned. Many talented and qualified individuals had been alienated from the government and an entire generation had become politically cynical. It was evident that change had become imperative and that, at a minimum, it would have to produce a measurable material improvement in the lives of the citizens of the PRC.

In the agricultural sector, the "responsibility system"—the restoration of familial and individual incentives—has generated significant improvements in agricultural yield. As in similar experiments in Eastern Europe, the relaxation of central controls released an immediate surge of productive energy. Unfortunately, it is unlikely that the rate of real productive growth achieved in the countryside in the early 1980s can be sustained. As productive yields plateau, there will probably be an increase in state intervention in the agricultural sector, and the old system will gradually be re-established.

In the industrial sector the reform has been more recent, and its ultimate impact is consequently less clear. Nevertheless, the leadership in Beijing has no intention of abandoning socialism. The command economy of the past may very well be "guided" by manipulation of economic "levers," but it is evident that the PRC is not traveling the road of "capitalist restoration."

When fears of capitalist restoration were raised by party members as early as 1982, party leaders assured them that "vigorous party leadership" would provide the anticipated order, stability, and continuity:

> Such worry is groundless. . . . [The] state sector of the economy is the dominant force of our country's socialist economy. The lifeline of our national economy is grasped in the hands of the state. . . . Individual economy occupies a small proportion in the whole picture, and it is there as a complement to the state-owned and collective economies. In no way could it affect the overall socialist public ownership. . . . [What] we are practicing is . . . planned economy. . . . The state incorporates the fundamental production and circulation into unified planning. The activities of all . . . come under the guidance and restraint . . . of the state.[64]

Neither capitalism nor democracy is in the offing for the People's Republic of China. Whatever reforms are yet to come, the system will, in all probability, prevail. It is sustained by a massive bureaucracy that has every corporate interest in its perpetuation—however flawed.

Some of the most recent reforms and the basic redirection of the economy were anticipated by Zhou Enlai while Mao was still alive. The reform process continued fitfully throughout the brief and contested tenure of Hua Guofeng, because it was evident that change was necessary. The reform of the system was not a result of the success or failure of one faction or another. Reform would have been undertaken in any case, by whoever was charged with the responsibilities of leadership. However, the extent of the reform was probably influenced by the more "pragmatic" and institutional orientation of Deng Xiaoping.

The retention of the prevailing system, disencumbered of the bizarre excesses of the Maoist period, can be anticipated whoever accedes to power in Beijing. Institutional inertia will ensure continuity. That is not to say that some of the future changes will not be fairly extensive. Communist Hungary has long since introduced economic reforms similar to those of Deng's China. But for all its reforms, communist Hungary remains one of the most politically repressive regimes in the world. There is very little reason to believe that the future of the PRC will be much different. The notion that the People's Republic of China was on the threshold of a systemic "transformation" in 1979 has shown itself to be devoid of substance. The wish was father to the thought.

8

The Elements of Policy

Enough time has elapsed since the first efforts were made to establish a rapprochement between the United States and the People's Republic of China to allow us to make some estimate of what can be expected of the "China connection." In the mid-1980s U.S.-China policy, originally shaped by specific concerns, seems to have taken on a momentum of its own. Washington now perceives the PRC, a large country inhabited by one-quarter of the world's population, as "counting" in some important, but indeterminate, sense.

In the mid-1970s, academics recommended the more intense cultivation of relations between the United States and the PRC because Communist China was "already . . . among the leading powers of the world," and its emergence as a "world power" could not be long delayed.[1] By the early 1980s, the estimate of the importance of the PRC was less positive. We have been told that "China is not a superpower and will not be in the future; China must be regarded as a second-ranking power."[2] But whatever the assessment of the PRC's present or future international role, it seems clear that for U.S. policymakers the die has been cast. No political leader in the United States can, for the foreseeable future, afford to be identified with the "loss" of China. Few Americans are prepared to countenance the possibility that hostility or complete indifference might once again separate Washington from Beijing. Every incumbent and aspirant to national office in the United States will seek to sustain "normal" relations between the two countries.

Even though normalized relations with the PRC can be considered a constant in U.S. foreign policy for the indeterminate future, there is a wide range of behaviors that will pass as "normal" bilateral relations. Those policy behaviors will be determined by factors too numerous to be confidently predicted. Nonetheless, we have learned enough about the ongoing relations between the United States and the People's Republic of China to make some preliminary estimates of what can be expected. From such assessments some policy recommendations will invariably emerge.

Policy recommendations focus on several loosely defined areas of concern that, taken together, are generally spoken of as "national interests." The national interests of any state usually include its survival (1) as a unified whole within clearly defined territorial boundaries, (2) under stable economic conditions, (3) in a benign and reasonably secure world. Such interests become objectives when national policy is formulated in a fashion conducive to their realization. National policy choices become instrumental to the attainment of national goals. Ill-considered policies fault aims. The result is that national objectives are not attained, and collective interests are unintentionally sacrificed. The only real defense (however frail) against policy failure is informed and responsible judgment.

Unfortunately, there are few policy areas concerning which we are less informed than U.S. policy toward the People's Republic of China. There has long been a serious shortfall in general information, and as a consequence Americans have experienced much befuddlement and self-delusion. The first sustained contacts between the United States and the PRC in the early 1970s, like the first contacts between imperial China and the West, precipitated a veritable avalanche of almost reverential statements about the People's Republic of China.[3] United States journalists and intellectuals, their motives obscure, tended to report on unreal Communist Chinese accomplishments and to attribute imaginary virtues to mainland China. As late as 1973, for example, some experts suggested that the PRC had a model political system that had overcome "a seemingly insurmountable set of problems." It was intimated that the United States might learn how to deal with its own problems of "bureaucratic practice, education, the patterns of urbanization, penology, public health, factory management, and civil-military affairs" from the communist leadership in Beijing.[4]

Everything about the PRC seemed to be described in superlatives. In 1975, a U.S. judge visited Communist China and returned immensely impressed. He reported that he had seen a "new society" in which "serious crime [was] a rarity, juvenile delinquency nearly nonexistent and lawyers virtually unnecessary. . . . Jails [were] few and their populations small. The trappings of a restrictive regime [were] absent."[5]

We now know that almost all such accounts were fanciful. The mainland Chinese themselves have dismissed them. They speak of the "new society" that Americans had perceived to be replete with virtue as one in which "feudal despotism [is] married to 20th-century fascism."[6] The Chinese, compelled to live under the system that the Americans had tended to celebrate, characterize the Communist Chinese bureaucracy as an "evil to be checked," composed of men who hold "unaccountable, centralized power in [their] hands" and who are "locked in a murderous internecine power struggle."[7]

The educational system of the PRC was, and remains, grievously impaired. About 15 percent of the population of Communist China is totally illiterate. Only 60 percent of the school-age population is enrolled in school, and more than 10 percent of the children of school age do not attend even primary school. One student per 1,000 in the population attends a college or university (compared with 19.4 students per 1,000 in Taiwan and 51 students per 1,000 in the United States). The PRC has fewer professors teaching in its colleges and universities in the mid-1980s than it had in 1949. Based on the percentage of its GNP allocated to education, the PRC ranks 130th of 149 countries surveyed.[8]

Mainland China's ongoing urbanization process hardly recommends itself as a model. Most of the PRC's major cities have serious problems of unemployment and crime, even though draconian controls have been imposed. Moreover, urbanization has resulted in devastating environmental damage, including extensive pollution. The PRC faces all the difficulties commonly encountered by developing countries.

Nor is there much to recommend the penological system of the PRC. The mainland Chinese have described the jails as "scum hole detention pens" and "butcheries," in which "savage corporeal punishment," "shackles [and] leather whips," "suppression, beating-up and executions" are commonplace.[9]

Only recently has the full extent of mainland China's public health problems become evident.[10] We know enough about factory management in the PRC to dismiss any claims that Beijing has discovered any new tactics that somehow render labor more satisfying, more efficient, or more "participatory." Civil-military relations are as stressful in the People's Republic of China as in any nation, and the legal system, which some Americans reported as epitomizing the "new society," is known to have been, and probably still is, characterized by governmental interference, arbitrary cruelty, and capricious infractions.[11]

The fact is that foreign analysts have often been grievously mistaken in their assessments of the politics, economics, and society of the People's Republic of China. Researchers have often accepted "Chinese Communist statements of ideals and principles as reliable indicators of the ways policies were actually implemented in China."[12] They have assumed the validity of fragmentary and often hopelessly flawed data and subjectively interpreted a complex reality that was little understood. There has been a wholesale tendency to adopt the political jargon of the authorities in Beijing—to speak of "elections" and "parliamentary bodies" in the People's Republic of China when there was little to legitimize the use of such familiar concepts. In the early 1970s, no less an authority than John K. Galbraith described Communist China's economy as "highly effective" and "remarkably efficient."[13]

Doubts about the political, economic, and social performance of the People's Republic of China arose only when the post-Maoist dispensation in Beijing legitimized such criticism. Only then were earlier criticisms accorded credence. One after another, all the extravagant claims made by many academic authorities were called into question—or completely discredited. To this day, there are few who are confident that foreigners have begun to fully grasp the complexity of the political, economic, and social system of Communist China.

Given at least these problems, it is easy to understand why the formulation of responsible U.S.-China policy has been extremely difficult. If such a significant number of academic authorities could so delude themselves concerning the People's Republic of China— authorities whose counseling had influenced U.S. policy toward the PRC since the early 1970s—errors in policy formation are to be expected. By the mid-1980s, professional judgments concerning the PRC had become more realistic, thus facilitating a more reasonable assessment of U.S. policy alternatives.

In 1983, there appeared to be a growing consensus, as indicated by the recommendations of the Atlantic Council's Committee on China Policy, that the United States and the People's Republic of China should seek "enhanced cooperation." Why increased cooperation should be desirable was not made clear. The People's Republic of China was simply acknowledged to be a "very large and underdeveloped country" in common with whom the United States had only "some . . . global and regional objectives."[14]

It remains unclear whether and to what extent "enhanced" cooperation between Washington and Beijing would increase the common global and regional objectives of the two nations, or would further the interests of the United States. In effect, it remains to be determined in just what sense cooperation between the United States and the PRC merits or requires "enhancement." Before such a recommendation can be considered relevant to U.S. policy, a review of the national interests of the

United States will be necessary to determine whether and to what extent enhanced cooperation with Beijing will further them.

SECURITY INTERESTS

In the mid-1980s, it is evident that the "parallel interests," in terms of security concerns, shared by the United States and the People's Republic of China derive from the preoccupation of each nation with the military threat posed by the Soviet Union. Beijing feels threatened by the Soviet forces deployed along its border. Washington perceives the Soviet buildup in East Asia a threat to its Pacific interests. Both the United States and the PRC, each for its own reasons, seek to complicate Moscow's military risk assessments.

As far as the United States is concerned, the very presence of the People's Republic of China complicates Moscow's military planning. By the early 1980s, it had become clear that those complications could not be further increased by anything either Washington or Beijing could conceivably do. Moreover, it had become equally obvious that whether the Soviet Union and the PRC remained hostile was a matter of relatively little consequence. The conflict between the two communist powers was so recent and had become so bitter that Moscow's military command could be expected not to make anything but cosmetic changes in the deployment of forces along the Sino-Soviet border, whatever the relations between the USSR and the PRC. Major Soviet forces would have to remain along the shared border in order to counter any moves by the armed forces of the PRC in the event of hostilities between the Soviet Union and the West—or to ensure the neutrality of Beijing in such an eventuality.[15]

Even if Beijing and Moscow should eliminate some of their most serious disagreement,[16] the USSR would have to retain a substantial multimission force in the East as a counterweight to the anti-Soviet forces, under U.S. command, that are arrayed in the West Pacific.[17] In effect, there is very little that Beijing can do that will alter the configuration of military forces in East Asia. The deficiencies of its military forces will prevent the PRC from exerting additional pressure on the Soviet Union. Because geostrategic considerations will change little during the remainder of this century, the PRC will continue to be a factor in Soviet risk assessment, whatever its relationship with the United States. Therefore, enhanced cooperation between Beijing and Washington would contribute little, if anything, to further U.S. security interests in East Asia.

The situations in Southeast Asia and South Asia are very similar.

Beijing has served as a major conduit for arms to the Afghan rebels resisting Soviet occupation of their nation. The PRC has been one of the major suppliers of modern weapons to the rebel forces in Afghanistan under a program probably orchestrated by the United States Central Intelligence Agency.[18] It is evident that the cooperation of the PRC in this enterprise is dictated by its national interests. Because of Afghanistan's proximity to the PRC, Beijing has every reason to oppose a strengthening of the Soviet Union's position in Afghanistan. In fact, Beijing has made withdrawal of Soviet troops from Afghanistan a condition for improved relations with the USSR—a condition that Moscow is not likely to agree to, given the strategic advantages afforded by the staging areas in Afghanistan. Afghanistan would be an ideal jumping-off place for action in the Persian Gulf region. Therefore, as long as the Persian Gulf remains critical to Moscow's contingency planning, it is unlikely that the USSR will evacuate Afghanistan in order to purchase Beijing's qualified friendship. Under the prevailing circumstances, it is hard to imagine any developments that would reduce Beijing's concern with regard to the presence of Soviet forces in Afghanistan. The PRC will continue to oppose that presence irrespective of the degree of cooperation between Beijing and Washington.

Similarly, Beijing will continue to apply pressure to the Socialist Republic of Vietnam as long as Hanoi continues its military relationship with Moscow. The PRC entertains perfectly comprehensible reservations concerning the presence of substantial, and potentially hostile, military forces along its southern border. Both the United States and the People's Republic of China would prefer a less belligerent and less Soviet-dependent Vietnam. Soviet military bases in Vietnam pose a strategic problem for both Washington and Beijing. From those staging areas, Moscow can launch attacks not only against vessels in the sea-lanes of communication that are critical to an adequate U.S. defense of noncommunist Asia, but against forces in the interior of the PRC as well.

To protect its national interests, therefore, Beijing will continue to share "parallel interests" with the United States in the containment of communist Vietnam. Beijing has involved itself in episodic violence along the Sino-Vietnamese border, and has provided considerable military assistance to anti-Vietnamese guerrilla forces in Laos and major military assistance to anti-Vietnamese forces in Kampuchea. The PRC has imposed disabling burdens on Hanoi in an effort to keep Vietnam destabilized and to increase the costs to Moscow of sustaining a Soviet-Vietnamese entente.

The PRC's behavior in Southeast Asia is clearly dictated by its national interests, and it is unlikely that the United States has, or will have, much influence over Beijing's policy decisions. As long as it is in the interests of the leadership in Beijing, the PRC will oppose Vietnamese attempts to achieve "hegemony" in Southeast Asia. Should Hanoi decide to seek rapprochement with Beijing, perhaps as a consequence of some sort of accommodation between the USSR and the PRC, Washington will have little influence over Communist Chinese policy in the region, however much it enhances its cooperation with the leadership on the mainland of China.

In effect, the security interests shared by Washington and Beijing are either (1) geostrategic (along the long Sino-Soviet border) and consequently do not require cultivation, (2) beyond the capacity of U.S. policymakers to significantly influence, or (3) contingent on the Beijing leadership's interpretation of the PRC's national interests. There is very little that U.S. policymakers could do with regard to the PRC that would materially affect U.S. security interests in the region.

As long as Washington's relations with Beijing remain "normal," enhanced cooperation between the two nations will probably not significantly further U.S. security interests in East Asia. The PRC will resist the Soviet Union as long as it is in its national interests to do so. The Soviet Union will maintain its military deployments along the Sino-Soviet border for the foreseeable future, and consequently Beijing will continue to share that security concern with the United States. Enhanced cooperation will not significantly increase those shared interests, nor will it materially augment any security benefits the United States has already received.

Aside from their immediate anti-Soviet concerns, Beijing and Washington have remarkably few "parallel interests" in East Asia. Their security interests are "parallel" only in some relatively specific areas, and there are a number of locales where those interests might someday clash. As a case in point, the PRC supports North Korea's claim against South Korea. Officially, Beijing supports Pyongyang's insistence on the withdrawal of U.S. troops from the Korean peninsula. The Democratic People's Republic of Korea is one of the main recipients of Communist Chinese military aid. At the Twelfth Congress of the Chinese Communist Party in September 1982, party General Secretary Hu Yaobang gave North Korea pride of place before the PRC's other socialist friends, Romania and Yugoslavia. Beijing has announced that it will provide North Korea with air combat assets to offset the U.S. supply of F-16 interceptors to Seoul.[19] In its effort to prevent an increase in Soviet influence on the Korean peninsula, Beijing must continue to court Pyongyang. As a consequence, it is readily conceivable that Washington and Beijing, in the not-too-distant future, could find themselves involved in a major confrontation in Korea, to the detriment of U.S. security interests in Northeast Asia.[20]

The security interests of Washington and Beijing do, in fact, clash in the Taiwan Strait. Beijing has insisted upon its own interpretation of the Taiwan issue, and the threat of military adventure by the PRC against the Republic of China on Taiwan remains real. Any such adventure would adversely affect U.S. interests and destabilize the entire region.

At best, the "parallel" security interests of the United States and the PRC derive from the long-term opposition of both nations to the Soviet threat in East Asia. At worst, there are no mutual interests, only potential conflicts. Other than that, there are some fragile security interests that are "parallel" because of some short-term national interest of Beijing. For example, both the United States and the PRC—in the mid-1980s—seek to maintain peace and stability among the nations belonging to the Association of Southeast Asian Nations (ASEAN). To that end, Beijing has sought to cultivate normal diplomatic relations with Brunei, Indonesia, Malaysia, Singapore, the Philippines, and Thailand and has announced that it will not interfere in the internal politics of the several sovereign ASEAN states. The PRC has either radically reduced or terminated entirely its arms aid and financial contributions to the insurrectionary communist movements in those countries. Yet the Chinese Communist Party continues to extend "moral" and "political" support to fraternal communist parties in those states in accordance with what Chinese Communist functionaries identify as "dual-track" diplomacy: "proper" state-to-state relations and "revolutionary" party-to-party affiliations.

At the second session of the Fifth National People's Congress in 1978, the director of the Foreign Liaison Department of the Central Committee of the Chinese Communist Party maintained that "we make a sharp distinction between governmental and party matters. We support the struggles of our brother parties in foreign countries, but this does not interfere with friendly interchange with the government and peoples of those countries." On the one hand, this means that the authorities in Beijing "would certainly never interfere in the internal affairs of any such country in order to support . . . brother parties there." On the other hand, it also means that "our brother parties who are still engaged in underground struggles, such as in Thailand, Malaysia and the Philippines, . . . will have direct contact with the Foreign Liaison Department. Except in exceptional circumstances, diplomatic personnel abroad will have no direct contact with them."[21]

What all this seems to indicate is that Beijing will continue to maintain informal relations with communist insurgents but will avoid formal contacts. The implication seems to be that whenever doing so serves its purposes, Beijing will restore formal relations and revive arms shipments and financial support to communist guerrilla units in all and any of the countries of Southeast Asia. Although the PRC's material assistance to the communist insurgents in the ASEAN countries on mainland China's periphery has ceased, the authorities in Beijing reserve the option to recommence such assistance whenever they see fit to do so.

In the early 1980s, the PRC made propaganda facilities available for the clandestine communist parties of Southeast Asia. In April 1980, the "Voice of the Malay Revolution," broadcasting from within southern China, carried congratulatory messages to the Communist Party of Malaysia from the communist parties of Burma, the Philippines, Indonesia, and Thailand as well as a lengthy statement by the leaders of the Communist Party of Malaysia. In May 1980, the Communist Party of Indonesia broadcast a virulent attack on the government of Indonesia from southern China. It is clear that even though its material assistance has apparently ceased, Beijing is keeping open its options. The consequence is that the governments of Indonesia and Malaysia entertain grave suspicions concerning the benignity of Beijing's effort to establish "normal" relations with them.[22]

The nations of Southeast Asia find little consolation in the fact that the PRC has terminated its material assistance to insurrectionary communist parties within their borders. Beijing's continued provision of military support to insurgents in Burma, irrespective of that country's long-established "normal" diplomatic relations with the PRC, is an example of unprincipled interference. The PRC's logistic, military, and political support of the bestial Khmer Rouge regime in Kampuchea, its armed invasion of Vietnam in February 1979, and its continued support of armed insurgents in Burma, Laos, and Kampuchea are seen by Southeast Asian nations as portents for the future, even if, in the short run, most of these initiatives have succeeded in containing an aggressive Vietnam and preventing an expansion of Soviet influence in the region. Beijing does not hesitate to use military force in the pursuit of what it considers to be its national interests, and its past record and present policies suggest to at least some of the nations in ASEAN that the PRC constitutes as much of a threat to their security as does the Soviet Union.

As we shall see, the potential for conflict in the South China Sea between the PRC and the nations of ASEAN contributes to those fears. For the United States those potential conflicts cast a long shadow over future U.S.-PRC relations. The fact is that the present strategic relationship between the two countries is strictly tactical[23] and does not promise long-term security to either the littoral or the insular neighbors of the PRC.

Beijing has done little, if anything, to contain Soviet initiatives in Southeast Asia, even though containment is in the interests of both the United States and the PRC. Chinese aggressiveness against Vietnam has, in fact, driven Hanoi closer to Moscow, allowing the USSR to exploit Vietnam's susceptibilities. As a consequence, the noncommunist nations of Southeast Asia find themselves not only burdened by the Soviet presence but threatened by Beijing's unpredictable behavior. It is difficult to determine whether and how enhanced cooperation between Washington and Beijing would alter those circumstances.

Beijing has made it clear that it does not seek enhanced cooperation with Washington in international affairs. The PRC has denounced U.S. foreign policy in Central America, the Caribbean, South Africa, and the Middle East. Beijing's continued support for the PLO, as well as its denunciations of Israel, directly conflict with Washington's security policies. Only in Africa north of the Limpopo River has Communist China provided aid, both military and economic (the latter in very limited quantities), in an effort to counter Soviet influence.

On the basis of these evident realities, in the mid-1980s most U.S. policy analysts are engaged in what can only be characterized as a "demythologizing" of the notion that the PRC can provide any further security benefits to the United States vis-à-vis the Soviet Union—that is, in addition to those obvious in the early 1970s.[24] If enhanced cooperation between Washington and Beijing includes the sale of lethal military equipment to the People's Republic of China (as seems to be the case), it will do little, if anything, to alter the balance of forces along the Sino-Soviet border, but it might very well disturb the tenuous balance in the Taiwan Strait and enable Beijing to supply advanced weaponry to the communist regime in North Korea—to the detriment of overall U.S. security interests. Many of the PRC's noncommunist neighbors have good reason to fear a better-armed and more mobile Communist Chinese military.[25]

The People's Republic of China is not in a position, nor does it have the capability, to significantly influence the military balance between the anti-Soviet coalition and the USSR. The Communist Chinese authorities are fully aware of the PLA's war-fighting disabilities with respect to the Soviet forces deployed along the shared border and are cognizant of how little can be done, in the short term, to redress those disabilities. Both Beijing and Moscow know that as a consequence, the PRC would join the anti-Soviet coalition in the event of an armed conflict with the USSR only if mainland China were under direct attack. Therefore, to deter Soviet military adventure in East Asia, Washington will have to steer a confederational alliance of noncommunist states. It can hardly count on the support of the PRC.

Beijing has made it eminently clear that it does not seek closer strategic ties with the anti-Soviet coalition. The PRC is content to allow the United States to continue to provide an effective counterweight to Soviet conventional and nonconventional firepower. This has enabled Beijing to reduce its military expenditures, in real terms, and to assign the modernization of its armed forces the lowest priority in its developmental program.

The security association between the United States and the PRC is one of mutual tactical convenience. The very existence of the PRC complicates Soviet military planning. The PRC profits from the forward deployment of U.S. armed forces in the West Pacific. Enhanced cooperation would contribute very little to the prevailing tactical arrangements and might very well complicate U.S. deterrence strategy.[26]

Economic Interests

With the dwindling of enthusiasm for a security relationship between the United States and the PRC, the advocates of enhanced cooperation between the two nations have turned their attention to the benefits potentially to be gained from increased trade and investment opportunities. There have been suggestions that the "China market" will provide incalculable bounty to U.S. industry and agriculture. As has been indicated, trade between the United States and the PRC increased from a scant $4.9 million in 1971 to about $5.5 billion in 1984. Between 1971 and 1982, the two nations exchanged about $22 billion in goods and services, and the United States enjoyed a favorable trade balance of approximately $8 billion. At a time when the United States is suffering some of the largest trade deficits in its history, such a surplus is not insignificant.

Beijing has indicated an interest in the annual purchase of about 6 million tons of U.S. grain. There has been talk in the United States of a $20 billion investment in the establishment of a nuclear industry in the PRC at a time when the U.S. nuclear industry literally finds itself without a domestic market. The PRC's drive for the offshore development of its oil reserves has kindled expectations, among foreigners, of $75 billion dollars of profitable investments in recovery projects. Since 1979, 33 foreign companies have undertaken seismic surveys of offshore geological formations and have bid for contract rights to recover an estimated 5 billion tons of oil reserves. Between 1980 and 1984, those companies drilled 42 exploratory wells, each requiring an investment of about $4–10 million, depending on the depth of the water column on the continental shelf. Arco, Esso, Occidental Petroleum, and Chevron have committed themselves to the construction of offshore drilling platforms, each of which requires an average outlay of about $50 million.

Along the entire coast of Communist China, the Beijing authorities have established special economic zones in which foreign joint-venture capital and direct equity investment are allowed special access. At first, four such zones were established in Guangdong and Fujian provinces. Subsequently, fourteen others were established in cities that had served as "treaty ports" in the late nineteenth and early twentieth centuries. By 1981, the first four zones had attracted about $1.7 billion in foreign investment, and by mid-1984 188 joint ventures had been established involving a total foreign investment of about $515 million. Typical of such joint ventures is the Beijing Jeep Corporation, established in 1983 by the Beijing Automobile Plant together with the American Motors Corporation. The U.S. company will provide the technology for the production of modified Jeeps to be assembled with Chinese labor. The investment of $16 million by the American Motors Corporation will allow that company to acquire a 49 percent interest in the Beijing Jeep Corporation.

These figures give an indication of the expanded trade and investment relations between the United States and the People's Republic of China. But they are not particularly informative unless they are placed in some perspective. Basic to that perspective is the fact that since the early 1970s, U.S. trade with Asian nations has exceeded that with the nations of the European Common Market, and in the mid-1980s exceeds it by about 50 percent. Trade with the nations in the Pacific Basin now totals $137 billion and constitutes about 30 percent of all U.S. foreign trade, disaggregated as follows: Japan, 45 percent; the Republic of China on Taiwan, about 12 percent; the Republic of Korea, about 9 percent; Hong Kong, abut 7 percent; Australia and New Zealand, about 6 percent; the ASEAN nations, about 13 percent; Southern Asia, about 4 percent; and the People's Republic of China, only 3 percent.[27]

The PRC will probably never be a major trading partner of the United States. Ever since its founding, the PRC has committed itself to the principle of economic self-reliance and has maintained imports at a fairly stable level of about 5–8 percent of its gross domestic product, even though it has sustained a high level of domestic capital formation (approximately 25 percent of total GNP since 1949).[28] In that respect, the "New China" has continued the traditional trading policies of the "old

China." At no time since the first contacts were made between the United States and China has U.S. trade with that nation ever exceeded 2 percent of the total foreign trade of the United States. Irrespective of the fascination the "vast China market" has had for generations of Americans, China has never been a major market or investment supplement for U.S. agriculture or industry.

Why this should be so is explained by a number of factors—among them the structure of the PRC's economy and the policy constraints imposed by the Communist Chinese leadership. In early September 1982, Chairman Hu Yaobang made his government's position eminently clear. Communist China will "actively import advanced technologies" that will be "helpful to the technical transformation of [the PRC's] own enterprises" in order to sustain its own "self-reliant stand." The entire purpose "in expanding economic and technological exchanges with foreign countries [is] to enhance [the PRC's] ability to be self-reliant and to promote . . . the development of [its] national economy." Hu added, "We must refrain from indiscriminate import of equipment, and particularly of consumer goods that can be manufactured and supplied at home. . . . In no circumstances must we forget that capitalist countries and enterprises will never change their capitalist nature simply because they have economic and technological exchanges with us."[29] In effect, the trade relations of the PRC with foreign countries are, and will continue to be, tactical; they are not motivated by any desire to foster "interdependency."

Huan Hsiang, vice-president of the PRC Academy of Social Science, reiterated essentially the same policy principles in April 1983: "China's industries cannot be based upon export trade; our production must be aimed at domestic needs and not foreign ones. . . . Economic progress must be based on self-reliance." Huan anticipated that the PRC's export trade would amount to no more than about 8–10 percent of the gross national product—and even that would be difficult to attain, sustain, and justify.[30]

Because of these policy constraints, the foreign trade of the PRC can be expected to increase at a rate of about 5–10 percent per annum in the remainder of this century—a rate that does not suggest that Communist China will ever become a major trading partner of the United States. The principle of self-reliance requires an ongoing development of import substitutes as the Communist Chinese economy grows and domestic capital investment increases. As domestic capital investment increases, the PRC will gradually reduce its economic dependence on foreign nations by adjusting its import schedule in order to mainain a fairly constant ratio of imports to total domestic output. The PRC will hew closely to the tradition of self-reliance as its economy modernizes, despite the short-run strategy of purchasing and borrowing from the West.

The objectives of the foreign trade policy of the People's Republic of China are: (1) one time importation of capital goods that embody advanced technology the PRC does not possess and that are required for its industrialization and modernization; (2) to compensate for any shortfall in domestic supplies; (3) to continue its long-term policy of self-reliance; and (4) to further its political objectives. The first two policy goals are currently contributing to an increase in the PRC's foreign trade. To what extent they will do so in the future is difficult to forecast. During the first phase of enthusiasm for the "opening to the West," it was estimated that $600 billion in capital investment would be required to produce the output scheduled for production by 1985. That would have necessitated not only the commitment of up to as much as 25 percent of the PRC's gross national product to capital investment, but the borrowing of large sums from abroad to close the domestic savings-investment gap. It would also have resulted in large trade deficits. By 1981, the estimate had been reduced (causing considerable embarrassment to Beijing and distress to those foreign firms that had signed contracts under the original plan) to $250 billion in capital investment over a five-year period, along with $80–100 billion in foreign credit.

By 1982, the PRC was a net importer of capital by a large margin and had received substantial grant aid and concessional loans from international financial institutions and numerous capitalist countries—the United States being prominent among them. About 25 percent of the concessional loans received by Beijing from the World Bank are actually funded by the United States. Washington has provided the PRC with direct economic assistance, and the U.S. Export-Import Bank has advanced more than $100 million to finance U.S. exports to Communist China. Even the grants and gifts the PRC has received from the United Nations and its agencies have been funded in substantial part by the United States. By the mid-1980s, U.S. Public Law 480 had been passed, approving food aid for the PRC, and the PRC has achieved "most-favored nation" status. There is also talk that 15–20 percent of Communist China's exports will soon be allowed free entry into the United States under the provisions of the Generalized System of Preferences.

Thus, whatever benefits Americans receive from U.S.-PRC trade are being subsidized, to a considerable extent, by U.S. taxpayers. Even the surplus enjoyed by the United States in its trade with the PRC would have to be discounted against the sizable "invisible" capital transfers that are the consequence of U.S. tariff exemptions, concessional loans, credits, and grants, as well as the money inflow resulting from the increasing U.S. tourist traffic to mainland China.[31] In 1984, U.S. trade with the PRC constituted about 1 percent of total U.S. foreign trade—hardly an amount that would have significant impact on the well-being of Americans.

The bulk of the PRC's future imports from the United States will probably be agricultural products (wheat, corn, raw cotton, soybeans, and soybean oil), high-technology items and energy-related capital goods (computers, microprocessors, data communications equipment, and oil- and gas-drilling ancillaries). Little foreign exchange will be spent on the importation of consumer goods, since Beijing's policy is to restrict such imports in order to encourage the growth of domestic import substitution industries.

The authorities in Beijing are primarily interested in the acquisition of advanced technology. The United States has been more generous in supplying such technology to the PRC than it has been to any other communist country. For the purposes of technology-related sales, the PRC has been categorized as a "friendly nonaligned nation," allowing Beijing to acquire technology denied the Soviet Union and its allies. In 1982, approximately 2,000 applications for licenses involving technology transfers to the PRC were approved by U.S. oversight agencies. By 1984, the number had escalated to 5,000.

The problem that attends such sales is that at least some of that technology has military applications. Dual-use technology (having both civilian and military applications) has already been supplied in the form of radar, communications, and surveillance equipment, as well as com- puters. The sale of antitank and antiaircraft weapons has been approved and preparations are being made to sell jet engines for fighter aircraft. Although none of this will alter the military balance along the Sino-Soviet border, there are foreseeable circumstances in which the PRC could utilize such technological enhancements of its armed forces in attacks against its littoral or insular neighbors—to the detriment of U.S. security interests. Such enhancements could very well provide the People's Lib- eration Army with a measure of advantage that might dispose Beijing to initiate a military adventure in Northeast, Southeast, or South Asia.

Technology-related sales to the PRC might generate serious prob- lems in a number of areas. One of the major markets for potential U.S. sales is energy related. Whereas investment for coal extraction and the construction of hydroelectric facilities in the PRC is relatively in- nocuous, investment in, and technology transfers to foster the growth of, Communist China's nuclear industry would bring a number of problems in their train.

U.S. involvement in the PRC's nuclear power program will make the United States at least partially responsible for seeing to it that Beijing conforms to international agreements on nuclear nonproliferation. That responsibility could be onerous. As long as the United States did not contribute to the development of the PRC's nuclear industry, Beijing, as a nonsignatory to the nuclear nonproliferation treaty, was free to deal with the issue of nuclear technology transfers as it saw fit. Once the U.S. had become party to the PRC's nuclear undertakings, Washington assumed oversight responsibilities.

Should the United States promote the growth of the PRC's nuclear industry, the close military and security relationships between the People's Republic of China and Pakistan would become particularly troublesome. Pakistan has long been identified as a "potential proliferator"—a nation with nuclear power capabilities on the threshold of manufacturing nuclear weapons. Its long-standing security relationship with the PRC has become increasingly intimate as a result of the Soviet invasion of Afghanistan and Moscow's apparent readiness to supply Indian armed forces with the most advanced weapon systems.

In the mid-1980s, Islamabad's intentions concerning the development of a nuclear weapons capability remain unclear, and both the United States government and the International Atomic Energy Agency maintain that the international inspection procedures of Pakistan's nuclear facilities are incomplete and ineffective. Pakistan has a fairly complex nuclear program that includes research. Its power reactors are supplied by a stock of plutonium that is estimated to have been 300 kilograms in 1980. Although its nuclear industrial infrastructure is fragile, Pakistan's nuclear equipment (mostly of Canadian origin) is sophisticated. It would not require a great deal of assistance from Beijing to provide nuclear arms capabilities to Islamabad. The Pakistani military has possessed delivery systems suitable for nuclear explosive devices since the early 1980s.[32] Pakistan's nuclear potential clearly exceeds that considered optimum for peaceful uses as estimated by the International Atomic Energy Agency.[33]

Although Beijing has shown restraint in the transfer of nuclear weapons technology, and considerable flexibility in the recent past with regard to arms control, its long opposition to the superpowers' nuclear weapons monopoly troubles those concerned with nonconventional arms proliferation. Most of Beijing's arms control postures are explicable in terms of its own perceived security needs, and it is certainly plausible that should its interests recommend such a course, the PRC might transfer nuclear arms technology to Pakistan.[34]

Beijing's position on nuclear arms control remains clouded. The PRC has acknowledged that any serious international agreement on nuclear weapons proliferation will probably require some method of "conclusive verification," including on-site inspection, to ensure compliance by participants. On the other hand, Beijing has also insisted that such procedures not be allowed to violate "national sovereignty"—which suggests the imposition of extensive constraints on effective inspection and verification of compliance. How the United States can confirm adherence by the PRC to any nonproliferation agreement is difficult to determine.

Should Beijing decide to transfer nuclear arms technology to Pakistan after collaborating with the United States in the development of its own nuclear industry, Washington would find itself embroiled in a number of complex problems. The United States would then be at least partly responsible for the nuclear arming of Pakistan—a Pakistan that would then constitute a potential threat in South Asia.

Pakistan is one of those developing countries that is "coup prone," having suffered at least three successful military coups since the mid-1950s (in 1958, 1969, and 1977). In such circumstances, the interaction between external security requirements, weak technological control, and tenuous political stability, influenced by competition among military factions, creates a heightened danger of unauthorized access to nuclear weapons, reckless deployment practices, and surreptitious nuclear weapons transfers, possibly leading to inadvertent or politically unintended nuclear risks.[35] Israel, the major U.S. security partner in the Middle East, is particularly apprehensive about the possible development of a Pakistani "Islamic bomb" and the possibility that one of Pakistan's military or political factions, after a successful coup, might contemplate the provision of nuclear weapons to anti-Israel nations.

If the United States, which is charged with some responsibility for oversight, were to promote the development of the Communist Chinese nuclear industry, it would be confronted by the kinds of problems whose solution has proven difficult in the past. Although the U.S. nuclear industry will doubtlessly continue to press the foreign policy establishment in Washington to support nuclear technology transfers to the People's Republic of China, it is clear that such transfers might not ultimately be in the best interests of the United States. Any economic benefits that might accrue to the United States from such enhanced cooperation with the PRC would not be cost free.

The same can be said about the profits expected to result from the involvement of U.S. oil companies in mainland China's offshore oil exploration and retrieval. This is acknowledged to be an expensive and risky undertaking. Moreover, Communist Chinese legislation governing joint ventures is so new (having been promulgated as recently as 1981) that its interpretation remains a matter of considerable dispute. Both general tax laws and contractual obligations have been subject to extensive revision and reinterpretation even in the course of their implementation. Not only do demands for training programs for Chinese personnel increase and currency exchange rates arbitrarily set by the Beijing authorities fluctuate, but many of the PRC's statutes governing investment and joint ventures remain "secret"—unavailable to foreign investors whose interests may be directly involved.[36]

More important in terms of the general interest of the United States is the fact that some of the offshore exploratory contract blocks awarded to foreign oil companies by Beijing overlap with the territorial claims made by other nations in the region. A contract block awarded to Mobil Oil, for example, borders on the waters of the Paracel Islands, which, although garrisoned by PRC forces, are claimed by the Socialist Republic of Vietnam. The Republic of China on Taiwan also claims the islands located 220 miles southeast of Hainan Island in the South China Sea. Until 1973, these islands were garrisoned by forces of the PRC and South Vietnam. In late 1973, when Saigon announced that it was granting foreigners oil exploration rights to its offshore shelf, Beijing reacted by sending a combined amphibious force to seize the islands. The United States, which was then deeply involved in the fighting in continental Southeast Asia, chose not to respond to Saigon's call for assistance.

After Hanoi's forces conquered South Vietnam, Hanoi asserted a claim to the Paracel islands—and has since repeated its claim to sovereign control. Beijing has responded by reinforcing the forces holding the Paracels and has refused to negotiate concerning islands it considers to be a "sovereign part of the motherland."

The PRC has awarded Amoco Oil a contract block to the west of Hainan Island that borders on waters contested by Vietnam. Although both the PRC and Vietnam agreed, in 1974, that a large area in the Tonkin Gulf between Hainan and the coast of Vietnam would not be developed by either country, Beijing claims that the borders of the region are not accurately defined. Hanoi has resisted Beijing's claims, and in July 1979, the Vietnamese fired on two Western-owned supply vessels in the contested zone. In March 1982, Communist Chinese and Vietnamese gunboats clashed in the area.[37] In June 1983, a Vietnamese naval vessel forced a French-operated oil-drilling rig to move eastward, out of the maritime region over which it claims jurisdiction.

A contract block awarded by the PRC to Phillips Petroleum encompasses the Pratas Islands (which are claimed by the Republic of China on

Taiwan) and the contested waters surrounding the Spratly Islands—about 100 islands, reefs, and shoals that extend across an area of about 7,000 square miles. The Central Spratly Group, the major concentration of islands, lies about 150 miles west of Palawan Province in the Philippines. Both the Republic of China on Taiwan and Vietnam lay claim to the entire Spratly group.

In 1968, the Republic of the Philippines occupied six of the Spratly Islands and still maintains a marine garrison and a complement of military aircraft there. Since 1976, the Philippines has been developing an oil field off the Reed Bank to the northwest of the Central Spratly Group, despite the protests of both Beijing and Hanoi. In 1983, the government of the Philippines announced that any "offensive action" by any of the claimants against the islands identified as national territory would be considered "an assault against the Republic of the Philippines."

Hanoi's armed forces occupy seven of the Spratly Islands located about 120 miles southwest of the Central Spratly Group. The Vietnamese have constructed hardened bunkers and an airstrip for the use of military aircraft on these islands. The Vietnamese forces are substantial, in large part because the Soviets have provided military supplies, as well as MiG fighters, *Foxtrot* attack submarines, and *Peyta*- and *Koni*-class frigates. As recently as April 1984, Hanoi affirmed its intention to "consolidate the Spratly archipelago into a stalwart steel fortress to defend the fatherland's sovereignty."[38]

For its part, the Republic of China on Taiwan maintains a military force on Taiping Island in the Spratlys and has communicated its intention to defend that island. Beijing has reaffirmed its determination to establish control over the entire Spratly archipelago and has also announced its intention to augment its blue water naval capability in the region, thus making the South Sea Fleet its largest. In early May 1984, a PRC naval squadron composed of two frigates, a troop ship, and a replenishment vessel circumnavigated the Spratly Islands and then undertook an amphibious landing exercise on Hainan Island. The PRC has constructed several harbors and a naval base in the Paracels to the northwest of the Spratly Islands. The naval base, built on Woody Island, is capable of supporting the activities of both frigates and missile-armed fast-attack craft, and can also serve as a staging area for a campaign against the Spratlys. In late May 1984, the Sixth National People's Congress, meeting in Beijing, proposed the incorporation of the Spratlys into the Hainan Island administrative region.

The result of all this has been the creation of a very hazardous situation in the South China Sea. The People's Republic of China has laid claim to all the islands, cays, sandbars and reefs in the region, and although Beijing has insisted that it is prepared to negotiate the conflicting claims, it will neither negotiate with Taipei (whose government it does not recognize) nor Hanoi (toward whom it harbors intense hostility). In the mid-1970s, Beijing announced that it would negotiate with Manila concerning the Philippine claim to the Spratlys, but no such negotiations have taken place. Since the early 1970s, there have been more armed confrontations in the South China Sea than there have been negotiations.

The Soviet Union supports Vietnamese claims in the area for reasons other than the military relationship between the two nations. Free passage through the South China Sea is critical to the supply and maintenance of Soviet Far Eastern forces. The overland logistical infrastructure between the European Soviet Union and the Asiatic Soviet Union is still too frail to support the extensive military forces deployed in East Asia. Shipborne supplies are essential to Soviet deployments, and those supplies must transit the waters and choke points in the South China Sea.

Because of the region's importance to the Soviet Union, there has been a rapid escalation of Soviet naval and air activity out of Danang and Camranh Bay. By November 1983, Soviet Tu-16 Badger medium-range bombers were operating out of Vietnamese airfields, and in mid-1984, Vietnamese landing vessels and frigates, together with the Soviet amphibious assault ship *Alexandr Nikoleyev*, escorted by the carrier *Minsk*, practiced combined operations and assault landings south of Haiphong Harbor.

It seems evident that Moscow is prepared to support Hanoi's claims in the South China Sea because it is interested in controlling ship passage through that vital region. It maintains reconnaisance flights over the area and has strengthened those naval forces that would be employed to militarily defend Vietnamese claims.

In effect, U.S. oil companies, and companies in which Americans have investment, have become involved with the People's Republic of China in high-cost commitments in the South China Sea. Not only does extensive U.S. investment in the PRC's offshore oil exploration and retrieval involve considerable economic risk, it puts U.S. oil-drilling platforms, personnel, supply ships, and seismic survey vessels in harm's way in one of the most hotly contested regions of the world.

In the past, Washington has counseled U.S. oil companies not to undertake oil exploration in offshore areas that are contested. In the early 1970s, in response to Beijing's objections, the Department of State advised U.S. oil companies not to participate in seismic surveys and oil exploration off the coasts of Japan, South Korea, and Taiwan on the grounds that it entailed too much risk.[39] In the mid-1980s, however, U.S.

oil companies are deeply involved in Beijing's effort to deal with its energy crisis by exploiting the subsea resources located far out in the continental shelf in contested waters.

The discovery of offshore petroleum resources in the East and South China Seas ensures that the nations of East Asia will continue to compete for exploration and exploitation rights in the continental shelf. The Republic of Korea, the Republic of China on Taiwan, and Japan have overlapping territorial claims with the People's Republic of China in the Sea of Japan and the East China Sea. In the South China Sea the conflicting claims are more complicated. Because of the increasing petroleum needs of the developing economies of ASEAN nations, there is a high probability of unintended or intended conflict over exploration and subsea oil and gas extraction rights in the disputed areas. Indonesia has economic zone boundary conflicts with Vietnam, Malaysia, and the People's Republic of China. Thailand has maritime claims conflicts with Vietnam, Malaysia, and Kampuchea.

Malaysia, Indonesia, and Thailand have negotiated agreements on maritime and territorial rights. Indonesia and Malaysia have reached an accord with Vietnam. However, Beijing appears reluctant to enter into any negotiation that might ultimately prejudice its maximum maritime claims. The U.S. involvement with the PRC in offshore exploration and exploitation lends credibility to Beijing's claims, although official U.S. recognition of those claims might result in a direct conflict between Washington and the other claimants in the region. Moreover, the United States has a mutual defense treaty with the Republic of the Philippines, and any conflict in the Spratlys might result in invocation of the response clauses of that agreement. The United States remains concerned with the security of the Republic of China on Taiwan, and it is unclear what Washington's reaction to a PRC attack on the Spratlys might be.

How extensively the United States should cooperate with the PRC in technology transfers, joint ventures, nuclear industry development, and offshore oil exploration and retrieval in the South China Sea is very difficult to determine. Certainly such cooperation includes more than simple business calculations—and the more that cooperation is "enhanced," the more complex the calculations become.

Even if U.S. cooperation with the People's Republic of China in these areas did not entail complicated security problems, it is problematic (1) whether Beijing will be able to attract sufficient foreign exchange to allow such investments and undertakings to continue, and (2) whether Beijing will allow U.S. companies to pursue economic opportunities on the mainland of China without making the United States government pay excessive political costs. Unless the People's Republic of China can sustain an appropriate level of export sales to produce the requisite foreign exchange to pay for technology transfers and capital goods imports, its planned purchases of those items from the West will have to be curtailed. The authorities in Beijing are committed to a conservative borrowing policy. They do not intend to allow the People's Republic of China to become heavily indebted to "capitalist" institutions. Moreover, Beijing has always attached political conditions to its foreign trade arrangements. Whenever a trading partner has failed to meet what the PRC has considered to be the proper conditions of reciprocity, Beijing has extracted political costs.

Communist China is a marginal supplier to the advanced Western countries. The top five categories of items sold by the PRC to the United States, in order of value, are textiles, footwear, rugs, artwork, and antiques. None of these items is important to the U.S. economy, all can be purchased at equivalent cost almost anywhere, and their demand elasticity, in general, is low. Most developing countries ship similar items to the United States, and PRC products are not particularly competitive. Irrespective of these considerations, Beijing is attempting to increase its share of the U.S. market in an effort to reduce its trade deficits. Unfortunately, Beijing is seeking a larger share of the U.S. market at a time when the U.S. textile industry is languishing.

About 18 percent of U.S. textile industry workers are unemployed in the mid-1980s, and the short-term prospects for that industry are not good. When Washington attempted to limit PRC textile sales to the United States and to maintain them at the level allowed other favored developing countries, Beijing retaliated by restricting its purchase of agricultural commodities. Until the United States relented, Beijing purchased from alternative suppliers. Pressure from U.S. farm groups, and a desire by the U.S. government to sustain what were considered important bilateral trade relations, resulted in an upward adjustment of the PRC's textile quota. Groups representing the U.S. textile industry then demanded more tariff controls.

The entire issue of Communist Chinese exports to the United States will doubtlessly continue to be a source of conflict. U.S. industries, finding themselves under price competition from PRC imports, can always argue that the prices for Communist Chinese commodities are arbitrarily and artificially low and that this amounts to unfair competition and international "dumping." It is quite possible that the prices fixed by the export authorities in the PRC only remotely reflect production costs for export items, since rent and interest charges generally are not included in those prices. Nor are the depreciation rates of agricultural assets counted as part of production costs. (Depreciation rates on fixed assets are notoriously low throughout the socialist economy of the PRC.) Moreover, since the domestic profitability of plant in the PRC does not necessarily enter into the calculations of the export authorities, export prices can be set artificially low in order to earn necessary foreign exchange. Appeals by U.S. companies against such practices can be based on the antimarket disruption and antidumping provisions of the Trade Act of 1974.

It is unlikely that the PRC will be able to export its labor-intensive commodities in sufficient quantities to maintain a trade balance that will allow it to meet its capital goods import needs. For a time it was argued that in the near future the PRC would become a major exporter of crude petroleum and could thereby earn the foreign exchange required to sustain its foreign purchases. But that appears to have been a forlorn hope. The comparisons, frequently made in the early 1970s, of the PRC's oil recovery potential with that of Saudi Arabia and other major oil producers were grossly exaggerated. According to most subsequent estimates, the PRC's oil exports will approach zero by the end of the 1980s and mainland China will be a net oil importer in the 1990s.[40] From all available indications, the PRC's oil exports will not cause a significant relaxation of mainland China's foreign-exchange constraints. To finance the large-scale foreign purchases the PRC's modernization drive requires will necessitate far more international borrowing than the conservative financial policies of the current leadership seem to countenance.

Ultimately, Beijing's political decisions will determine how the PRC manages its foreign trade. But whatever those decisions, foreign trade will be restricted largely to the import of technology and capital goods. Political considerations and effective demand will severely limit the importation of commodity goods for the domestic market. As a consequence, it is unlikely that U.S.-PRC trade, in the foreseeable future, will exceed trade between the United States and the Republic of China on Taiwan. Even if U.S.-PRC trade should triple by the turn of the century (an unlikely prospect), it would still constitute only approximately 2 percent of total U.S. foreign trade.

Beijing has occasionally chosen not to purchase from U.S. suppliers for reasons other than buyers' preferences, prices, or quality. In the early 1980s, Beijing increased its purchases in Western Europe by almost 40 percent; its imports from France and Great Britain increased 127 percent and 117 percent, respectively. One reason for doing so was to force the United States to reconsider the restrictions that had been imposed on Communist Chinese textile imports as part of Washington's effort to avoid market disruption and to reduce high unemployment in the textile-producing regions of the United States. Similar behavior by the PRC can be anticipated in the future and may be of more strategic significance. As mentioned, the involvement of U.S. oil companies in the PRC's petroleum recovery program in the South China Sea and the sharing of nuclear technology with the PRC may have political and strategic costs that are not yet fully ascertainable.

Whatever the ultimate costs, U.S. trade with the PRC is predicated on continued political stability in that nation. Washington assumes that the leadership that follows octogenarian Deng Xiaoping will not stage another Cultural Revolution, Great Leap Forward, or even a series of lesser campaigns in the foreseeable future. Unfortunately, the People's Republic of China has never in its entire history known such tranquility. The inevitable struggle for succession that will follow Deng's demise will doubtlessly cause new upheavals and result in "reversals of verdicts." Without a strong consensus among the leadership of the People's Republic of China—and there is evidence suggesting that such a consensus does not now exist—the mainland Chinese may once again, in the near future, experience economically disruptive domestic turmoil. The costs to U.S. business, not to speak of U.S. strategic and political costs, could be great. Whether "enhanced" economic cooperation between the United States and the PRC will limit that damage is difficult to predict.

POLITICAL INTERESTS

So many interacting variables influence political outcomes in Communist China that prediction is extremely difficult at best. Several conclusions can be drawn, however. It is very likely that the political system of the People's Republic of China, for the foreseeable future and barring cataclysmic developments, will remain bureaucratic—not only because of the long and deeply ingrained tradition of Chinese bureaucratic rule but because of the requirements of a command economy. Currently, it appears that the PRC has exhausted the "easy" ways to achieve economic growth. It is clear that returns are diminishing relative to investment. Virtually all of the prime arable soil in mainland China is already under cultivation, and per capita availability is declining because of population pressure and the widespread conversion of farm land to nonagricultural uses. Other economies subject to such constraints have turned to export trade, an option the authorities in Beijing currently exclude—and one that would be difficult for the PRC to pursue for reasons that have already been briefly considered. Moreover, should the PRC attempt to enter the international markets as a major exporter of labor-intensive commodities, it would find itself competing with other developing countries that were at a similar stage of economic development—a situation that would jeopardize its effort to be a leader of the Third World.

What this suggests is that the PRC, because of prevailing constraints, will be forced to continue its economic strategy of requiring high rates of domestic savings to provide the funds needed for increased investments—and that will only result in declining yields. The state will assume the responsibility of increasing savings and mobilizing investments. The required rate of saving will probably require a continuation of restrictions on consumption. That, in turn, will require a renewal of extensive propaganda campaigns to dampen consumer demand and convince the population to remain content with modest, and gradual, increments in the level of consumption. Controlled consumption, the inculcation of a work and sacrifice ethic, and the marshaling of resources and mobilization of investments for exacting projects, as well as the identification and suppression of dissidence, all require an elaborate state apparatus. Consequently, it is unlikely that any policy that attempts to limit state power will be very extensive or permanent.[41] It is also clear that control of that apparatus will remain securely in the hands of the Chinese Communist Party. In the mid-1980s, both "liberalism" and the pursuit of "abstract democracy" are deemed "counterrevolutionary," and the "democratic faction," so prominent in the late 1970s, has disappeared.[42] Although any institutional changes made in the government of the PRC and in the Chinese Communist Party will probably result in more clearly defined and less concentrated power, the state system of Communist China will continue to bear more resemblance to that of the Soviet Union than to any other alternative.[43]

As a communist power, the People's Republic of China, whatever its economic relations with the West, will assume an international posture predicated on some variant of Marxism-Leninism. Not only will its foreign policy be "independent," but the PRC will follow "a long-term strategy"[44] that is intended to defeat "imperialism and hegemonism" and to contribute to the realization of "communism . . . throughout the world."[45]

The authorities in Beijing fully intend to continue their trade and investment relations with the West, but they will continue to perceive imperialism, whose foremost representative is the United States, as one of the "main forces" jeopardizing the future of the world community and impeding progress toward communism. Building on the Leninist convictions that inspired Mao, the intellectual leadership of the People's Republic of China maintains that one of the major "contradictions" in the modern world is that between the imperialist countries and the "large number of developing countries" that remain "fettered . . . within the capitalist sphere." The industrial democracies, according to this argument, have "caused the greatest damage to the national economic interests of the developing countries." They have imposed a modern form of colonialism on the developing countries "and continue to make developing countries serve as sources of raw materials, markets for sales and sites for investment, in order to attain monopoly profits far in excess of what they would gain domestically."[46]

For the political leadership in Beijing, this translates into a foreign policy that supports the demands made by the less-developed countries—demands often made at the expense of the United States—which are also supported by the Soviet Union.[47] In effect, given its aspiration to be a leader of the Third World, Beijing will pursue its interests at the expense of the United States. This has been reflected in the voting record of the PRC in the General Assembly of the United Nations. During the meetings of the 38th U.N. General Assembly (September to December 1983), for example, the People's Republic of China voted against the United States about 80 percent of the time—only marginally less than did the Soviet Union, which recorded opposing votes 87 percent of the time.[48]

Deng Xiaoping had provided the rationale for this position as early as 1974, when he developed themes that Mao had included in his "anti-imperialist" doctrine of the "Three Worlds." At that time, Deng perceived the developing countries as one of the principal forces destined to defeat "world capitalism." As a consequence, he committed the PRC to support "the actions of the developing countries to bring all foreign capital, and particularly 'transnational corporations,' under their control and management, up to and including nationalization. . . . The Chinese Government and people," he went on, "warmly endorse and firmly support all just propositions made by Third World countries . . . [that] demand that the present extremely unequal international economic relations be changed."[49]

Irrespective of the PRC's involvement with "international imperialism" since that time, the same themes have been repeated and are still being heard in the mid-1980s. How secure that leaves foreign investors in the PRC is difficult to determine. The authorities in Beijing are apparently convinced that the ambition of capitalists to seek profits everywhere is not dampened by even the most candid recitation of potential risk. The PRC anticipates that Americans will invest in Communist China no matter what. The ideologues of the People's Republic of China argue that "the closer imperialism approaches destruction the more it struggles for survival."[50] The U.S. imperialists will continue to thrash about searching out investment opportunities and trade outlets—even in those nations that are committed to the destruction of capitalism.

By the beginning of 1983, Beijing's "independent foreign policy" had taken on overtones of opposition to the foreign policies of the United States. Official foreign policy statements had begun to refer to the United States once again as a "hegemonic" and "imperialist" power and to cite instances of U.S. arrogance whenever it criticized the arrogance of the Soviet Union. In late 1982, Beijing had explicitly joined Moscow in opposing Washington's "support of Israeli aggression and the South African apartheid rule."[51] Beijing subsequently recited the PRC's objections to U.S. policy on the Korean peninsula, and in the Taiwan Strait, in Central America, in the Middle East, in Latin America, and in the Third World in general. Moreover, the authorities in Beijing now blame the increase in domestic political dissent, defections of mainland Chinese citizens to foreign countries, and even an accelerating crime rate at least in part on the PRC's contacts with the capitalist world. Restrictions are increasingly being imposed on contacts between PRC nationals and foreigners, and Chinese seeking educational opportunities in the industrial democracies are being more closely scrutinized than in the past.

None of this suggests that Beijing will alter its involvement with the West in the near term. It seems evident that it expects to gain much from its new multilateral connections. Such relations are necessary if the PRC is to strengthen itself sufficiently to satisfy its domestic needs as well as defend itself against any foreign encroachment.

Until the early 1970s, the leaders of Communist China attempted to avoid any sustained contact with the "bourgeois" West. A consequence was the flawed policy of self-reliance. The "pragmatists" who have succeeded the more doctrinaire Maoists now consider economic cooperation with the industrial democracies a prerequisite for the rapid modernization of the nations's economy and of its military forces. They are convinced that a determined government, led by a disciplined communist party, can avoid dependency and ideological corruption and can marshal the citizens of the People's Republic of China for the final struggle against hegemonism and inperialism.

Conclusions

The domestic and foreign policies of the People's Republic of China have been influenced by China's past as well as the imported Western anti-Western creed we identify with Marxism-Leninism. Like the rulers dynastic China, the leaders of Maoist and post-Maoist China have controlled the population through bureaucratic instrumentalities. The Chinese people are expected to exemplify the traditional virtures of obedience and discipline. It is difficult not to recognize the Confucian concept of "fraternal submission" in the subordination required by the "democratic centralism" of the Chinese Communist Party. The notion that rulers, possessed of wisdom augmented by the study of classical texts, merit the obedience of their subordinates and the common people was held not only by Mengzi and the neo-Confucians, but by the Maoist mandarins as well. The Maoist enthusiasm for mass mobilization and collective projects can be traced to the use of corvée labor and the tradition of state supervision of public works.

The Maoist and the post-Maoist state battens on the Chinese traditional political model, originally fashioned for a system that anticipated severely limited political participation. The contemporary communist variant of traditional population management techniques involves the participation of citizens, but only if their activities do not "impair the interests of the state, society and the collective." Under no circumstances will "hostile, anti-socialist elements be given any freedom." The post-Maoists allow popular participation in the political processes only under the supervision of the "leadership of the Party," which is inspired by the "truths" embodied in the "scientific theories of Marxism-Leninism and Mao Zedong Thought."[52] Like "old China," the "new China" will apparently be ruled by an exiguous leadership that is expected to attain wisdom by the conscientious study of classical texts.

In its external relations, Communist China has always been preoccupied with universalism. It perceives the world as an interdependent whole with a single doctrine of governance and organized by relationships that can be classified under a single system. Like dynastic China, Communist China sees itself as an actor in a cosmic moral drama that will determine the future of humanity.

For the Maoists and post-Maoists, the universal doctrine that explains the world and reveals its moral configurations, and on the basis of which the future of mankind can be predicted, is Marxism-Leninism. According to the Communist Chinese interpretation of Marxism-Leninism, the history of international politics is one of struggle: the imperialist powers attempt to impose their will on the weaker nations in the pursuit of profit, and the oppressed inevitably resist the oppressor. In this Manichaean worldview, imperialism is the embodiment of evil and "proletarian socialism" is the promise of virtue.

Communist China's preoccupation with imperialism is perfectly comprehensible, given its experience with the European powers during the nineteenth century. It is unfortunate that the preoccupation has now become a permanent feature of mainland China's political culture. The borrowing of concepts and language from Marxism-Leninism all but ensures that relations between the People's Republic of China and the nations of the "capitalist West" will remain fundamentally adversarial. The behaviors of the United States and other industrialized democracies will forever be "interpreted" by authorities in Beijing who are convinced that they "understand the essential nature of imperialism."

Since the inception of the Chinese Communist Party, "imperialism" has been the touchstone of its domestic and foreign policy. During the revolutionary struggle, their presumed relationship to "imperialism" determined the lot of the Chinese population. Beijing's official foreign policy has always been "anti-imperialist." Nonetheless, the PRC has, at various times, had relations with traditional monarchies, sheikhdoms, military juntas, and overtly anticommunist regimes. For the theoreticians in Beijing, such flexibility is part of historical and revolutionary "dialectics." Revolutionary struggle requires the flexibility that permits collaboration with those with whom one has a common interest, however temporary, in order to mobilize resistance against one's principal adversary. These tactical accommodations are dictated by the peculiarities of any given situation. As long as the United States was the principal adversary of "proletarian China," Beijing made common cause with a variety of political regimes—so long as those regimes were prepared to oppose U.S. imperialism.

When the Soviet Union became "social imperialist" and replaced the United States as the principal adversary of Communist China, the United States became a potential member of a prospective "united front" against Moscow's hegemonic intentions. Now that the Soviet Union appears prepared to negotiate some kind of settlement with the PRC, and the United States seems disposed to serve as a counterweight to Soviet military forces in East Asia, Beijing apparently has opted for foreign policy "independence." It seeks an alliance with the "progressive forces" in the Third World to accelerate the collapse of all forms of imperialism and hegemony and to facilitate the advent of world communism, anticipated by the philosophers of dynastic China as the "Great Harmony" of Confucius.

What all this seems to indicate is that Beijing's relations with imperialist and hegemonic powers will be cautious and manipulative. Many of the interests Beijing shares with such powers are transient. In judging where its interests lie, Beijing will, in the last analysis, keep its own counsel—which is not at all surprising. Sovereign nations have been doing just that since time immemorial.

It should be borne in mind, however, that the national and revolutionary interests of the People's Republic of China are not often compatible with the national and foreign policy interests of the United States. Consequently, relations between the two nations should be conducted on the basis of cautious cost accounting. A reasonable assessment should be made of both potential benefits and anticipated costs. Principles of strict reciprocity should govern bilateral trade, and the U.S. national interest should determine whether technology transfers to the PRC should continue. Unfortunately, such an assessment is not easy to make. There is considerable evidence that suggests that U.S. policymakers have been influenced by judgments of academics and media professionals that could most charitably be characterized as sinocentric.

Allen Whiting has identified as "unduly sinocentric" the notion that the PRC might either divert Soviet forces in East Asia from their anti-Western pursuits or free them for just such use. The PRC is incapable of accomplishing either. The People's Republic of China will remain a regional military power. Unlike Japan, it lacks virtually all the qualities necessary to enable it to serve as a swing-weight between the United States and the Soviet Union.[53]

Americans tend to overlook the fact that Beijing has the potential for working considerable mischief among the East Asian allies of the United States. As we have seen, Beijing has used force in the South China Sea to secure what it considers the "sovereign territory of the motherland." It has threatened violence against the Japanese in the dispute over the Senkaku Islands in the Asian continental shelf. Its claims in the South China Sea also conflict with those of the Philippines, Indonesia, Malaysia, Brunei, and Vietnam, not to mention the Republic of China on Taiwan. Beijing's insistence that all the maritime territory of the region constitutes part of the PRC "may foreshadow military action there once the PLA acquires the capability. . . . Strengthening Beijing's ability to pursue its territorial claims . . . in the South China Sea is antithetical to [the United States'] larger interests, whatever [the] particular problems [of the U.S.] with Vietnam, Laos, and Kampuchea may be. . . . In short, the American judgment that a strong China will serve the cause of peace and stability in Asia is not shared by all [U.S.] allies and friends there."[54]

Beijing's insistence upon the "reunification" of Taiwan with the regime on the mainland threatens to destabilize a region critical to the defense of East Asia. Beijing's continued formal support of North Korea's demands on South Korea complicates the planning necessary for the strategic defense of Japan. Any nonpeaceful change on the Korean peninsula that would reduce the U.S. presence there would make the defense of the West Pacific far more difficult.

As for economic relations between the United States and the PRC, it appears that neither nation will be vital to the other for the remainder of this century. Beijing has diversified its export markets and utilizes various suppliers; consequently, U.S. trade, technology, investments, and loans—although convenient and useful—are not essential to the PRC's ongoing development. United States trade with, and investment in, the People's Republic of China will remain marginal. A number of U.S.-based international corporations will probably enjoy substantial profit from their relations with the PRC, but it is doubtful whether Communist China will make any real contribution to the material well-being of Americans in general. In fact, Americans have underwritten, with their tax dollars, at least part of the economic and political reconstruction now going on in the People's Republic of China. U.S. government appropriations constitute about 25 percent of all capital loans made available to the PRC by the World Bank and the International Monetary Fund and about 25 percent of the grants and financial assistance made available to the PRC by United Nations agencies. U.S government guarantees for export-import transactions and relief from tariff duties—Washington's designation of the PRC as a most-favored nation, and the benefits that derive from the relaxation of restrictions on technology transfers to the PRC—have all contributed to Communist China's welfare and were made possible, directly or indirectly, by U.S. taxpayers.

Relations between the United States and the People's Republic of China have probably reached a stage at which a general review of those relations would be salutary. How much is the United States prepared to invest in the rehabilitation of the neo-Stalinist political system that prevails in the People's Republic of China? What are the real benefits—strategic, economic, and political—that Washington can reasonably expect from its "China connection"? In order to obtain those benefits, will the United States have to mortgage the interests of the noncommunist nations of Asia?

In the mid-1980s, it has become evident to a great many Americans that the United States does not have a principled China policy. Washington seems simply to have made ad hoc responses to issues and opportunities as they have arisen, and relations between Washington and Beijing have simply "developed." As relations between the two countries developed, constituencies formed in the United States, composed of individuals who benefited from those relations. Military men found themselves associating with their counterparts in the People's Liberation

Army; academics became involved in exchange programs; businessmen became increasingly enthusiastic about the prospect of access to the "world's single largest market"; and farmers began to profit from the sale of wheat and soybeans.

What seems to have been lost in all this is the general interest. It is unlikely that "enhanced" strategic cooperation with the PRC—possibly to the detriment of long-standing U.S. relations with allies in East Asia— will serve the security interests of the United States, however much it might serve the interest of some constituency in the military. It is equally unlikely that most Americans will find it in their ultimate best interests to support the perpetuation of a Marxist-Leninist bureaucracy and agree to the rehabilitation of a neo-Stalinist China with capital and technology transfers, however much U.S. business interests might profit from such cooperation.

The United States has sought to foster the establishment and maintenance of pluralistic societies and open-market systems in East Asia and throughout the world. The People's Republic of China may seem dedicated to "reform," but it is most unlikely that the Chinese Communist Party will ever surrender its bureaucratic control of China—or abandon its legitimating commitment to "Marxism-Leninism–Mao Zedong Thought." The leadership in Beijing might modify its political creed, but it is not likely that the ensconced bureaucracy will surrender its privileges in the pursuit of "bourgeois democracy" or capitalism.

In the last analysis, the future of Asia and the best interests of the United States depend not on the cultivation of relations with the People's Republic of China, but on Washington's success in balancing its relations with the PRC and with those nations with which Americans share more in terms of political and economic modalities and security interests. Ultimately, Japan, the Republic of Korea, the Republic of China on Taiwan, the Republic of the Philippines, Malaysia, Singapore, Thailand, and Indonesia will have a more determinate influence on the future of East Asia than will the People's Republic of China. In that sense, maintenance of the "China connection" may ultimately prove to be of secondary importance to the West Pacific policy of the United States.

Notes

CHAPTER ONE

1. Voltaire, "The Philosophy of History," in *Collected Works of Voltaire* (New York: Walter J. Black, 1927), 7:408–12. See also John K. Fairbank, *The United States and China* (Cambridge, Mass.: Harvard University Press, 1979), pp. 155–57.

2. Quoted in Foster Rhea Dulles, *China and America* (Princeton, N.J.: Princeton University Press, 1946), p. 13.

3. Quoted in John K. Fairbank and Ssu-yu Teng, eds. *China's Response to the West: A Documentary Survey* (Cambridge, Mass.: Harvard University Press, 1954), p. 19.

4. John G. Stoessinger, *Nations in Darkness: China, Russia, and America* (New York: Random House, 1981), pp. 15–16.

5. See James C. Thomson, Jr., Peter W. Stanley, and John Curtis Perry, *Sentimental Imperialists: The American Experience in East Asia* (New York: Harper & Row, 1981), chap. 1.

6. For a summary of these assessments, see Paul Hollander, *Political Pilgrims: Travels of Western Intellectuals to the Soviet Union, China, and Cuba* (New York: Harper & Row, 1981), chap. 7.

7. For an instructive discussion of China's geography and population, see John F. Copper, *China's Global Role* (Stanford: Hoover Institution Press, 1980), chap. 2. Data can also be found in *China Handbook* (Hong Kong: Kung Pao, 1980).

8. See Sun Yat-sen, *The International Development of China* (Taipei: China Cultural Service, 1953), pp. 177, 184, 196–97, 198.

9. George B. Cressey, *China's Geographic Foundations* (New York: Columbia University Press, 1934), p. 106.

10. Victor P. Petrov, *China: Emerging World Power* (New York: Van Nostrand, 1976), p. 157.

11. Mihajlo Mesarović and Eduard Pestel, *Mankind at the Turning Point* (New York: Dutton, 1974) Table III, B-3, p. 176.

12. "China Oil: Strategy and Spinoff," *Asian Finance* 8, no. 6 (June 15, 1982):59.

13. Yuan-li Wu, *Economic Development and the Use of Energy Resources in Communist China* (New York: Praeger, 1963), p. 187.

14. Hua Guofeng, *Report on the Work of the Government*, June 18, 1979, Xinhua News Agency, news bulletin no. 11120, June 26, 1979, p. 12.

15. Nicholas Lardy, "Chinese Agricultural Development Policy," in *Mainland China's Modernization: Its Prospects and Problems* (Berkeley: University of California, Institute of International Studies and Institute of East Asian Studies, 1981), pp. 176–79.

16. See Ramon Myers, *The Chinese Economy, Past and Present* (Belmont, Calif.: Wadsworth, 1980), pp. 228–30.

17. Ibid., p. 234.

18. Guy Pauker, "The Security Implications of Regional Energy and Natural Resource Exploitation," in Richard H. Solomon, ed., *Asian Security in the 1980s: Problems and Policies for a Time of Transition* (Boston, Mass.: Oelgeschlager, Gunn & Hain, 1980), pp. 245, 250.

19. See Kim Woodard, "China and Offshore Energy," *Problems of Communism* 30, no. 6 (November–December 1981):36.

20. Pauker, "Regional Energy and Natural Resource Exploitation," pp. 250–51.

21. For estimates of the rate of growth of the Chinese population, see E. A. Wrigley, *Population and History* (New York: McGraw-Hill, 1969), pp. 205–7; Leo A. Orleans, "The Population of Communist China," in Ronald Freeman, ed., *Population: The Vital Revolution* (New York: Doubleday, Anchor Press, 1964) pp. 227–39.

22. Friedrich Engels, "Umrisse zu einer Kritik der Nationalökonomie," *Marx Engels Werke* (Berlin: Dietz, 1961), 1:517.

23. Ibid., p. 520.

24. As quoted in Steven W. Mosher, *Broken Earth: The Rural Chinese* (New York: Free Press, 1983), p. 231; and Han Suyin, "Birth Control in China: Recent Aspects," *Eugenics Review* 52, no. 1 (1960):20.

25. Jan S. Prybyla, "Economic Problems of Communism: Mainland China—A Case Study," in King-yuh Chang, ed., *The Emerging Teng System: Orientation, Policies, and Implications* (Taipei: Institute of International Relations, 1982), p. III-1–13.

26. Mosher, *Broken Earth*, pp. 257–58.

27. See S.D. Richardson, *Forestry in Communist China* (Baltimore, Md.: Penguin Books, 1966), p. 65.

28. Dwight Perkins, "Development of Agriculture," in Michel Oksenberg, ed., *China's Developmental Experience* (New York: Praeger, 1973), p. 62.

29. Charles Hoffman, *The Chinese Worker* (Albany: State University of New York Press, 1974).

30. See the discussion in Wang Hsueh-wen, *Legalism and Anti-Confucianism in Maoist Politics* (Taipei: Institute of International Relations, 1975), chap. 7.

31. Jian Bozan, Shao Xunzheng, and Hu Hua, *A Concise History of China* (Beijing: Foreign Languages Press, 1981), pp. 20–22.

32. Karl A. Wittfogel, *Oriental Despotism: A Comparative Study of Total Power* (New Haven, Conn.: Yale University Press, 1963), particularly pp. 22–33; p. 33, n. b.

33. "The Great Appendix," in Z. D. Sung, ed., *The Text of Yi King* (Taipei: n.p., n.d.), chap. 2; and "Orderly Sequence of the Hexagrams," in ibid., sec. 2.

34. Leonard Shihlien Hsu, *The Political Philosophy of Confucianism* (London: George Routledge, 1932), pp. 66–67.

35. Confucius, "The Great Learning," in *The Four Books*, trans. James Legge (Taipei: Culture Books, 1975), bk. 1, chap. 9, sec. 1; see also secs. 5, 6, and 9.

36. Confucius, "The Analects," in ibid., bk. 1, chap. 2, sec. 1, para. 1.

37. Ibid., bk. 1, chap. 7.

38. Mencius, "The Works of Mencius," in ibid., bk. 4, pt. 1, chap. 5; Confucius, "The Analects," bk. 12, chap. 19. See also bk. 16, chap. 1, sec. 10.

39. Confucius, "The Analects," bk. 16, chap. 2, sec. 3.

40. Mencius, "The Works of Mencius," bk. 3, pt. 1, chap. 4, sec. 6.

41. Ibid., bk. 1, chap. 3, sec. 4.

42. See Hsu, *Political Philosophy of Confucianism*, pp. 78–80.

43. Confucius, "The Analects," bk. 6, chap. 28, sec. 2.

44. A. James Gregor, "Confucianism and the Political Thought of Sun Yat-sen," *Philosophy East and West* 31, no. 1 (January 1981): 55–70.

45. See the discussion in Wittfogel, *Oriental Despotism*, chap. 5.

46. Ch'u Chai and Winberg Chai, *Confucianism* (Woodbury, N.Y.: Barron's Educational Series, 1973), chap. 9.

47. See Wang, *Legalism and Anti-Confucianism*, chap. 7.

48. Lucien W. Pye, *The Spirit of Chinese Politics* (Cambridge, Mass.: MIT Press, 1968), p. 12.

CHAPTER TWO

1. There are a number of informative biographies of Mao Zedong. Among the most useful are Stuart Schram, *Mao Tse-tung* (Baltimore, Md.: Penguin Books,

1967); Jerome Ch'en, *Mao and the Chinese Revolution* (New York: Oxford University Press, 1967); Han Suyin, *The Morning Deluge* (Boston: Little, Brown, 1972); Edgar Snow, *Red Star over China* (New York: Grove Press, 1961); Robert Payne, *Mao Tse-tung* (New York: Pyramid Books, 1966).

2. Schram, ibid., pp. 24–25; Snow, ibid., pp. 134–135.

3. Snow, ibid., p. 157.

4. See Maurice Meissner, *Li Ta-chao and the Origins of Chinese Marxism* (Cambridge, Mass.: Harvard University Press, 1967), pp. 93, 125.

5. A. James Gregor, *The Fascist Persuasion in Radical Politics* (Princeton, N.J.: Princeton University Press, 1974), chap. 6.

6. Franz Schurmann, *Ideology and Organization in Communist China* (Berkeley and Los Angeles: University of California Press, 1968), p. 42.

7. See the selections in Stuart Schram, ed., *The Political Thought of Mao Tse-tung* (New York: Praeger, 1969), pp. 153, 158, 206–10.

8. See the Introduction to ibid., pp. 39–42.

9. Ibid., pp. 206, 208.

10. Ibid., p. 269.

11. *Mao Tse-tung's Thought Is the Invincible Weapon* (Beijing: Foreign Languages Press, 1968), p. 3.

12. Lin Biao, Foreword to the Second Edition, *Quotations from Chairman Mao Tse-tung* (Beijing: Foreign Languages Press, 1966), p. xxx.

13. See the discussion in Nigel Harris, *The Mandate of Heaven: Marx and Mao in Modern China* (London: Quartet, 1978), pp. 285–86.

14. Mao discussed the importance of the "superstructure" in the transformation of society. See Mao Zedong, *A Critique of Soviet Economics* (New York: Monthly Review Press, 1977), p. 51; compare the editor's comment on p. 18.

15. See the representative essays in George Urban, ed., *The Miracles of Chairman Mao* (Los Angeles, Calif.: Nash, 1971).

16. Frederic Wakeman, Jr., *History and Will: Philosophical Perspectives of Mao Tse-tung's Thought* (Berkeley and Los Angeles: University of California Press, 1973), pp. 306–7.

17. *The Constitution of the People's Republic of China* (Beijing: Foreign Languages Press, 1975), Preamble, p. 8; *The Constitution of the People's Republic of China* (Beijing: Foreign Languages Press, 1978), Preamble, p. 3.

18. *The Constitution of the Communist Party of China* (Beijing: Foreign Languages Press, 1965), "General Programme," pp. 6, 7.

19. Editorial, "Long Live the Great Proletarian Cultural Revolution," *Hongqi*, no. 5 (1966); reprinted in *The Great Socialist Cultural Revolution in China* (Beijing: Foreign Languages Press, 1966), 4:18.

20. *The Whole Country Should Become a Great School of Mao Tse-tung's Thought* (Beijing: Foreign Languages Press, 1966), p. 17.

21. "Long Live the Great Proletarian Cultural Revolution," p. 13.

22. See A. James Gregor and Maria H. Chang, "Marxism, Sun Yat-sen, and the Concept of 'Imperialism'," *Pacific Affairs* 55, no. 1 (Spring 1982): 56–62.

23. Alfred G. Meyer, *Communism* (New York: Random House, 1984), pp. 48–54; A. James Gregor, *A Survey of Marxism* (New York: Random House, 1965), pp. 227–37.

24. Yeh Ch'ing, *Inside Mao Tse-tung's Thought: An Analytic Blueprint of His Actions* (Hicksville, N.Y.: Exposition Press, 1975), p. 3.

25. Mao Zedong, "The Chinese Revolution and the Chinese Communist Party," *Selected Works* (Beijing: Foreign Languages Press, 1965), 2:315.

26. Ibid., pp. 319–25.

27. See Harris, *Mandate of Heaven*, chap. 19.

28. M. I. Sladkovsky, Y. F. Kovalyov, and V. Y. Sidikhmenov, eds., *Leninism and Modern China's Problems* (Moscow: Progress Publishers, 1972), p. 30; O. E. Vladimirov, ed., *Maoism as It Really Is* (Moscow: Progress Publishers, 1981), pp. 9, 11, 12, 37; B. Zanegin, A. Mironov, and Y. Mikhailov, *Developments in China* (Moscow: Progress Publishers, 1968), p. 16; Boris Leibson, *Petty-Bourgeois Revolutionism* (Moscow: Progress Publishers, 1970), pp. 114–15; V. I. Krivtsov, ed., *Maoism Through the Eyes of Communists* (Moscow: Progress Publishers, 1970), pp. 46–47.

29. *Mao Tse-tung's Thought*, p. 2.

30. Mao Zedong, "On the People's Democratic Dictatorship," *Selected Works* 4:417–18.

31. Ibid., pp. 412, 418, 422.

32. Ibid., pp. 414, 418, 419, 421.

33. Liu Shaoqi, *On the Party* (Beijing: Foreign Languages Press, 1951), pp. 27, 33, 55; see also pp. 29–34, 43.

34. Ibid., pp. 83, 84, 85.

35. John Wilson Lewis, *Major Doctrines of Communist China* (New York: Norton, 1964), p. 193.

36. Richard Walker, *China Under Communism: The First Five Years* (New Haven, Conn.: Yale University Press, 1955), pp. 30–31.

37. John Wilson Lewis, *Leadership in Communist China* (Ithaca, N.Y.: Cornell University Press, 1963), pp. 169–175.

38. For a discussion of this issue, see A. James Gregor and Maria Hsia Chang, *The Republic of China and U.S. Policy* (Washington, D.C.: Ethics and Public Policy Center, 1983).

39. *The Constitution of the People's Republic of China*, Art. 2, 14, 18, and 56.

40. Ibid., Art. 56.

41. See Gordon White, "The Postrevolutionary Chinese State," in Victor Nee and David Mozingo, eds., *State and Society in Contemporary China* (Ithaca, N.Y.: Cornell University Press, 1983), pp. 27–52.

42. Edward Friedman, "The Societal Obstacle to China's Socialist Transition: State Capitalism or Feudal Fascism?" in ibid., pp. 150–51.

43. Mao Zedong, "On the Struggle Against the 'Three Evils' and the 'Five Evils'," *Selected Works* 5:64–66; see also Mao, "Combat Bureaucracy, Commandism, and Violations of the Law and of Discipline," ibid., pp. 84–86.

44. Mao, "On the Ten Major Relationships," ibid., p. 297.

45. See Richard Kraus, "The Chinese State and Its Bureaucrats," in Nee and Mozingo, *State and Society*, pp. 134–36.

46. Leonard Schapiro and John Wilson Lewis, "The Roles of the Monolithic Party Under the Totalitarian Leader," in John Wilson Lewis, ed., *Party Leadership and Revolutionary Power in China* (New York: Cambridge University Press, 1970), pp. 127–37.

47. See John Wilson Lewis, "Leader, Commissar, and Bureaucrat," in Ping-ti Ho and Tang Tsou, eds., *China's Heritage and the Communist Political System* (Chicago: University of Chicago Press, 1968), 1:449–81.

48. See the introduction to Stuart Schram, ed., *Chairman Mao Talks to the People: Talks and Letters, 1956–1971* (New York: Pantheon Books, 1974), pp. 11–18.

49. As translated from *Guangyin Hongqi*, in U.S. Consulate General (Hong Kong), *Survey of China Mainland Press*, no. 4190 (June 4, 1968), p. 3.

50. "Sweep Away All Monsters," *People's Daily*, June 1, 1966, reprinted in *Great Socialist Cultural Revolution*, 3:5.

51. "A Great Revolution that Touches People to Their Very Souls," *People's Daily*, June 2, 1966; reprinted in ibid., p. 10.

52. "Mao Zedong's Thought Is the Telescope and Microscope of Our Revolutionary Cause," *Liberation Army Daily*, June 7, 1966; reprinted in ibid., p. 13.

53. Ibid., p. 15.

54. Mao Zedong, "China Is Poor and Blank," in Schram, *Political Thought of Mao Tse-tung*, p. 352.

55. See the quotations cited in Vladimirov, *Maoism as It Really Is*, pp. 222–23.

56. There are many studies of the economic history of the People's Republic of China. One of the most informative is Chu-yuan Cheng, *China's Economic Development: Growth and Structural Change* (Boulder, Colo.: Westview Press, 1982).

57. Albert Feuerwerker, "Relating to the International Community," in Michel Oksenberg, ed., *China's Developmental Experience* (New York: Praeger, 1973), pp. 42–54. See also Mao Zedong, "New Democratic Constitutional Government," *Selected Works* 2:407.

58. Mao Zedong, "The Chinese Revolution and the Chinese Communist Party," *Selected Works* 2:327.

59. Mao, "On New Democracy," ibid., p. 353.

60. *Ten Great Years* (Beijing: State Statistical Bureau, 1960).

61. Mao Zedong, "On the People's Democratic Dictatorship," *Selected Works* 4:423.

62. Cheng, *China's Economic Development*, p. 29; Vladimirov, *Maoism as It Really Is*, p. 56.

63. See the discussion of the complexity of this situation in industry in Stephen Andors, *China's Industrial Revolution: Politics, Planning, and Management, 1949 to the Present* (New York: Pantheon Books, 1977), pp. 53–62; see also Jan S. Prybyla, "The Economic System of the People's Republic of China," *Asian Thought and Society*, 9, no. 25 (March 1984): 3–10.

64. See the post-Mao comments by Xu Dixin in "Transformation of China's Economy," in Xu Dixin, ed., *China's Search for Economic Growth: The Chinese Economy Since 1949* (Beijing: New World Press, 1982), p. 9.

65. As quoted in Fedor Burlatsky, *Mao Tse-tung: An Ideological and Psychological Portrait* (Moscow: Progress Publishers, 1980), p. 138.

66. Mao, *A Critique of Soviet Economics*, p. 58.

67. Chu-yuan Cheng, "Economic Development in Taiwan and Mainland China: A Comparison of Strategies and Performance," *Asian Affairs: An American Review*, Spring 1983, p. 65.

68. See *World Development Report, 1980* (New York: Oxford University Press, 1980), Table 1, p. 110.

69. Cheng, *China's Economic Development*, p. 424.

70. Xu, "Transformation of China's Economy," p. 18.

71. Cheng, *China's Economic Development*, p. 356.

72. A. Doak Barnett, *China's Economy in Global Perspective* (Washington, D.C.: Brookings Institution, 1981), p. 305.

73. See the discussion in Steven W. Mosher, *Broken Earth: The Rural Chinese* (New York: Free Press, 1983), chap. 3.

74. Benjamin I. Schwartz, "The Reign of Virtue: Some Broad Perspectives on Leader and Party in the Cultural Revolution," in Lewis, *Party Leadership and Revolutionary Power*, p. 154.

75. See the Preamble to *The Constitution of the People's Republic of China, 1982* (Beijing: Foreign Languages Press, 1982).

Chapter Three

1. See the discussion in Melvin Gurtov and Byong-Moo Hwang, *China Under Threat: The Politics of Strategy and Diplomacy* (Baltimore, Md.: Johns Hopkins University Press, 1980), chap. 1.

2. See the stenographic record in Chang Chien, "Imperialism Is the Eve of the Social Revolution of the Proletariat: Notes on Studying Lenin's *Imperialism, the*

Highest Stage of Capitalism," in *Beijing Review,* no. 39 (1973); reprinted in *Social Imperialism* (Berkeley, Calif.: Yenan Books, n.d.), pp. 1, 2.

3. Chang quoting Lenin, ibid., p. 2.

4. Ibid., p. 3.

5. See the analysis in Hu Sheng, *Imperialism and Chinese Politics* (Beijing: Foreign Languages Press, 1955).

6. Mao Zedong, "The Present Situation and Our Tasks," *Selected Works* (Beijing: Foreign Languages Press, 1965), 4:167; and Mao, "The Foolish Old Man Who Removed the Mountains," ibid., 3:321–24.

7. Mao, "Stalin, Friend of the Chinese People, *Selected Works* 2:335.

8. Mao, "On New Democracy," ibid., pp. 343–44, 346.

9. Mao, "On Policy," ibid., p. 444.

10. Mao, "Talk with the American Correspondent Anna Louise Strong," ibid., 4:99.

11. See Mao, "Some Points in Appraisal of the Present International Situation," ibid., pp. 87–88.

12. Mao, "Revolutionary Forces of the World Unite, Fight Against Imperial Aggression!" ibid., pp. 283–86.

13. Mao, "Report to the Second Plenary Session of the Seventh Central Committee of the Communist Party of China," ibid., p. 372; see also J. D. Armstrong, *Revolutionary Diplomacy: Chinese Foreign Policy and the United Front Doctrine* (Berkeley and Los Angeles: University of California Press, 1977), pp. 38–39.

14. Mao Zedong, "On the People's Democratic Dictatorship," *Selected Works* 4:415, 417.

15. See Richard C. Thornton, *China: A Political History, 1917–1980* (Boulder, Colo.: Westview Press, 1982), chaps. 8 and 9.

16. "Foreign Policies Toward Asia: A Television Interview with Secretary Acheson," *Department of State Bulletin* (Washington, D.C.: Government Printing Office, September 18, 1950).

17. Alexander L. George, *The Chinese Communist Army in Action: The Korean War and Its Aftermath* (New York: Columbia University Press, 1967), chap. 1.

18. John G. Stoessinger, *Nations in Darkness: China, Russia, and America* (New York: Random House, 1981), chap. 4.

19. See Allen S. Whiting, *China Crosses the Yalu* (New York: Macmillan, 1960).

20. Samuel B. Griffith, *The Chinese People's Liberation Army* (New York: McGraw-Hill, 1967), p. 118.

21. Mao Zedong, "Present Situation and Our Tasks," *Selected Works,* pp. 158–59.

22. Mao, "Revolutionary Forces of the World Unite," ibid., pp. 284–85.

23. Whiting, *China Crosses the Yalu,* p. 154.

24. Mao Zedong, "Greet the New High Tide of the Chinese Revolution," *Selected Works* 4:120–21.

25. Armstrong, *Revolutionary Diplomacy*, p. 69.

26. Liu Shaoqi, *Speech at Trade Union Conference of Asian and Australian Countries, November 16, 1949*, New China News Agency, Beijing, November 25, 1949.

27. Mao Zedong, "On New Democracy," *Selected Works*, p. 364.

28. Mao Zedong, "There Is No Third Way," in Stuart R. Schram, ed., *The Political Thought of Mao Tse-tung* (New York: Praeger, 1969), p. 377.

29. Yitzhak Shichor, *The Middle East in China's Foreign Policy, 1949–1977* (New York: Cambridge University Press, 1979), p. 30.

30. Zhou Enlai, "Political Report to the Third Session of the First National Committee of the Chinese People's Political Consultative Conference," October 23, 1951, as reprinted in *New China Forges Ahead* (Beijing: Foreign Languages Press, 1952), p. 12.

31. See Chae-Jin Lee, *Communist China's Policy Toward Laos: A Case Study, 1954–1967* (Lawrence: University of Kansas, Center for East Asian Studies, 1970).

32. As quoted in Wei Liang-tsai, *Peking Versus Taipei in Africa, 1960–1978* (Taipei: Asia and World Institute, 1982), p. 41.

33. As cited in Shichor, *Middle East in China's Foreign Policy*, p. 73.

34. Soong Qingling, "The Basis of Eternal Friendship," in Winbert Chai, ed., *The Foreign Relations of the People's Republic of China* (New York: Capricorn Books, 1972), pp. 130–38.

35. All of these arguments and quotations are included in the brochure *Long Live Leninism!* (Beijing: Foreign Languages Press, 1964). Three essays in the brochure ("Long Live Leninism!" "Forward Along the Path of the Great Lenin," and "Unite Under Lenin's Revolutionary Banner!") appeared in *Red Flag* and the *People's Daily* in April 1960.

36. See *Leninism and Modern Revisionism* (Beijing: Foreign Languages Press, 1963), p. 8.

37. *The Polemic on the General Line of the International Communist Movement* (Beijing: Foreign Languages Press, 1963), p. 13.

38. Ibid., p. 202.

39. David Mozingo, *Chinese Policy Toward Indonesia, 1949–1967* (Ithaca, N.Y.: Cornell University Press, 1976), p. 146.

40. See the primary documents in J. Chester Cheng, ed., *The Politics of the Red Chinese Army* (Stanford: Hoover Institution Press, 1966), p. 484.

41. For documentation concerning the PRC involvement, see *Nkrumah's Subversion in Africa* (Accra: Ministry of Information, Republic of Ghana, 1966), pp. 18–20.

42. B. D. Larkin, *China and Africa* (Berkeley and Los Angeles: University of California Press, 1971), p. 27.

43. *On Khrushchev's Phoney Communism and Its Historical Lessons for the World* (Beijing: Foreign Languages Press, 1964), pp. 2, 7, 9, 24–25, 27, 28.

44. See A. Kruchinin and V. Olgin, *Territorial Claims of Mao Tse-tung: History and Modern Times* (Moscow: Novosti, n.d.), p. 36.
45. For a comprehensive discussion, see Armstrong, *Revolutionary Diplomacy*, pp. 142–46; and Mozingo, *Chinese Policy Toward Indonesia*, pp. 216–24.
46. Lin Biao, *Long Live the Victory of People's War!* (Beijing: Foreign Languages Press, 1965).
47. Mao Zedong as quoted by Lin, ibid., p. 97.
48. As quoted in *The True Facts of Chinese Communist Accelerated Aggression Against Foreign Countries at the Present Stage* (Taipei: World Anti-Communist League, 1970), p. 39.
49. See Lin, *Long Live the Victory*, pp. 82–92.
50. Peter Van Ness, *Revolution and Chinese Foreign Policy* (Berkeley and Los Angeles: University of California Press, 1970), pp. 189, 245.
51. As quoted in Golam W. Choudhury, *China in World Affairs: The Foreign Policy of the PRC Since 1970* (Boulder, Colo.: Westview Press, 1982), p. 34.

CHAPTER FOUR

1. John W. Garver, *China's Decision for Rapprochement with the United States, 1968–1971* (Boulder, Colo.: Westview Press, 1982), chap. 1.
2. See the discussion in Thomas M. Gottlieb, *Chinese Foreign Policy Factionalism and the Origins of the Strategic Triangle* (Santa Monica, Calif.: Rand Corporation, 1977).
3. Michael Y. M. Kau and Pierre Perrolle, "The Politics of Lin Biao's Abortive Military Coup," *Asian Survey* 14, no. 6 (June 1974):572.
4. Sydney J. Jammes, "The Chinese Defense Burden, 1965–1974," in *China: A Reassessment of the Economy. Joint Economic Committee, United States Congress, 94th Session* (Washington, D.C.: Government Printing Office, 1975), p. 463.
5. Harold C. Hinton, *The Sino-Soviet Confrontation: Implications for the Future* (New York: Crane, Russak, 1976), p. 18.
6. For a general review of this period, see Claude A. Buss, *China: The People's Republic of China and Richard Nixon* (San Francisco: W.H. Freeman, 1974), pp. 90–100.
7. Zhou Enlai, "Why Did Our Country Accede to Nixon's Request for a Visit?" in King C. Chen, ed., *China and the Three Worlds: A Foreign Policy Reader* (White Plains, N.Y.: M. E. Sharpe, 1979), p. 133.
8. "A Powerful Weapon to Unite the People and Defeat the Enemy: A Study of 'On Policy,' " in ibid., pp. 74–77.
9. See the confidential "Kunming Documents" of mid-1973, appendix 1 of *Chinese Communist Internal Politics and Foreign Policy Reviews on Reference Mate-*

rials Concerning Education on Situation Issues by the Kunming Military Region (Taipei: Institute of International Relations, 1974), p. 126.

10. *Down with the New Tsars!* (Beijing: Foreign Languages Press, 1969), p. 3.

11. Chang Chien, "Imperialism Is the Eve of the Social Revolution of the Proletariat: Notes on Studying Lenin's *Imperialism, the Highest Stage of Capitalism*," *Beijing Review*, no. 39 (1973); Ming Sung, "Dire Consequences of Soviet Revisionists' All-Round Capitalist Restoration," *Beijing Review*, no. 42 (October 18, 1974). Both reprinted in *Social Imperialism* (Berkeley, Calif.: Yenan Books, n.d.).

12. Hsin Feng, "Mighty Ideological Weapon in the Struggle Against Revisionism—A Study of Lenin's *Imperialism, the Highest Stage of Capitalism*," *Beijing Review*, no. 20 (May 17, 1974); reprinted in *Social Imperialism*.

13. "Third World Struggle Against Hegemony," *Beijing Review*, no. 38 (1973); "Aid or Control and Plunder?" in ibid., no. 45 (1973). Both reprinted in *Social Imperialism*.

14. "Soviet Social Imperialism—Most Dangerous Source of War,"*Beijing Review*, no. 5 (January 30, 1976), reprinted in *Social Imperialism*.

15. Representative of this kind of analysis is *Ugly Features of Soviet Social Imperialism* (Beijing: Foreign Languages Press, 1976).

16. "Kunming Documents," pp. 116, 126, 130–31.

17. Ibid., p. 135.

18. See "Chairman Mao's Theory of the Differentiation of the Three Worlds Is a Major Contribution to Marxism-Leninism," *Beijing Review*, no. 45 (November 4, 1977).

19. Deng Xiaoping, "China and the Three Worlds," in Chen, *China and the Three Worlds*, pp. 86–87.

20. "Teng Hsiao-ping Talks on U.S.-China Relations," in *Inside China Mainland* 1 (January 1979):1.

21. Geng Biao, "Speech to the Foreign Liaison Department," ibid., p. 3.

22. Harry Harding, "Change and Continuity in Chinese Foreign Policy," *Problems of Communism* 32, no. 2 (March–April 1983):1–19.

23. See Jonathan D. Pollack, *Security, Strategy, and the Logic of Chinese Foreign Policy* (Berkeley: University of California, Institute of East Asian Studies, 1981), pp. 40–41.

24. *U.S. Policy with Respect to Mainland China. Hearings Before the Senate Foreign Relations Committee.* (Washington, D.C.: Government Printing Office, 1966). Major portions of the hearings are reprinted in Akira Iriye, ed., *U.S. Policy Toward China* (Boston: Little, Brown, 1968).

25. Richard Nixon, "Asia After Vietnam," *Foreign Affairs* 46, no. 1 (October 1967): 111–25.

26. *United States Foreign Policy—1971: A Report of the Secretary of State* (Washington, D.C.: Government Printing Office, 1972), p. 49.

27. A. Doak Barnett, *China Policy* (Washington, D.C.: Brookings Institution, 1977), p. 4.

28. Robert G. Sutter, *The China Quandary: Domestic Determinants of U.S. China Policy, 1972–1982* (Boulder, Colo.: Westview Press, 1983), pp. 19–20.

29. See Stanley B. Lubman, "Trade and Sino-American Relations," in Michel Oksenberg and Robert B. Oxnam, eds., *Dragon and Eagle: United States–China Relations, Past and Future* (New York: Basic Books, 1973), pp. 187–212.

30. Richard H. Solomon, *China Policy and America's Public Debate: Ten Arguments in Search of Normalized U.S.-PRC Relations* (Santa Monica, Calif.: Rand Corporation, December 1977, Mimeographed), p. 23.

31. A. Doak Barnett, *China and the Major Powers in Asia* (Washington, D.C.: Brookings Institution, 1977), p. 197; Golam W. Choudhury, *China in World Affairs: The Foreign Policy of the PRC Since 1970* (Boulder, Colo.: Westview Press, 1982), pp. 76–77; Sutter, *The China Quandary*, pp. 72–73.

32. Justin Galen, "U.S.'s Toughest Message to the USSR," *Armed Forces Journal International*, February 1979, pp. 30, 32, 35–36.

33. See Pauly Parakal, *Peking's Betrayal of Asia* (New Delhi: Sterling, 1976), p. vi.

34. "NATO—Need for Improved Military Forces," *Beijing Review*, no. 21 (December 1973); and *New York Times*, July 2, 1974.

35. Parakal, *Peking's Betrayal of Asia*, p. 62.

36. *New York Times*, November 27, 1975.

37. Ibid., December 14, 1975.

38. Ibid., November 14, 1975, and August 24, 1975.

39. Ibid., November 29, 1975.

40. For a more comprehensive discussion, see Yitzhak Shichor, *The Middle East in China's Foreign Policy, 1949–1977* (New York: Cambridge University Press, 1979), chap. 4; Parakal, *Peking's Betrayal of Asia*, chap. 10.

41. Robert E. Osgood, "Containment, Soviet Behavior, and Grand Strategy," in Robert E. Osgood, ed., *Containment, Soviet Behavior, and Grand Strategy* (Berkeley: University of California, Institute of International Studies, 1981), pp. 4, 9; see also the comments by Ernst B. Haas, "Toward a Workable Grand Strategy," ibid., p. 43.

42. See, for example, Kenneth R. McGruther, "Two Anchors in the Pacific: A Strategy Proposal for the U.S. Pacific Fleet," *United States Naval Institute Proceedings*, May 1979, p. 134; and Peter W. Soverel, "Problems of Sea Power in the Western Pacific as We Approach the Twenty-First Century," in J. L. George, ed., *Problems of Sea Power as We Approach the Twenty-First Century* (Washington, D.C.: American Enterprise Institute, 1978), pp. 164–66.

43. Randall W. Hardy, *China's Oil Future: A Case of Modest Expectations* (Boulder, Colo.: Westview Press, 1978), pp. 21–22.

44. See the report of Seeley Lodwick, under secretary of agriculture for international affairs, in *The New Era in East Asia. Hearings Before the Subcommittee on*

Asian and Pacific Affairs of the Committee on Foreign Affairs, House of Representatives. (Washington, D.C.: Government Printing Office, 1981), pp. 332–39.

45. Mary H. Copper, "China: Quest for Stability and Development," *China: Quest for Stability and Development* 1, no. 14 (April 13, 1984):271.

46. Sutter, *The China Quandary*, p. 20.

47. William Watts, *The United States and Asia: Changing Attitudes and Policies* (Lexington, Mass.: D. C. Heath, 1982), pp. 5–6.

48. See William Clarke, "Commercial Implications of Normalization," *International Trade Law Journal* 5, no. 1 (Fall–Winter 1979):93.

49. McGruther, *Two Anchors in the Pacific*," p. 128.

Chapter Five

1. Paul W. Wolfowitz, "Sino-American Relations: Eleven Years After the Shanghai Communiqué," prepared statement presented to U.S. House of Representatives, Committee on Foreign Affairs, Subcommittee on Asian and Pacific Affairs, February 28, 1983, pp. 1, 3 (manuscript).

2. A. A. Sidorenko, *The Offensive*, translated and published under the auspices of the U.S. Air Force (Washington, D.C.: Government Printing Office, n.d.).

3. See the discussion in Banning N. Garrett and Bonnie S. Glaser, *War and Peace: The Views from Moscow and Beijing* (Berkeley: University of California, Institute of International Studies, 1984), chap. 4.

4. Robert Arnett, "Soviet Attitudes Toward Nuclear War: Do They Really Think They Can Win?" *Journal of Strategic Studies* 2, no. 2 (1979):181.

5. Garrett and Glaser, *War and Peace*, pp. 108–9; see also Robert B. Foster and William M. Carpenter, "Development of the Washington-Moscow-Peking Triangular Relationship During the Last Three Years," in King-yuh Chang, ed., *The Emerging Teng System: Orientation, Policies, and Implications* (Taipei: Institute of International Relations, 1982), pp. V-1–V-7.

6. See Thomas C. Schelling, *The Strategy of Conflict* (Cambridge, Mass.: Harvard University Press, 1960), pp. 3–20.

7. Harlan W. Jencks, *From Muskets to Missiles: Politics and Professionalism in the Chinese Army, 1945–1981* (Boulder, Colo.: Westview Press, 1982), p. 144.

8. See Alexander L. George, *The Chinese Communist Army in Action: The Korean War and Its Aftermath* (New York: Columbia University Press, 1967), p. 165; see also p. 70.

9. King C. Chen, *China's War Against Vietnam, 1979: A Military Analysis* (Baltimore: University of Maryland School of Law, 1983), p. 15.

10. William V. Kennedy, "The Defense of China's Homeland," in Ray Bonds, ed., *The Chinese War Machine* (New York: Crescent Books, 1979), p. 94.

11. See the discussion in Harlan W. Jencks, *The Politics of Chinese Military Develop-*

ment, 1945–1977 (Ann Arbor, Mich.: University Microfilms International, 1978), 2:443–448.

12. See Paul H. B. Godwin, "China's Defense Modernization: Of Tortoise Shells and Tigers' Tails," *Air University Review* 33, no. 1 (November–December 1981):8–15; Ralph L. Powell, *Maoist Military Doctrines* (New York: American-Asian Educational Exchange, n.d.).

13. Ellis Joffe, "The Chinese Army: A Balance Sheet," *Quadrant* 22, no. 11 (November 1978):7 (reprint; Jerusalem: Hebrew University, Truman Institute, n.d.).

14. See Angus M. Fraser, *The People's Liberation Army: Communist China's Armed Forces* (New York: Crane, Russak, 1973), pp. 33–34.

15. Kennedy, "Defense of China's Homeland," p. 103.

16. Ibid., p. 110.

17. Ibid., p. 94.

18. For a more detailed discussion, see A. James Gregor, "Western Security and the Military Potential of the PRC," *Parameters* 14, no. 1 (Spring 1984):35–48; Kenneth Hung, "Sino-Soviet Theater Force Comparisons," in Douglas T. Stuart and William T. Tow, eds., *China, the Soviet Union, and the West* (Boulder, Colo.: Westview Press, 1982), pp. 103–114.

19. Edward Luttwak, "The PRC in Soviet Grand Strategy," in *China, the Soviet Union, and the West*, p. 269.

20. Noel Gayler, "Security Implications of the Soviet Military Presence in Asia," in Richard H. Solomon, ed., *Asian Security in the 1980s: Problems and Policies for a Time of Transition* (Cambridge, Mass.: Oelgeschlager, Gunn & Hain, 1980), p. 59.

21. A. James Gregor, "The People's Republic of China as a Western Security Asset," *Air University Review* 34, no. 5 (July–August 1983):19–20.

22. William V. Kennedy, "China's Role in a New U.S. Deterrence Strategy," in Stuart and Tow, *China, the Soviet Union, and the West*, p. 253.

23. Strobe Talbott, "The Strategic Dimension of the Sino-American Relationship," in Richard H. Solomon, ed., *The China Factor: Sino-American Relations and the Global Scene* (Englewood Cliffs, N.J.: Prentice-Hall, 1981), p. 96.

24. See Ray Bonds, ed., *Russian Military Power* (New York: Crown Publishers, Bonanza Books, 1980), p. 148.

25. See Steven I. Levine, "The Soviet Perspective," in John Bryan Starr, ed., *The Future of U.S.-China Relations* (New York: New York University Press, 1981), pp. 84–85.

26. See Joseph J. Collins, "The Soviet-Afghan War: The First Four Years," *Parameters* 14, no. 2 (Summer 1984):53.

27. Juergen Domes, "Domestic Sources of PRC Policy Toward the USSR," in Stuart and Tow, *China, the Soviet Union, and the West*, p. 32.

28. Lawrence Freedman, "Sino-Soviet Economic and Technological Factors," ibid., p. 85.

29. William C. Green and David S. Yost, "Soviet Military Options Regarding China," in ibid., p. 143.

30. See Green and Yost, "Soviet Military Options," and Luttwak, "PRC in Soviet Grand Strategy," in ibid., pp. 136, 268; William Hyland, "The Sino-Soviet Conflict: A Search for New Security Strategies," *Strategic Review* 7 (Fall 1979):61.

31. As cited in Garrett and Glaser, *War and Peace*, p. 26.

32. See David G. Muller, Jr., *China as a Maritime Power* (Boulder, Colo.: Westview Press, 1983), pp. 226–27.

33. See Allen S. Whiting, *Siberian Development and East Asia: Threat or Promise?* (Stanford: Stanford University Press, 1981).

34. See the discussion in Drew Middleton, *The Duel of the Giants: China and Russia in Asia* (New York: Scribner's, 1978), chap. 6.

35. Dennis J. Doolin, *Territorial Claims in the Sino-Soviet Conflict* (Stanford: Hoover Institution Press, 1977); Maud Russell, *The Sino-Soviet Ussuri River Border Clash: The Historical Background and Current Implications* (New York: Far East Reporter, n.d.).

36. Allen S. Whiting, "The Karakhan Declaration," in his *Soviet Policies in China, 1917–1924* (New York: Columbia University Press, 1954), p. 273.

37. As quoted in Middleton, *Duel of the Giants*, p. 152.

38. Edward N. Luttwak, "Why We Need More 'Waste, Fraud, and Mismanagement' in the Pentagon," *Commentary*, February 1982, p. 17.

39. Richard H. Solomon, "American Defense Planning and Asian Security: Policy Choices for a Time of Transition," in Richard Solomon, ed., *Asian Security in the 1980s*, p. 26.

40. Michael Y. M. Kau, "Teng's Quest for Military Modernization and National Security," in *Mainland China's Modernization: Its Prospects and Problems* (Berkeley: University of California, Institute of International Studies and Institute of East Asian Studies, 1981), pp. 229–33.

41. Drew Middleton, "Pentagon Studies Prospects of Military Links with China," *New York Times*, January 4, 1980, p. A2.

42. Thomas W. Robinson, "Notes on Chinese Military Modernization," in *Mainland China's Modernization*, p. 212 n. 26; Jencks, *Politics of Chinese Military Development*, pp. 197–98.

43. Freedman, "Economic and Technological Factors," p. 76.

44. Luttwak, "PRC in Soviet Grand Strategy," p. 267.

45. Leslie H. Gelb, "U.S. Defense Policy, Technology Transfers, and Asian Security," in Solomon, *Asian Security in the 1980s*, pp. 264–65.

46. Gayler, "Soviet Military Presence in Asia," p. 64; see also p. 59.

47. Garret and Glaser, *War and Peace*, pp. 23–24.

48. See the testimony of Banning Garrett in *The United States and the People's Republic of China: Issues for the 1980s. Hearings Before the Subcommittee on Asian and Pacific Affairs of the Committee on Foreign Affairs, U.S. House of Representatives* (Washington, D.C.: Government Printing Office, 1980), p. 98.

49. As quoted in Jonathan D. Pollack, "Rebuilding China's Great Wall: Chinese Security in the 1980s," in Paul H. B. Godwin, ed., *The Chinese Defense Establishment: Continuity and Change in the 1980s* (Boulder, Colo.: Westview Press, 1983), p. 8.

50. See Shigeo Hiramatsu, "A Chinese Perspective on Sino-Soviet Relations," *Journal of Northeast Asian Studies* 2, no. 3 (September 1983):52–53.

51. See Allen S. Whiting, "Sino-American Relations: The Decade Ahead," *Orbis* 26, no. 3 (Fall 1982):700–701.

52. Edmund Lee, "Beijing's Balancing Act," *Foreign Policy* 51 (Summer 1983):27.

53. Richard Lowenthal, "The Degeneration of an Ideological Dispute," in Stuart and Tow, *China, the Soviet Union, and the West*, pp. 59–72.

54. "Oppose Hegemonism for the Sake of World Peace," in Zhou Guo, ed., *China and the World* (Beijing: Beijing Review, 1983), 4:30–31.

55. Xing Shugang, Li Yunhua, and Liu Yingna, "A Study of the Relative Strength Between United States and the Soviet Union," in Zhou, *China and the World*, pp. 67–84.

56. "Oppose Hegemonism," ibid., p. 34.

57. See Huan Xiang, "Adhere to Independent Foreign Policy," *Beijing Review*, November 15, 1982, pp. 21–23.

58. William E. Griffith, "Sino-Soviet Rapprochement?" *Problems of Communism* 32, no. 2 (March–April 1983):24; Kenneth Lieberthal, "China in 1982: A Middling Course for the Middle Kingdom," *Asian Survey* 23, no. 1 (January 1983):27.

59. See Allen S. Whiting, "Assertive Nationalism in Chinese Foreign Policy," *Asian Survey* 23, no. 8 (August 1983):917.

60. The speeches of Seng Ziaping and Hu Yaobang to the Twelfth Congress of the Chinese Communist Party were reported in *Beijing Review*, September 6 and 13, 1982.

61. See Martin Lasater, "The Limits to U.S.-China Strategic Cooperation," *Backgrounder* (Washington, D.C.: Asian Studies Center, Heritage Foundaton, April 20, 1984, Mimeographed).

Chapter Six

1. See *United States–Soviet Union–China: The Great Power Triangle. Summary of Hearings Conducted by the Subcommittee on Future Foreign Policy Research and*

Development of the Committee on International Relations (Washington, D.C.: Government Printing Office, 1977).

2. *Playing the China Card: Implication for United States–Soviet–Chinese Relations. Report Prepared for the Subcommittee on Asian and Pacific Affairs of the Committee on Foreign Affairs, U.S. House of Representatives* (Washington, D.C.: Government Printing Office, 1979), p. 19.

3. See the comments by Robert Scalapino in *Normalization of Relations with the People's Republic of China: Practical Implications. Hearings Before the Subcommittee on Asian and Pacific Affairs of the Committee on International Relations.* (Washington, D.C.: Government Printing Office, 1977), pp. 27–28.

4. See the comments of Harold Hinton in ibid., p. 215.

5. For a brief history of Taiwan, see W. G. Goddard, *Formosa: A Study in Chinese History* (Edinburgh: R & R Clarke, n.d.).

6. Frank S. T. Hsiao and Lawrence R. Sullivan, "The Chinese Communist Party and the Status of Taiwan, 1928–1943," *Pacific Affairs* 52, no. 3 (Fall 1979):446–51.

7. Ibid., p. 465.

8. See John F. Copper, "China's View of Taiwan's Status: Continuity and Change," *Asia Pacific Community*, Spring 1980, p. 124.

9. For the text of the Shanghai Communiqué, see the appendix to Claude A. Buss, *China: The People's Republic of China and Richard Nixon* (San Francisco: W. H. Freeman, 1974), p. 104.

10. *Taiwan Enabling Act* (Washington, D.C.: Government Printing Office, 1979), p. 7.

11. See the Testimony of Ray Cline and A. James Gregor in *Taiwan Communiqué and Separation of Powers. Hearings Before the Subcommittee on Separation of Powers of the Committee on the Judiciary, United States Senate* (Washington, D.C.: Government Printing Office, 1983), pp. 25, 31, 57.

12. Hungdah Chiu, "The Question of Taiwan in Sino-American Relations," in Hungdah Chiu, ed., *China and the Taiwan Issue* (New York: Praeger, 1979), pp. 161–62.

13. Frank P. Morello, *The International Legal Status of Formosa* (The Hague: Martinus Nijhoff, 1966), p. 92. This claim would not extend to the offshore islands, which have been under bombardment by the forces of the PRC almost since establishment of the Communist Chinese authorities in Beijing.

14. Chiu, "The Question of Taiwan," pp. 163–64.

15. See L. Oppenheim, *International Law*, 8th ed. (London: Longmans, Green, 1955), p. 873, cited Hungdah Chiu, "The Future of U.S.-Taiwan Relations," *Asian Affairs: An American Review*, September–October 1981, p. 26.

16. See David Ta-Wei Lee, "Presidential-Congressional Relations: A Case Study of the Taiwan Relations Act," in *Emerging Western Pacific Community: Problems and Prospects* (Taipei: Freedom Council, 1979), pp. 183–84.

17. Nicholas deB. Katzenbach, *Communist China: A Realistic View* (Washington, D.C.: Department of State, 1968), p. 4.

18. As quoted in Robert L. Downen, *The Taiwan Pawn in the China Game: Congress to the Rescue* (Washington, D.C.: Georgetown University Press, 1979), p. 15.

19. See Edwin K. Snyder, A. James Gregor, and Maria Hsia Chang, *The Taiwan Relations Act and the Defense of the Republic of China* (Berkeley: University of California, Institute of International Studies, 1980), chap. 2.

20. See Harry Harding, *China and the U.S.: Normalization and Beyond* (New York: Foreign Policy Association, 1979), p. 11.

21. See Hua's statement in the appendixes to Lester L. Wolff and David L. Simon, eds., *Legislative History of the Taiwan Relations Act: An Analytic Compilation with Documents on Subsequent Developments* (New York: American Association for Chinese Studies, 1982), p. 305.

22. As quoted in Harding, *China and the U.S.*, pp. 10, 12.

23. Wolff and Simon, *Legislative History of the Taiwan Relations Act*, pp. 12, 15.

24. For the full text of the Taiwan Relations Act, see Snyder, Gregor, and Chang, *Taiwan Relations Act*, appendix D, pp. 104–111.

25. See A. James Gregor, "The United States, the Republic of China, and the Taiwan Relations Act," *Orbis* 24, no. 3 (Fall 1980).

26. For the text of the communiqué of August 17, 1982, see *U.S.-China Joint Communiqué, August 1982*, Current Policy Series no. 413 (Washington, D.C.: Bureau of Public Affairs, 1982), p. 2.

27. John Holdridge, *U.S.-China Joint Communiqué*, p. 3.

28. Ibid.

29. Several detailed studies have been made of the economic development of the Republic of China on Taiwan. Two of the most informative are John C. H. Fei, Gustav Ranis, and Shirley W.Y. Kuo, *Growth with Equity: The Taiwan Case* (New York: Oxford University Press, 1979); and Walter Galenson, ed., *Economic Growth and Structural Change: The Postwar Experience of the Republic of China* (Ithaca, N.Y.: Cornell University Press, 1979).

30. Neil Jacoby, *U.S. Aid to Taiwan* (New York: Praeger, 1966), pp. 225–26.

31. For a more complete summary of these data, see *Economic Indicators: Taiwan, Republic of China* (Taipei: Ministry of Economic Affairs, 1978).

32. Shirley W. Y. Kuo, Gustav Ranis, and John C. H. Fei, *The Taiwan Success Story: Rapid Growth with Improved Distribution in the Republic of China, 1952–1979* (Boulder, Colo.: Westview Press, 1981), p. 5.

33. Chu-yuan Cheng, "Economic Development in Taiwan and Mainland China: A Comparison of Strategies and Performance," *Asian Affairs: An American Review*, Spring 1983, pp. 62–67.

34. See Jan S. Prybyla, *The Societal Objective of Wealth, Growth, Stability, and Equity in Taiwan* (Baltimore: University of Maryland School of Law, 1978), pp. 28–31; Yuan-li Wu, *Income Distribution in the Process of Economic Growth of the Republic*

of China (Baltimore: University of Maryland School of Law, 1977), pp. 33–42.

35. See the discussion in Shirley W. Y. Kuo, *The Taiwan Economy in Transition* (Boulder, Colo.: Westview Press, 1983).

36. There is an abundance of literature devoted to dependency theory. Some of the most popular studies are James D. Cockcroft, André Gunder Frank, and Dale L. Johnson, *Dependence and Underdevelopment: Latin America's Political Economy* (New York: Anchor Press, 1972); Harry Magdoff, *The Age of Imperialism: The Economics of U.S. Foreign Policy* (New York: Monthly Review Press, 1969); Pierre Jalée, *The Third World in World Economy* (New York: Monthly Review Press, 1969); Samir Amin, *Accumulation on a World Scale: A Critique of the Theory of Underdevelopment* (New York: Monthly Review Press, 1974); Samir Amin, *Imperialism and Unequal Development* (New York: Monthly Review Press, 1977); and Samir Amin, *Unequal Development: An Essay on the Social Formations of Peripheral Capitalism* (New York: Monthly Review Press, 1977); Arghiri Emmanuel, *Unequal Exchange: A Study of the Imperialism of Trade* (New York: Monthly Review Press, 1972).

37. A. James Gregor, Maria Hsia Chang, and Andrew B. Zimmerman, *Ideology and Development: Sun Yat-sen and the Economic History of Taiwan* (Berkeley: University of California, Center for Chinese Studies, 1981), chap. 5.

38. A. James Gregor and Maria Hsia Chang, *The Republic of China and U.S. Policy: A Study in Human Rights* (Washington, D.C.: Ethics and Public Policy Center, 1983).

39. A. James Gregor and Maria Hsia Chang, "Marxism, Sun Yat-sen, and the Notion of 'Imperialism,' " *Pacific Affairs* 55, no. 1 (Spring 1982):54–79.

40. See the comments of Julien Weiss in *Taiwan: One Year After United States–China Normalization* (Washington, D.C.: Government Printing Office, 1980), p. 86.

41. Text of the communiqué of August 17, 1982, p. 3.

42. William T. Tow, "U.S. Alliance Policies and Asian Pacific Security: A Transregional Approach," in William T. Tow and William R. Feeney, *U.S. Foreign Policy and Asian-Pacific Security: A Transregional Approach* (Boulder, Colo.: Westview Press, 1982), p. 24.

43. Charles T. Cross, "Taipei's Identity Crisis," *Foreign Policy*, no. 51 (Summer 1983), p. 43.

44. See A. James Gregor and Maria Hsia Chang, *The Iron Triangle: A U.S. Security Policy for Northeast Asia* (Stanford: Hoover Institution Press, 1984), pp. 46, 79–80; A. James Gregor, "U.S. Interests in Northeast Asia and the Security of Taiwan," *Strategic Review* 13, no. 1 (Winter 1985).

45. See Edmund Lee, "Beijing's Balancing Act," *Foreign Policy*, no. 51 (Summer 1983), p. 43.

46. For a discussion of the ROC's air defense requirements, see Martin L. Lasater, *Taiwan: Facing Mounting Threats* (Washington, D.C.: Heritage Foundation, 1984).

47. The ROC commitment to a Western defense strategy is briefly described in Wego W. K. Chiang, *The Strategic Significance of Taiwan—in the Global Strategic Picture* (Taipei: World Anti-Communist League, 1978). General Chiang is the son of Chiang Kai-shek and the half-brother of the present president of the ROC. The ROC commitment has been regularly reiterated since 1949 by the political leadership in Taipei.

48. Zhang Hongzeng, "U.S. 'Taiwan Relations Act' Viewed Against International Law," in the *Chinese Yearbook of International Law*, reprinted in *Selected Articles from Chinese Yearbook of International Law* (Beijing: China Translation and Publishing Co., 1983), p. 190.

49. Holdridge, *U.S.-China Joint Communiqué*, p. 4.

50. *Taiwan Enabling Act*, p. 7.

51. "Answers to Questions Regarding Taiwan Arms Sales," in *Taiwan Communiqué and Separation of Powers*, p. 140.

52. Zhang, "U.S. 'Taiwan Relations Act,' " pp. 202–3.

53. "Answers to Questions Regarding Arms Sales," in *Taiwan Communiqué and Separation of Powers*, p. 141.

54. Holdridge, *U.S.-China Joint Communiqué*, p. 3.

55. Zhang, "U.S. 'Taiwan Relations Act,' " pp. 197–98.

56. *New York Times*, February 28, 1981, p. E19 (Op-Ed page).

57. See Donald S. Zagorian's significantly qualified judgments in "China's Quiet Revolution," *Foreign Affairs* 62, no. 4 (Spring 1984):879–904.

CHAPTER SEVEN

1. Richard M. Nixon, "Asia After Vietnam," *Foreign Affairs* 46, no. 1 (October 1967):118.

2. As cited in *China Business Review*, January–February 1984, p. 29.

3. Xu Dixin, "Transformation of China's Economy," in Xu Dixin, ed., *China's Search for Economic Growth: The Chinese Economy Since 1949* (Beijing: New World Press, 1982), pp. 17, 20.

4. Mao Zedong, *A Critique of Soviet Economics* (New York: Monthly Review Press, 1977), p. 134.

5. *Economy* (Beijing: Foreign Languages Press, 1984), p. 63.

6. He Jianzhang, "The Current Economic Policies of China," in George C. Wang, ed., *Economic Reform in the PRC in Which China's Economists Make Known What Went Wrong, Why, and What Should Be Done About It* (Boulder, Colo.: Westview Press, 1982), pp. 69–70.

7. Reeitsu Kojima, "China's New Agricultural Policy," *Developing Economies*, 20, no. 4 (December 1982):391–92.

8. Dong Furen, "The Chinese Economy in the Process of Great Transformation," in Wang, *Economic Reform in the PRC*, p. 125.

9. Strobe Talbott, "The Strategic Dimension of the Sino-American Relationship," in Richard H. Solomon, ed., *The China Factor: Sino-American Relations and the Global Scene* (Englewood Cliffs, N.J.: Prentice-Hall, 1981), p. 112.

10. See Shigeru Ishikawa, "China's Economic Growth Since 1949—An Assessment," *China Quarterly*, no. 94 (June 1983), p. 245, Table 1.

11. Ren Tao and Zheng Jingsheng, "Why a Shift in Emphasis?" in Su Wenning, ed., *Modernization—The Chinese Way* (Beijing: Beijing Review, 1983), p. 11.

12. Lu Baifu, "Agriculture's Way Ahead," in Su, *Modernization—The Chinese Way*, p. 48.

13. Vaclav Smil, *The Bad Earth: Environmental Degradation in China* (Armonk, N.Y.: M.E. Sharpe, 1984), p. 69.

14. Lu, "Agriculture's Way Ahead," p. 47.

15. Ibid., p. 48; Chu-yuan Cheng, *China's Economic Development: Growth and Structural Change* (Boulder, Colo.: Westview Press, 1982), p. 408.

16. Wen Lang Li, "Population and Prospects of Social Change in People's Republic of China," Communication at the Thirteenth Sino-American Conference on Mainland China, Taipei, June 12–15, 1984.

17. Lu, "Agriculture's Way Ahead," p. 48.

18. Cheng, *China's Economic Development*, p. 355.

19. Dong Fureng, "Relationship Between Accumulation and Consumption," in Xu, *China's Search for Economic Growth*, pp. 90–91.

20. Jan S. Prybyla, "The Economic System of the People's Republic of China," *Asian Thought and Society*, 9, no. 25 (March 1984):17; see also *Economy*, p. 48.

21. *Economy*, p. 49; see also Liu Sinian, "Economic Planning," Xu, in *China's Search for Economic Growth*, p. 37.

22. Dong, "Accumulation and Consumption," in Xu, *China's Search for Economic Growth*, p. 67.

23. Ibid., p. 66.

24. Zhang Shuguang, "Two Keys to Industrial Development," in Su, *Modernization—The Chinese Way*, p. 62.

25. See the discussion in Benedict Stavis, "The Dilemma of State Power: The Solution Becomes the Problem," in Victor Nee and David Mozingo, eds., *State and Society in Contemporary China* (Ithaca, N.Y.: Cornell University Press, 1983), p. 185.

26. Xu Dixin, "Transformation of China's Economy," in Xu, *China's Search for Economic Growth*, p. 17.

27. Ren Tao, "Reform Holds the Key to Success," in Su, *Modernization—The Chinese Way*, p. 135.

28. "An Exposure of the True Face of Fixing Output Quotas for Individual Households," *People's Daily*, November 2, 1959, p. 4; cited by Chen Ting-

Chung in "Agriculture in Mainland China: Reform and Problems," communication at the Thirteenth Sino-American Conference on Mainland China, Taipei, June 12–15, 1984. See also "New Switch in Peiping's Agricultural Policy," in *Mainland China's Modernization: Its Prospects and Problems* (Berkeley: University of California, Institute of International Studies and Institute of East Asian Studies, 1981), pp. 187–88.

29. Smil, *The Bad Earth*, p. 192.

30. Ren and Zheng, "Why a Shift in Emphasis?," p. 134; Xu, "Transformation of China's Economy," p. 8.

31. "Zhao Ziyang Speech at Industry Conference," Foreign Broadcast Information Service *Daily Report* (hereafter cited as *FBIS*), April 1, 1982, pp. K6–K8.

32. See Robert F. Dernberger, "Communist China's Industrial Policies: Goals and Results," in *Mainland China's Modernization*, p. 152.

33. Robert F. Dernberger, "Mainland China's Economic System: A New Model or Variations on an Old Theme?" communication at the Thirteenth Sino-American Conference on Mainland China, Taipei, June 12–15, 1984.

34. Liu Guoguang and Zhao Renwei, "Relationship Between Planning and the Market Under Socialism," in Wang, *Economic Reform in the PRC*, p. 90.

35. Ibid.

36. Ren and Zheng, "Why a Shift in Emphasis?," p. 138.

37. Liu and Zhao, "Planning and the Market Under Socialism," pp. 99, 100.

38. Ibid., p. 102.

39. As quoted by Xu Dixin, "China's Modernization and the Prospects for Its Economy," in Wang, *Economic Reform in the PRC*, p. 47; and Ren Tao and Wang Shunsheng, "What's It Like?" in Su, *Modernization—The Chinese Way*, p. 29.

40. Yao Yilin, "Report on the 1983 Plan for National Economic and Social Development," in *The First Session of the Sixth National People's Congress (June 1983)* (Beijing: Foreign Languages Press, 1983), pp. 68–69, 72.

41. See He Hianzhang, "Current Economic Policies of China," in Wang, *Economic Reform in the PRC*, pp. 73–74.

42. Liu and Zhao, "Planning and the Market Under Socialism," p. 97.

43. See Peter Van Ness and Satish Raichur, "Dilemmas of Socialist Development: An Analysis of Strategic Lines in China, 1949–1981," in *China from Mao to Deng* (Armonk, N.Y.: M. E. Sharpe, 1983), pp. 77–89.

44. See the rendering in Edward Friedman, "The Original Chinese Revolution Remains in Power," in *China from Mao to Deng*, pp. 22–23.

45. Hua Guofeng, "Political Report to the Eleventh National Congress of the Communist Party of China" in *The Eleventh Congress of the Communist Party of China* (Beijing: Foreign Languages Press, 1977), pp. 49–53.

46. For a fuller discussion, see Lowell Dittmer, "Ideology and Organization in Post-Mao China," *Asian Survey*, 24, no. 3 (March 1984): 349–69.

47. T. C. Chang, C. F. Chen, and Y. T. Lin, eds., *Catalog of Chinese Underground Literatures*, 2 vols. (Taipei: Institute of Current China Studies, 1981).

48. As quoted in ibid., 1:3, 11, 71. For complete translations of some of the major publications, see Lin Yih-tang, ed., *What They Say: A Collection of Current Chinese Underground Publications* (Taipei: Institute of Current China Studies, n.d.).

49. See the discussion in "China Spring," translated in *Freedom at Issue*, no. 74 (September–October 1983), pp. 36–41.

50. See Ralph Croizer, "The Thorny Flowers of 1979: Political Cartoons and Liberalization in China," in *China from Mao to Deng*, pp. 29–38.

51. "Transcript of Wei Ching-sheng's Trial," in *Inside China Mainland*, January 1980, pp. 1–12.

52. Translated in *Inside China Mainland*, April 1980, pp. 7–13.

53. See the Preamble of *The Constitution of the People's Republic of China (Promulgated for Implementation on December 4, 1982)* (Beijing: Foreign Languages Press, 1983).

54. "Deng Xiaoping's Speech at the Second Plenary Session of the Twelfth Central Committee of the Chinese Communist Party," *Issues and Studies*, 20, no. 4 (April 1984):100, 102, 107, 109.

55. Mao Zedong, "Combat Liberalism," *Selected Works* (Beijing: Foreign Languages Press, 1965), 2:33.

56. See Hungdah Chiu, *Chinese Law and Justice: Trends over Three Decades* (Baltimore: University of Maryland School of Law, 1982).

57. Hungdah Chiu, *Socialist Legalism: Reform and Continuity in Post-Mao People's Republic of China* (Baltimore: University of Maryland School of Law, 1982), p. 4. For the English-language text of the Law on Counterrevolutionary Acts, see *Inside China Mainland*, January 1980, pp. 13–14.

58. As quoted in Chiu, *Socialist Legalism*, p. 16.

59. For the English-language text of the Labor Reform Statute, see *Inside China Mainland*, January 1980, pp. 14–15.

60. Wei Jingsheng was prosecuted under Art. 56 of the Constitution of 1978, which states: "Citizens must support the leadership of the Communist Party of China [and] support the socialist system." See "Transcript of Wei Ching-sheng's Trial," p. 9.

61. See the section on the People's Republic of China in *Country Reports on Human Rights and Practices for 1983* (Washington, D.C.: Government Printing Office, February 1984), pp. 740–755.

62. "Deng Xiaoping's Speech," pp. 104–5.

63. Ibid., pp. 106, 109.

64. As quoted in Ho Chih-cheng, *The Fourth Constitution of Communist China* (Taipei: World Anti-Communist League, May 1983), pp. 24–25.

CHAPTER EIGHT

1. Victor P. Petrov, *China: Emerging World Power* (New York: Van Nostrand, 1976), pp. 156–57.

2. John Franklin Copper, *China's Global Role* (Stanford: Hoover Institution Press, 1980), p. 132.

3. See Paul Hollander, *Political Pilgrims: Travels of Western Intellectuals to the Soviet Union, China, and Cuba* (New York: Harper & Row, 1981), chap. 7.

4. Michel Oksenberg, "On Learning from China," in Michel Oksenberg, ed., *China's Developmental Experience* (New York: Praeger, 1973), p. 2.

5. As quoted in Hungdah Chiu, *Socialist Legalism: Reform and Continuity in Post-Mao People's Republic of China* (Baltimore: University of Maryland School of Law, 1982), p. 1.

6. "Quarterly Chronicle and Documentation (October–December 1978)," *China Quarterly*, no. 77 (March 1979), p. 172.

7. Edward Friedman, "The Societal Obstacle to China's Socialist Transition: State Capitalism or Feudal Fascism?" in Victor Nee and David Mozingo, eds., *State and Society in Contemporary China* (Ithaca, N.Y.: Cornell University Press, 1983), p. 161, 151.

8. Cited in Beijing's English-language *China Daily*, as reported in *Chung-kuo shih-pao* (*China Times*), October 1, 1984 (U.S. edition), p. 3; "Red China's Education and Its Problems," *Inside China Mainland*, June 1984, pp. 11–12; and Alan P. L. Liu, *Social Change on Mainland China and Taiwan, 1949–80* (Baltimore: University of Maryland School of Law, 1982), pp. 14–15.

9. See Friedman, "China's Socialist Transition," p. 151.

10. Vaclav Smil, *The Bad Earth: Environmental Degradation in China* (Armonk, N.Y.: M.E. Sharpe, 1984), pp. 141, 143, 153–67.

11. See Hungdah Chiu, *Chinese Law and Justice: Trends over Three Decades* (Baltimore: University of Maryland School of Law, 1982).

12. Chalmers Johnson, "What's Wrong with the Chinese Political Studies?" in King-yuh Chang, ed., *The Emerging Teng System: Orientation, Policies, and Implications* (Taipei: Institute of International Relations, 1982), p. VII-1–3.

13. John K. Galbraith, *China Passage* (Boston: Beacon Press, 1973), pp. 104, 115.

14. *China Policy for the Next Decade: Report of the Atlantic Council's Committee on China Policy* (Washington, D.C.: Atlantic Council of the United States, October 1983), pp. 13–14.

15. Harry Gelman, *The Soviet Far East Buildup and Soviet Risk-Taking Against China* (Santa Monica, Calif.: Rand Corporation, August 1982).

16. See Allen S. Whiting, "The Great Triangle: China, the U.S.S.R., and Japan," in Harrison Brown, ed., *China Among the Nations of the Pacific* (Boulder, Colo.: Westview Press, 1982), pp. 49–51.

17. A. James Gregor and Maria Hsia Chang, *The Iron Triangle: A U.S. Security Policy for Northeast Asia* (Stanford: Hoover Institution Press, 1984), pp. 98–99.

18. Carl Bernstein, "Arms for Afghanistan," *New Republic*, 18 (July 1981):8.

19. See Fin-Sup Shinn, "North Korea in 1982: Continuing Revolution Under Kim Jog-Il," *Asian Survey*, January 1983, p. 105.

20. Gregor and Chang, *The Iron Triangle*, chap. 5.

21. "New Tactics in Foreign Policy," in *Inside China Mainland*, March 1980, p. 4.

22. See Denis D. Gray, "Suspicion of Chinese Hangs On in Southeast Asia," *Los Angeles Times*, November 26, 1982; Guy J. Pauker, "Southeast Asia Looks at China," in Brown, *Nations of the Pacific*, pp. 115–25; Justus M. van der Kroef, *Communism in Southeast Asia* (Berkeley and Los Angeles: University of California Press, 1980), chap. 5.

23. Murrey Marder, "The China Policy That Isn't," *Washington Post*, June 14, 1981, p. C1.

24. See Leslie H. Gelb, "U.S.-China Ties: Lower Expectations," *New York Times*, February 2, 1983, p. 3.

25. Drew Middleton, "Arms for China: Experts See Little Benefit," *New York Times*, April 12, 1982, p. 8.

26. See the extended discussion in Todd R. Starbuck, *China and the Great Power Balance* (Carlisle Barracks, Penn.: Strategic Studies Institute, August 1983).

27. Antony Preston, "The Changing Balance in the Pacific," *Jane's Defense Weekly*, September 29, 1984, p. 547.

28. Peter C. Y. Chow, "U.S.-China Trade: Old Myths and New Realities," paper presented at the Forty-ninth Annual Conference of the Southern Economic Association, Atlanta, Ga., November 7–9, 1979, mimeographed, p. 4.

29. Text of Hu Yaobang's Report to Twelfth CPC Congress, *FBIS*, September 8, 1982, p. K11.

30. Huan Hsiang, "Where Communist China Stands," *Inside China Mainland*, April 1983, pp. 2, 3.

31. *Briefing Book: President Reagan's Trip to Asia, Part II* (Washington, D.C.: Heritage Foundation, April 1984), pp. 31–36.

32. Marvin G. Weinberg and Stephen B. Cohen, "Pakistan in 1982: Holding On," *Asian Survey* 23, no. 2 (February 1983):130–31.

33. Joanne Finegan, *Policy, Proliferation, and the Nuclear Proliferation Treaty: U.S. Strategies and South Asian Prospects* (Baltimore: University of Maryland School of Law, 1980), pp. 40–41.

34. See David Salem, *The People's Republic of China, International Law, and Arms Control* (Baltimore: University of Maryland School of Law, 1983), pp. 47–58.

35. Lewis A. Dunn, "Military Politics, Nuclear Proliferation, and the Nuclear Coup d'état," *Journal of Strategic Studies*, 1, no. 1 (May 1978):31–50.

36. Nancy Langston, "Wells of Uncertainty," *Far Eastern Economic Review*, June 28, 1984, pp. 50–52.

37. "Where the Guns May Be Turned on Oil Drillers," *Business Week*, May 9, 1983, p. 44.
38. *FBIS*, Asia and Pacific, May 2, 1984, p. K14.
39. Gregor and Chang, *The Iron Triangle*, chap. 7.
40. Randall W. Hardy, *China's Oil Future: A Case of Modest Expectations* (Boulder, Colo.: Westview Press, 1978), chap. 8.
41. Benedict Stavis, "The Dilemma of State Power: The Solution Becomes the Problem," in Nee and Mozingo, *State and Society*, pp. 175–93.
42. See the comments in the official PRC press, as translated by the Xinhua News Agency, August 15, 1984, in *Inside China Mainland*, September 1984, p. 2; and text of Hu Yaobang's Report to the Twelfth CPC Congress, September 8, 1982, *FBIS*, September 8, 1982, pp. K15–K17, K22–K24.
43. Edmund Lee, "Beijing's Balancing Act," *Foreign Policy*, no. 51 (Summer 1983), pp. 29, 31.
44. See Wang Bingnan, "China's Independent Foreign Policy," speech of January 30, 1983, reprinted in *FBIS*, January 31, 1983, pp. A1–A7.
45. Hu, Report to the Twelfth CPC Congress, p. K18.
46. "Neocolonialism," *Jingji Yanjiu*, no. 4 (1984), as translated in *Inside China Mainland*, September 1984, pp. 8–9.
47. Hu, Report to the Twelfth CPC Congress, p. K20.
48. See appendix B of *Report on the U.S. and the U.N.: A Balance Sheet* (Washington, D.C.: Heritage Foundation, 1984), p. 57.
49. "Speech by Chairman of the Delegation of the People's Republic of China, Teng Hsiao-ping, at the Special Session of the U.N. General Assembly (April 10, 1974)," in Chi Hsin, *Teng Hsiao-ping: A Political Biography* (Hong Kong: Cosmos, 1978), p. 173.
50. "Neocolonialism," p. 11.
51. "Liaowang Publishes Article on China's Independent and Initiatory Diplomacy," speech of October 20, 1982, reprinted in *FBIS*-Chi, October 21, 1982, pp. A1–A2.
52. Hu, Report to the Twelfth CPC Congress, pp. K15, K16, K18.
53. See Allen S. Whiting, "Sino-American Relations: The Decade Ahead," *Orbis* 26, no. 3 (Fall 1982):697–719.
54. Ibid., pp. 705, 706, 707.

Bibliography

Amin, Samir. *Accumulation on a World Scale: A Critique of the Theory of Underdevelopment*. New York: Monthly Review Press, 1974.

———. *Imperialism and Unequal Development*. New York: Monthly Review Press, 1977.

———. *Unequal Development: An Essay on the Social Formations of Peripheral Capitalism*. New York: Monthly Review Press, 1977.

Andors, Stephen. *China's Industrial Revolution: Politics, Planning, and Management, 1949 to the Present*. New York: Pantheon Books, 1977.

———, ed. *Workers and Workplaces in Revolutionary China*. White Plains, N.Y.: M. E. Sharpe, 1977.

Armstrong, J. D. *Revolutionary Diplomacy: Chinese Foreign Policy and the United Front Doctrine*. Berkeley and Los Angeles: University of California Press, 1977.

Barnett, A. Doak. *China and the Major Powers in Asia*. Washington, D.C.: Brookings Institution, 1977.

———. *China Policy*. Washington, D.C.: Brookings Institution, 1977.

———. *China's Economy in Global Perspective*. Washington, D.C.: Brookings Institution, 1981.

———. *Communist China in Perspective*. New York: Praeger, 1962.

Barrymaine, Norman. *The Time Bomb: Today's China from the Inside*. New York: Taplinger Publishing Co., 1971.

A Basic Understanding of the Communist Party of China. Toronto: Norman Bethune Institute, 1976.

Bedeski, Robert E. *The People's Republic of China's Relations in Asia: The Strategic Implications*. Ottawa: Department of National Defense, July 1984.

Bennett, Gordon, ed. *China's Finance and Trade: A Policy Reader*. White Plains, N.Y.: M. E. Sharpe, 1978.

Bianco, Lucien. *Origins of the Chinese Revolution, 1915–1949*. Stanford: Stanford University Press, 1971.

Bonds, Ray. *Russian Military Power*. New York: Crown Publishers, Bonanza Books, 1980.

————, ed. *The Chinese War Machine*. New York: Crescent Books, 1979.

Briefing Book: President's Trip to Asia, Part II. Washington, D.C.: Heritage Foundation, April 1984.

Brown, Harrison, ed. *China Among the Nations of the Pacific*. Boulder, Colo.: Westview Press, 1982.

Burlatsky, Fedor. *Mao Tse-tung: An Ideological and Psychological Portrait*. Moscow: Progress Publishers, 1980.

Bush, Richard C., ed. *China Briefing, 1982*. Boulder, Colo.: Westview Press, 1983.

Buss, Claude A. *China: The People's Republic of China and Richard Nixon*. San Francisco: W. H. Freeman, 1974.

Camilleri, Joseph. *Chinese Foreign Policy: The Maoist Era and Its Aftermath*. Seattle: University of Washington Press, 1980.

Chai, Ch'u, and Winberg Chai. *Confucianism*. Woodbury, N.Y.: Barron's Educational Series, 1973.

Chai, Winberg, ed. *The Foreign Relations of the People's Republic of China*. New York: Capricorn Books, 1972.

Chang, King-yuh. *A Communist Nationalism?* Taipei: Government Information Office, 1984.

————, ed. *The Emerging Teng System: Orientation, Policies, and Implications*. Taipei: Institute of International Relations, 1982.

Chang, Maria Hsia. *The Chinese Blue Shirt Society: Fascism and Developmental Nationalism*. Berkeley: University of California, Institute of East Asian Studies, 1985.

Chang, Parris H. *Power and Policy in China*. 2d ed., rev. and enl. University Park: Pennsylvania State University Press, 1981.

Chang, T. C., C. F. Chen, and Y. T. Lin, eds. *Catalog of Chinese Underground Literatures*. 2 vols. Taipei: Institute of Current China Studies, 1981.

Chen, Frederick Tse-shyang, ed. *China Policy and National Security*. Dobbs Ferry, N.Y.: Transnational Publishers, 1984.

Ch'en, Jerome. *Mao and the Chinese Revolution*. New York: Oxford University Press, 1967.

Chen, King C. *China's War Against Vietnam, 1979: A Military Analysis*. Baltimore: University of Maryland School of Law, 1983.

————, ed. *China and the Three Worlds: A Foreign Policy Reader*. White Plains, N.Y.: M. E. Sharpe, 1979.

Cheng, Chu-yuan. *China's Economic Development: Growth and Structural Change.* Boulder, Colo.: Westview Press, 1982.

Cheng, J. Chester, ed. *The Politics of the Red Chinese Army.* Stanford: Hoover Institution Press, 1966.

Chi, Hsin. *Teng Hsiao-ping: A Political Biography.* Hong Kong: Cosmos Books, 1978.

Chiang, Wego W. K. *The Strategic Significance of Taiwan—in the Global Strategic Picture.* Taipei: World Anti-Communist League, 1978.

China: A Reassessment of the Economy. Joint Economic Committee, United States Congress, 94th Session. Washington, D.C.: Government Printing Office, 1975.

China Handbook. Hong Kong: Kung Pao, 1980.

China from Mao to Deng. Armonk, N.Y.: M. E. Sharpe, 1983.

China Policy for the Next Decade: Report of the Atlantic Council's Committee on China Policy. Washington, D.C.: Atlantic Council of the United States, October 1983.

Chinese Communist Internal Politics and Foreign Policy Reviews on Reference Materials Concerning Education on Situation Issues by the Kunming Military Region. Taipei: Institute of International Relations, 1974.

Chiu, Hungdah. *Chinese Law and Justice: Trends over Three Decades.* Baltimore: University of Maryland School of Law, 1982.

————.*The People's Republic of China and the Law of Treaties.* Cambridge, Mass.: Harvard University Press, 1972.

————.*Socialist Legalism: Reform and Continuity in Post-Mao People's Republic of China.* Baltimore: University of Maryland School of Law, 1982.

————, ed. *China and the Taiwan Issue.* New York: Praeger, 1979.

Chiu, Hungdah, and Shao-chuan Leng, eds. *China: Seventy Years After the 1911 Hsin-hai Revolution.* Charlottesville: University Press of Virginia, 1984.

Choudhury, Golam W. *China in World Affairs: The Foreign Policy of the PRC Since 1970.* Boulder, Colo.: Westview Press, 1982.

Classified Chinese Communist Documents: A Selection. Taipei: Institute of International Relations, 1978.

Cockcroft, James D., André Gunder Frank, and Dale L. Johnson. *Dependence and Underdevelopment: Latin America's Political Economy.* New York: Doubleday, Anchor Press, 1972.

Cohen, Warren I. *New Frontiers in American–East Asian Relations.* New York: Columbia University Press, East Asia Institute, 1983.

Collis, Maurice. *Foreign Mud: The Opium Imbroglio at Canton in the 1830s and the Anglo-Chinese War.* New York: Norton & Co., 1946.

Confucius. *The Four Books.* Translated by James Legge. Taipei: Culture Books, 1975.

The Constitution of the People's Republic of China. Beijing: Foreign Languages Press, 1975.

The Constitution of the People's Republic of China. Beijing: Foreign Languages Press, 1978.

The Constitution of the People's Republic of China. Beijing: Foreign Languages Press, 1982.

Copper, John F. *China's Foreign Aid in 1978.* Baltimore: University of Maryland School of Law, 1979.

———. *China's Foreign Aid in 1979–80.* Baltimore: University of Maryland School of Law, 1981.

———. *China's Global Role.* Stanford: Hoover Institution Press, 1980.

Country Reports on Human Rights and Practices for 1983. Washington, D.C.: Government Printing Office, February 1984.

Cressey, George B. *China's Geographic Foundations.* New York: Columbia University Press, 1934.

The Criminal Law and the Criminal Procedure Law of China. Beijing: Foreign Languages Press, 1984.

Deng, Xiaoping. *Selected Works.* Beijing: Foreign Languages Press, 1984.

Dernberger, Robert F. *China's Development Experience in Comparative Perspective.* Cambridge, Mass.: Harvard University Press, 1980.

Doolin, Dennis J. *Territorial Claims in the Sino-Soviet Conflict.* Stanford: Hoover Institution Press, 1977.

Down with the New Tsars! Beijing: Foreign Languages Press, 1969.

Downen, Robert L. *The Taiwan Pawn in the China Game: Congress to the Rescue.* Washington, D.C.: Georgetown University Press, 1979.

Dulles, Foster Rhea. *China and America.* Princeton, N.J.: Princeton University Press, 1946.

Eckstein, Alexander. *China's Economic Revolution.* New York: Cambridge University Press, 1977.

Economic Indicators: Taiwan, Republic of China. Taipei: Ministry of Economic Affairs, 1978.

Economy. Beijing: Foreign Languages Press, 1984.

The Eleventh Congress of the Communist Party of China. Beijing: Foreign Languages Press, 1977.

Emerging Western Pacific Community: Problems and Prospects. Taipei: Freedom Council, 1979.

Fairbank, John K. *The United States and China.* Cambridge, Mass.: Harvard University Press, 1979.

———, ed. *The Chinese World Order.* Cambridge, Mass.: Harvard University Press, 1968.

Fairbank, John K., and Ssu-yu Teng, eds. *China's Response to the West: A Documentary Survey.* Cambridge, Mass.: Harvard University Press, 1954.

Fei, John C. H., Gustav Ranis, and Shirley W. Y. Kuo. *Growth with Equity: The Taiwan Case.* New York: Oxford University Press, 1979.

Finegan, Joanne. *Policy, Proliferation, and the Nuclear Proliferation Treaty: U.S.*

Strategies and South Asian Prospects. Baltimore: University of Maryland School of Law, 1980.

The First Session of the Sixth National People's Congress (June 1983). Beijing: Foreign Languages Press, 1983.

Fraser, Angus M. *The People's Liberation Army: Communist China's Armed Forces.* New York: Crane, Russak, 1973.

Freeman, Ronald, ed. *Population: The Vital Revolution*. New York: Doubleday, Anchor Press, 1964.

Galbraith, John K. *China Passage*. Boston: Beacon Press, 1973.

Galenson, Walter, ed. *Economic Growth and Structural Change: The Postwar Experience of the Republic of China*. Ithaca, N.Y.: Cornell University Press, 1979.

Garrett, Banning N., and Bonnie S. Glaser. *War and Peace: The Views from Moscow and Beijing*. Berkeley: University of California, Institute of International Studies, 1984.

Garver, John W. *China's Decision for Rapprochement with the United States, 1968–1971*. Boulder, Colo.: Westview Press, 1982.

Gasster, Michael. *Chinese Intellectuals and the Revolution of 1911: The Birth of Modern Chinese Radicalism*. Taipei: Rainbow Bridge Book Co., 1969.

Gelber, Harry G. *Technology, Defense, and External Relations in China, 1975–1978*. Boulder, Colo.: Westview Press, 1979.

Gelman, Harry. *Soviet Expansionism and the Sino-Soviet-U.S. Triangle*. Marina del Rey, Calif.: Security Conference on Asia and the Pacific, March 1983.

———. *The Soviet Far East Buildup and Soviet Risk-Taking Against China*. Santa Monica, Calif.: Rand Corporation, August 1982.

George, Alexander L. *The Chinese Communist Army in Action: The Korean War and Its Aftermath*. New York: Columbia University Press, 1967.

George, J. L., ed. *Problems of Sea Power as We Approach the Twenty-First Century*. Washington, D.C.: American Enterprise Institute, 1978.

Goddard, W. G. *Formosa: A Study in Chinese History*. Edinburgh: R & R Clarke, n.d.

Godwin, Paul H. B., ed. *The Chinese Defense Establishment: Continuity and Change in the 1980s*. Boulder, Colo.: Westview Press, 1983.

Goodman, David S. G., ed. *Groups and Politics in the People's Republic of China*. Armonk, N.Y.: M. E. Sharpe, 1984.

Gottlieb, Thomas M. *Chinese Foreign Policy Factionalism and the Origins of the Strategic Triangle*. Santa Monica, Calif.: Rand Corporation, 1977.

The Great Socialist Cultural Revolution in China. 10 vols. Beijing: Foreign Languages Press, 1966.

Gregor, A. James. *The Fascist Persuasion in Radical Politics*. Princeton, N.J.: Princeton University Press, 1974.

———. *A Survey of Marxism*. New York: Random House, 1965.

———. *Three Essays on China Policy and U.S. Security Interests in East Asia*. Berkeley:

University of California, Institute of International Studies, Pacific Basin Project, 1984.

————, and Maria Hsia Chang. *The Iron Triangle: A U.S. Security Policy for Northeast Asia*. Stanford: Hoover Institution Press, 1984.

————, and Maria Hsia Chang. *The Republic of China and U.S. Policy: A Study in Human Rights*. Washington, D.C.: Ethics and Public Policy Center, 1983.

————, and Maria Hsia Chang, and Andrew B. Zimmerman. *Ideology and Development: Sun Yat-sen and the Economic History of Taiwan*. Berkeley: University of California, Center for Chinese Studies, 1981.

Grieder, Jerome B. *Intellectuals and the State in Modern China: A Narrative History*. New York: The Free Press, 1981.

Griffith, Samuel B. *The Chinese People's Liberation Army*. New York: McGraw-Hill, 1967.

Grobe, Karl. *Chinas Wegnach Westen*. Frankfurt-am-Main: China Studien- und Verlagsgesellschaft, 1980.

Gurtov, Melvin. *China and Southeast Asia—The Politics of Survival: A Study of Foreign Policy Interaction*. Baltimore, Md.: The Johns Hopkins University Press, 1975.

————, and Byong-Moo Hwang. *China Under Threat: The Politics of Strategy and Diplomacy*. Baltimore, Md.: The Johns Hopkins University Press, 1980.

Han, Suyin. *The Morning Deluge*. Boston: Little, Brown, 1972.

Harding, Harry. *China and the U.S.: Normalization and Beyond*. New York: Foreign Policy Association, 1979.

————. *Organizing China: The Problem of Bureaucracy, 1949–1976*. Stanford: Stanford University Press, 1981.

Hardy, Randall W. *China's Oil Future: A Case of Modest Expectations*. Boulder, Colo.: Westview Press, 1978.

Harris, Nigel. *The Mandate of Heaven: Marx and Mao in Modern China*. London: Quartet, 1978.

Harrison, James P. *The Communists and Chinese Peasant Rebellions: A Study in the Rewriting of Chinese History*. New York: Atheneum, 1969.

Harrison, Selig S. *China, Oil, and Asia: Conflict Ahead?* New York: Columbia University Press, 1977.

Henry, Ernst. *What Are They After in Peking?* Moscow: Progress Publishers, 1979.

Hinton, Harold C. *China's Turbulent Quest: An Analysis of China's Foreign Relations Since 1949*. New and enl. ed. Bloomington: Indiana University Press, 1972.

————. *The Sino-Soviet Confrontation: Implications for the Future*. New York: Crane, Russak, 1976.

Ho, Chih-cheng. *The Fourth Constitution of Communist China*. Taipei: World Anti-Communist League, May 1983.

————, and Tang Tsou, eds. *China's Heritage and the Communist Political System*. Chicago: University of Chicago Press, 1968.

Ho, Samuel P. S., and Ralph W. Huenemann. *China's Open Door Policy: The Quest for Foreign Technology and Capital.* Vancouver: University of British Columbia Press, 1984.

Hoffman, Charles. *The Chinese Worker.* Albany: State University of New York Press, 1974.

Holcombe, Arthur N. *The Spirit of the Chinese Revolution.* Reprint. Westport, Conn.: Hyperion Press, 1973.

Hollander, Paul. *Political Pilgrims: Travels of Western Intellectuals to the Soviet Union, China, and Cuba.* New York: Harper & Row, 1981.

Hsu, Leonard Shihlien. *The Political Philosophy of Confucianism.* London: George Routledge, 1932.

Hu, Sheng. *Imperialism and Chinese Politics.* Beijing: Foreign Languages Press, 1955.

———. *The 1911 Revolution: A Retrospective After Seventy Years.* Beijing: New World Press, 1983.

Huang, Sung-k'ang. *Li Ta-chao and the Impact of Marxism on Modern Chinese Thinking.* The Hague: Mouton & Co., 1965.

Iriye, Akira, ed. *U.S. Policy Toward China.* Boston: Little, Brown, 1968.

Jacoby, Neil. *U.S. Aid to Taiwan.* New York: Praeger, 1966.

Jalée, Pierre. *The Third World in World Economy.* New York: Monthly Review Press, 1969.

Jencks, Harlan W. *From Muskets to Missiles: Politics and Professionalism in the Chinese Army, 1945–1981.* Boulder, Colo.: Westview Press, 1982.

———. *The Politics of Chinese Military Development, 1945–1977.* Ann Arbor, Mich.: University Microfilms International, 1978.

Jian, Bozan, Xunzheng Shao, and Hua Hu. *A Concise History of China.* Beijing: Foreign Languages Press, 1981.

Joseph, William A. *The Critique of Ultra-Leftism in China, 1958–1981.* Stanford: Stanford University Press, 1984.

Katzenbach, Nicholas deB. *Communist China: A Realistic View.* Washington, D.C.: Department of State, 1968.

On Khrushchev's Phoney Communism and Its Historical Lessons for the World. Beijing: Foreign Languages Press, 1964.

Krivtsov, V. I., ed. *Maoism Through the Eyes of Communists.* Moscow: Progress Publishers, 1970.

Kruchinin, A., and V. Olgin. *Territorial Claims of Mao Tse-tung: History and Modern Times.* Moscow: Novosti, n.d.

Kuo, Shirley W. Y. *The Taiwan Economy in Transition.* Boulder, Colo.: Westview Press, 1983.

———, Gustav Ranis, and John C. H. Fei. *The Taiwan Success Story: Rapid Growth with Improved Distribution in the Republic of China, 1952–1979.* Boulder, Colo.: Westview Press, 1981.

Kuo, Warren. *Analytic History of the Chinese Communist Party.* 4 vols. Taipei: Institute of International Relations, 1968–1971.

———, ed. *Foreign Policy Speeches by Chinese Communist Leaders, 1963–1975.* Taipei: Institute of International Relations, 1976.

Lall, Arthur. *How Communist China Negotiates.* New York: Columbia University Press, 1968.

Larkin, B. D. *China and Africa.* Berkeley and Los Angeles: University of California Press, 1971.

Lasater, Martin L. *Taiwan: Facing Mounting Threats.* Washington, D.C.: Heritage Foundation, 1984.

Lawrance, Alan, ed. *China's Foreign Relations Since 1949.* London: Routledge & Kegan Paul, 1975.

Lee, Chae-Jin. *Communist China's Policy Toward Laos: A Case Study, 1954–1967.* Lawrence: University of Kansas Center for East Asian Studies, 1970.

Leibson, Boris. *Petty-Bourgeois Revolutionism.* Moscow: Progress Publishers, 1970.

Leninism and Modern Revisionism. Beijing: Foreign Languages Press, 1963.

Lewis, John Wilson. *Leadership in Communist China.* Ithaca, N.Y.: Cornell University Press, 1963.

———. *Major Doctrines of Communist China.* New York: Norton, 1964.

———, ed. *Party Leadership and Revolutionary Power in China.* New York: Cambridge University Press, 1970.

Li, Tien-min. *Mao's First Heir-Apparent: Liu Shao-Ch'i.* Taipei: Institute of International Relations, 1975.

Lin, Biao. *Long Live the Victory of People's War!* Beijing: Foreign Language Press, 1965.

Lin, John Y. *Secret Documents: Red China's U.S. Policy.* Taipei: Institute of Current China Studies, n.d.

Lin, Yih-tang, ed. *What They Say: A Collection of Current Chinese Underground Publications.* Taipei: Institute of Current China Studies, n.d.

Liu, Alan P. L. *Social Change on Mainland China and Taiwan, 1949–80.* Baltimore: University of Maryland School of Law, 1982.

Liu, Shaoqi. *On the Party.* Beijing: Foreign Languages Press, 1951.

———. *Selected Works.* Beijing: Foreign Languages Press, 1984.

Liu, Ta-chung, and Kung-chia Yeh. *The Economy of the Chinese Mainland: National Income and Economic Development, 1933–1959.* Princeton: Princeton University Press, 1965.

Long Live Leninism! Beijing: Foreign Languages Press, 1964.

Louis, Victor. *The Coming Decline of the Chinese Empire.* New York: Times Books, 1979.

Magdoff, Harry. *The Age of Imperialism: The Economics of U.S. Foreign Policy.* New York: Monthly Review Press, 1969.

Mainland China's Modernization: Its Prospects and Problems. Berkeley: University of California, Institute of International Studies and Institute of East Asian Studies, 1980.

Mao Tse-tung's Thought Is the Invincible Weapon. Beijing: Foreign Languages Press, 1968.

Mao Zedong. *A Critique of Soviet Economics*. New York: Monthly Review Press, 1977.

———. *Quotations from Chairman Mao Tse-tung*. 2d ed. Beijing: Foreign Languages Press, 1966.

———. *Selected Works*. 5 vols. Beijing: Foreign Languages Press, 1967–77.

Marx, Karl. *Marx on China: Articles from the New York Daily Tribune, 1853–1860*. London: Lawrence & Wishart, 1968.

Mehnert, Klaus. *China Returns*. New York: New American Library, 1972.

Meissner, Maurice. *Li Ta-chao and the Origins of Chinese Marxism*. Cambridge, Mass.: Harvard University Press, 1967.

Mesarović, Mihajlo, and Eduard Pestel. *Mankind at the Turning Point*. New York: Dutton, 1974.

Meyer, Alfred G. *Communism*. New York: Random House, 1984.

Middleton, Drew. *The Duel of the Giants: China and Russia in Asia*. New York: Scribner's, 1978.

Moorsteen, Richard, and Morton Abramowitz. *Remaking China Policy: U.S.-China Relations and Governmental Decisionmaking*. Cambridge, Mass.: Harvard University Press, 1971.

Morello, Frank P. *The International Legal Status of Formosa*. The Hague: Martinus Nijhoff, 1966.

Morse, Ronald A., ed. *The Limits of Reform in China*. Boulder, Colo.: Westview Press, 1983.

Mosher, Steven W. *Broken Earth: The Rural Chinese*. New York: Free Press, 1983.

Mozingo, David. *Chinese Policy Toward Indonesia, 1949–1967*. Ithaca, N.Y.: Cornell University Press, 1976.

Muller, David G., Jr. *China as a Maritime Power*. Boulder, Colo. Westview Press, 1983.

Munro, Donald J. *The Concept of Man in Contemporary China*. Ann Arbor: University of Michigan Press, 1977.

Myers, Ramon. *The Chinese Economy, Past and Present*. Belmont, Calif.: Wadsworth, 1980.

Nee, Victor, and David Mozingo, eds. *State and Society in Contemporary China*. Ithaca, N.Y.: Cornell University Press, 1983.

New China Forges Ahead. Beijing: Foreign Languages Press, 1952.

The New Era in East Asia. Hearings Before the Subcommittee on Asian and Pacific Affairs of the Committee on Foreign Affairs, House of Representatives. Washington, D.C.: Government Printing Office, 1981.

The New Look in China's Rural Areas. Beijing: Great Wall Books, 1983.

Nkrumah's Subversion in Africa. Accra: Ministry of Information, Republic of Ghana, 1966.

Normalization of Relations with the People's Republic of China: Practical Implications. Hearings Before the Subcommittee on Asian and Pacific Affairs of the Committee on International Relations. Washington, D.C.: Government Printing Office, 1977.

North, Robert C. *The Foreign Relations of China.* 3d ed. North Scituate, Mass.: Duxbury Press, 1978.

Ojha, Ishwer C. *Chinese Foreign Policy in an Age of Transition: The Diplomacy of Cultural Despair.* Boston: Beacon Press, 1969.

Oksenberg, Michel, ed. *China's Developmental Experience.* New York: Praeger, 1973.

————, and Robert B. Oxnam, eds. *Dragon and Eagle: United States–China Relations, Past and Future.* New York: Basic Books, 1973.

O'Leary, Greg. *The Shaping of Chinese Foreign Policy.* New York: St. Martin's Press, 1980.

The Opium War. Beijing: Foreign Languages Press, 1976.

Oppenheim, L. *International Law.* 8th ed. London: Longmans, Green, 1955.

Osgood, Robert E., ed. *Containment, Soviet Behavior, and Grand Strategy.* Berkeley: University of California, Institute of International Studies, 1981.

Parakal, Pauly. *Peking's Betrayal of Asia.* New Delhi: Sterling, 1976.

Payne, Robert. *Mao Tse-tung.* New York: Pyramid Books, 1966.

Petrov, Victor P. *China: Emerging World Power.* New York: Van Nostrand, 1976.

Playing the China Card: Implications for United States–Soviet–Chinese Relations. Report Prepared for the Subcommittee on Asian and Pacific Affairs of the Committee on Foreign Affairs, U.S. House of Representatives. Washington, D.C.: Government Printing Office, 1979.

The Polemic on the General Line of the International Communist Movement. Beijing: Foreign Languages Press, 1963.

Pollack, Jonathan D. *Security, Strategy, and the Logic of Chinese Foreign Policy.* Berkeley: University of California, Institute of East Asian Studies, 1981.

Powell, Ralph L. *Maoist Military Doctrines.* New York: American-Asian Educational Exchange, n.d.

Prybyla, Jan S. *The Chinese Economy: Problems and Policies.* Columbia: University of South Carolina Press, 1978.

————. *Readjustment and Reform in the Chinese Economy.* Baltimore: University of Maryland School of Law, 1981.

————. *The Societal Objective of Wealth, Growth, Stability, and Equity in Taiwan.* Baltimore: University of Maryland School of Law, 1978.

Pye, Lucien W. *The Spirit of Chinese Politics.* Cambridge, Mass.: MIT Press, 1968.

The Reform Movement of 1898. Beijing: Foreign Languages Press, 1976.

Report on the U.S. and the U.N.: A Balance Sheet. Washington, D.C.: Heritage Foundation, 1984.

The Revolution of 1911. Beijing: Foreign Languages Press, 1976.

Richardson, S. D. *Forestry in Communist China.* Baltimore, Md.: Penguin Books, 1966.

Russell, Maud. *The Sino-Soviet Ussuri River Border Clash: The Historical Background and Current Implications.* New York: Far East Reporter, n.d.

Salem, David. *The People's Republic of China, International Law, and Arms Control.* Baltimore: University of Maryland School of Law, 1983.

Schelling, Thomas C. *The Strategy of Conflict.* Cambridge, Mass.: Harvard University Press, 1960.

Schram, Stuart. *Mao Tse-tung.* Baltimore, Md.: Penguin Books, 1967.

————, ed. *Chairman Mao Talks to the People: Talks and Letters, 1956–1971.* New York: Pantheon Books, 1974.

————, ed. *The Political Thought of Mao Tse-tung.* New York: Praeger, 1969.

Schurmann, Franz. *Ideology and Organization in Communist China.* Berkeley and Los Angeles: University of California Press, 1968.

Selected Articles from Chinese Yearbook of International Law. Beijing: China Translation and Publishing Co., 1983.

Senese, Donald J. *Asianomics: Challenge and Change in Northeast Asia.* Washington, D.C.: Council on American Affairs, 1981.

Shichor, Yitzhak. *The Middle East in China's Foreign Policy, 1949–1977.* New York: Cambridge University Press, 1979.

Sidorenko, A. A. *The Offensive.* Washington, D.C.: Government Printing Office, n.d.

The Sixth Five-Year Plan of the People's Republic of China for Economic and Social Development (1981–1985). Beijing: Foreign Languages Press, 1984.

Sladkovsky, M. I., Y. F. Kovalyov, and V. Y. Sidikhmenov, eds. *Leninism and Modern China's Problems.* Moscow: Progress Publishers, 1972.

Smil, Vaclav. *The Bad Earth: Environmental Degradation in China.* Armonk, N.Y.: M. E. Sharpe, 1984.

Snow, Edgar. *Red Star over China.* New York: Grove Press, 1961.

Snyder, Edwin K., A. James Gregor, and Maria Hsia Chang. *The Taiwan Relations Act and the Defense of the Republic of China.* Berkeley: University of California, Institute of International Studies, 1980.

Social Imperialism. Berkeley, Calif.: Yenan Books, n.d.

Solomon, Richard H. *China Policy and America's Public Debate: Ten Arguments in Search of Normalized U.S.-PRC Relations.* Santa Monica, Calif.: Rand Corporation, December 1977. Mimeo.

————, ed. *Asian Security in the 1980s: Problems and Policies for a Time of Transition.* Cambridge, Mass.: Oelgeschlager, Gunn & Hain, 1980.

————, ed. *The China Factor: Sino-American Relations and the Global Scene.* Englewood Cliffs, N.J.: Prentice-Hall, 1981.

Stacey, Judith. *Patriarchy and Socialist Revolution in China.* Berkeley and Los Angeles: University of California Press, 1983.

Starbuck, Todd R. *China and the Great Power Balance.* Carlisle Barracks, Penn.: Strategic Studies Institute, August 1983.

Starr, John Bryan, ed. *The Future of U.S.-China Relations.* New York: New York University Press, 1981.

Stoessinger, John G. *Nations in Darkness: China, Russia, and America.* New York: Random House, 1981.

Stuart, Douglas T., and William T. Tow, eds. *China, the Soviet Union, and the West.* Boulder, Colo.: Westview Press, 1982.

Su, Wenning, ed. *Modernization—The Chinese Way.* Beijing: Beijing Review, 1983.

Sun, Yat-sen. *The International Development of China.* Taipei: China Cultural Service, 1953.

Sung, Z. D., ed. *The Text of Yi King.* Taipei: n.p., n.d.

Sutter, Robert G. *The China Quandary: Domestic Determinants of U.S. China Policy, 1972–1982.* Boulder, Colo.: Westview Press, 1983.

Swanson, Bruce. *Eighth Voyage of the Dragon: A History of China's Quest for Seapower.* Annapolis, Md.: Naval Institute Press, 1982.

The Taiping Revolution. Beijing: Foreign Languages Press, 1976.

Taiwan Communiqué and Separation of Powers. Hearings Before the Subcommittee on Separation of Powers of the Committee on the Judiciary, United States Senate. Washington, D.C.: Government Printing Office, 1983.

Taiwan Enabling Act. Washington, D.C.: Government Printing Office, 1979.

Taiwan: One Year After United States–China Normalization. Washington, D.C.: Government Printing Office, 1980.

Tan, Su-cheng. *The Expansion of Soviet Seapower and the Security of Asia.* Taipei: Asia and the World Forum, April 1977.

Tang, Anthony M., and Bruce Stone. *Food Production in the People's Republic of China.* Research Report 15. Washington, D.C.: International Food Policy Research Institute, May 1980.

Teiwes, Frederick C. *Leadership, Legitimacy, and Conflict in China: From a Charismatic Mao to the Politics of Succession.* Armonk, N.Y.: M. E. Sharpe, 1984.

Ten Great Years. Beijing: State Statistical Bureau, 1960.

Thomson, James C., Jr., Peter W. Stanley, and John Curtis Perry. *Sentimental Imperialists: The American Experience in East Asia.* New York: Harper & Row, 1981.

Thorton, Richard C. *China: A Political History, 1917–1980.* Boulder, Colo.: Westview Press, 1982.

Tikhvinsky, S. L., ed. *China and Her Neighbors from Ancient Times to the Middle Ages.* Moscow: Progress Publishers, 1981.

Tow, William T., and William R. Feeney. *U.S. Foreign Policy and Asian-Pacific Security: A Transregional Approach*. Boulder, Colo.: Westview Press, 1982.

The True Facts of Chinese Communist Accelerated Aggression Against Foreign Countries at the Present Stage. Taipei: World Anti-Communist League, 1970.

Ugly Features of Soviet Social Imperialism. Beijing: Foreign Languages Press, 1976.

Ulyanovsky, R. A., ed. *The Cominterm and the East: A Critique of the Critique*. Moscow: Progress Publishers, 1981.

U.S.-China Joint Communiqué, August 1982. Current Policy Series no. 413. Washington, D.C.: Bureau of Public Affairs, 1982.

United States Foreign Policy—1971: A Report of the Secretary of State. Washington, D.C.: Government Printing Office, 1972.

The United States and the People's Republic of China: Issues for the 1980s. Hearings Before the Subcommittee on Asian and Pacific Affairs of the Committee on Foreign Affairs, U.S. House of Representatives. Washington, D.C.: Government Printing Office, 1980.

U.S. Policy with Respect to Mainland China. Hearings Before the Senate Foreign Relations Committee. Washington, D.C.: Government Printing Office, 1966.

United States–Soviet Union–China: The Great Power Triangle. Summary of Hearings Conducted by the Subcommittee on Future Foreign Policy Research and Development of the Committee on International Relations. Washington, D.C.: Government Printing Office, 1977.

Urban, George, ed. *The Miracles of Chairman Mao*. Los Angeles, Calif.: Nash, 1971.

van der Kroef, Justus. *Communism in Southeast Asia*. Berkeley and Los Angeles: University of California Press, 1980.

Van Ness, Peter. *Revolution and Chinese Foreign Policy*. Berkeley and Los Angeles: University of California Press, 1970.

Vladimirov, O. E., ed. *Maoism as It Really Is*. Moscow: Progress Publishers, 1981.

Wakeman, Frederic, Jr. *History and Will: Philosophical Perspectives of Mao Tse-tung's Thought*. Berkeley and Los Angeles: University of California Press, 1973.

Walker, Richard. *China Under Communism: The First Five Years*. New Haven, Conn.: Yale University Press, 1955.

Wang, George C., ed. *Economic Reform in the PRC in Which China's Economists Make Known What Went Wrong, Why, and What Should Be Done About It*. Boulder, Colo. Westview Press, 1982.

Wang, Hsueh-wen. *Legalism and Anti-Confucianism in Maoist Politics*. Taipei: Institute of International Relations, 1975.

Wang, N. T. *China's Modernization and Transnational Corporations*. Lexington, Mass.: D. C. Heath, Lexington Books, 1984.

Wang, Y. C. *Chinese Intellectuals and the West, 1872–1949*. Chapel Hill: University of North Carolina Press, 1966.

Watts, William. *The United States and Asia: Changing Attitudes and Policies*. Lexington, Mass.: D. C. Heath, 1982.

Wei, Liang-tsai. *Peking Versus Taipei in Africa, 1960–1978.* Taipei: Asia and World Institute, 1982.

Wei, Lin, and Arnold Chao, eds. *China's Economic Reforms.* Philadelphia: University of Pennsylvania Press, 1982.

Whiting, Allen S. *China Crosses the Yalu.* New York: Macmillan, 1960.

———. *The Chinese Calculus of Deterrence: India and Indochina.* Ann Arbor: University of Michigan Press, 1975.

———. *Siberian Development and East Asia: Threat or Promise?* Stanford: Stanford University Press, 1981.

———. *Soviet Policies in China, 1917–1924.* New York: Columbia University Press, 1954.

The Whole Country Should Become a Great School of Mao Tse-tung's Thought. Beijing: Foreign Languages Press, 1966.

Wittfogel, Karl A. *Oriental Despotism: A Comparative Study of Total Power.* New Haven, Conn.: Yale University Press, 1963.

Wolff, Lester L., and David L. Simon, eds. *Legislative History of the Taiwan Relations Act: An Analytic Compilation with Documents on Subsequent Developments.* New York: American Association for Chinese Studies, 1982.

Wrigley, E. A. *Population and History.* New York: McGraw-Hill, 1969.

Wu, Yuan-li. *Economic Development and the Use of Energy Resources in Communist China.* New York: Praeger, 1963.

———. *Income Distribution in the Process of Economic Growth in the Republic of China.* Baltimore: University of Maryland School of Law, 1977.

Xu, Dixin, ed. *China's Search for Economic Growth: The Chinese Economy Since 1949.* Beijing: New World Press, 1982.

Xue, Muqiao. *China's Socialist Economy.* Beijing: Foreign Languages Press, 1981.

Yahuda, Michael. *Towards the End of Isolationism: China's Foreign Policy After Mao.* New York: St. Martin's Press, 1983.

Yeh, Ch'ing. *Inside Mao Tse-tung's Thought: An Analytic Blueprint of His Actions.* Hicksville, N.Y.: Exposition Press, 1975.

Zanegin, B., A. Mironov, and Y. Mikhailov. *Developments in China.* Moscow: Progress Publishers, 1968.

Zhao, Ziyang. *China's Economy and Development Principles.* Beijing: Foreign Languages Press, 1982.

Index